Voices in Harmony

SONGBOOK

Voices in Harmony Songbook

ISBN: 978-0-9841624-6-8
Second Edition - Tevet 5778 / December 2018

Copyright © 2018 by Jewish Girls Unite

Jewish Girls Unite
12 Thompson Hill Rd
East Greenbush, NY 12061
www.JewishGirlsUnite.com

Design & Layout by Carasmatic Design
www.CarasmaticDesign.com

Cover & interior artwork by Chanie Chanin.

Note: Pictures were not photographed on Shabbos.

Printed in the USA

THIS SONGBOOK IS DEDICATED TO

Our daughters, our Jewish future!

*The net proceeds of this book will be used to support
and connect our Jewish daughters around the world.*

*You are already a part of the beautiful global community of Jewish daughters!
We welcome YOU to connect with us and with each other at Jewish Girls Unite!*

PRESENTED AS A GIFT TO:

FROM:

*May our precious heritage be passed on to you with the love
and joy expressed through the gift of Jewish song.*

INTRODUCTION

From the very beginning of creation, music and song have been essential parts of our heritage. Adam, the first man, realized that each of G-d's creations has a unique song of praise for *Hashem*. He called out to all the creatures in the world, *"Lechu Nerannena LaHashem* – Let us sing to *Hashem."* [Psalms 95:1] When our ancestors crossed the Red Sea and witnessed the miracles of G-d, they sang out in praise of G-d and His miraculous salvation. Throughout our history there have been in total nine songs composed by our people to thank and praise G-d for His miracles. Our Sages teach us that the tenth song will be called, "The New Song of Redemption."

Songs of prayer, songs of hope and faith, folk songs and lullabies: through song, we express the essence of our people, the longing for peace and a brighter future, the yearning of the soul to be close to G-d and to be freed from life's struggles. *Chassidic* philosophy explains that song is the language of the soul and a *niggun* — a melody without words — is the prayer of the heart.

We can look to our foremothers and fathers to see how they used song and dance to connect to *Hashem* and ask for His assistance in times of trouble. Leah *Imeinu*, Devorah, and Chana, along with Miriam and *Dovid Hamelech*, expressed gratitude, hope, and strength through their songs and prayers.

Music and song also provide an easy way to learn and remember concepts and verses from our prayers and Torah study. The learning process is greatly enhanced and becomes enjoyable when we are taught with a melody.

In this songbook, we present to you the gift of song. It is a compilation of our favorite songs, gathered from original compositions created for the Jewish Girls Retreat and Jewish Girls Unite online community, as well as many beautiful melodies by famous Jewish artists from around the world.

Discover your voice and add your unique song to *Hashem*. Enjoy singing these songs with your friends and family and pass them on to the next generation. We pray that very soon we will all gather together from around the world with our "Voices in Harmony" to sing the song of redemption! May your life always be filled with joy and song.

Nechama Dina Laber
JGU Global Director

HOW TO USE THIS SONGBOOK

Can You Picture?

A noisy family car trip is transformed into musical bliss as many enthusiastic individuals, who couldn't distance themselves far enough away from each other just moments before, press in closer as they lift up their voices with a beloved song.

Can You Imagine?

An educator or youth group leader puzzles over the perfect icebreaker for their young charges. He looks to his bookshelf, or she checks her pocketbook or briefcase, and draws forth the songbook as their solution; for few things other than song possess the spirit, the magic, to dissolve barriers, warm hearts, and breed harmony.

Can You Visualize?

A frazzled parent takes a deep breath after a wearying day of hard work. The layers of stress melt away as they enter the room of their child anticipating "tuck-in time," and the two settle down together to sing and tell a story. A song sustains their heartfelt longing to reconnect at the end of a long day, through a beautiful, peaceful tradition.

Can You See?

A special women's group or girls' Shabbaton hums with holy feminine energy, joined by the Shabbos Queen herself. You might choose a song which reflects the week's signature message imparted through the Torah portion, piercing the heart with the timely yet timeless wisdom. The range of voices lift in captivating harmony; and when the time arrives, the company parts ways reinvigorated to greet the new week in all its colors.

Can You Envision?

Your *Shabbos* table atmosphere is graced with a unique soulfulness and spirit as a meaningful book is passed around. Everyone has their moment to shine, to impart their voice of inspiration through a song precious to them, and you all sing your way to weekly redemption. Your table is a sacred space, a paradisaical island of holiness, and a true taste of the World to Come.

These are but a few of the infinite array of instances in which the **Voices in Harmony** songbook will serve us. It is a multifaceted tool — a ladder to reach new levels of joy and unity; a key to unlock your real soul-expression; a valuable resource for all Jewish parents, educators, leaders, and anyone searching for a meaningful and innovative way to impart vital messages that will not be forgotten.

TABLE OF CONTENTS

NIGGUNIM

PRAYER

JEWISH GIRLS unite

SHINE YOUR INNER LIGHT!

JGU is a united, safe, online global community...

A community where girls feel loved and accepted by peers and mentors...

A safe online forum and blogs where girls share ideas, thoughts and feelings...

A variety of online programs and contests where girls connect through creativity and self-expression...

A place where girls meet, laugh, learn and share together in person at retreats...

A place where every girl can truly shine her inner light...

WELCOME TO JEWISH GIRLS UNITE!

www.JewishGirlsUnite.com

VISION STATEMENT:

We see all Jewish girls in the world connected online in a safe, loving, happy Jewish place at Jewish Girls Unite.

MISSION STATEMENT:

Our mission is to create a global community of empowered Jewish leaders and mothers, using innovative approaches in education, technology, and leadership development.

CHAPTER 1:
JGU All-Time Favorites

![Where Heaven and Earth Meet! Jewish Girls Retreat]

The Jewish Girls Retreat, founded in 2004, evolved into the global Jewish Girls Unite community with online classes, and the JGU Press that produces resources to uplift the souls of women and girls today.

It ain't camp without songs! Songs are essential to the vibrant camp magic, creating melodies and memories that abide in girls' minds and hearts forever. Campers sing around a roaring fire, during cleanups, in a talent show, en route on the bus, at midnight when they're supposed to be asleep, and have even been heard singing in the showers!

Have a seat once more and revive that classic spirit; take a deep breath of nostalgia; reminisce about those golden days with your cherished friends and counselors; let the camp soul sweep you away!

TURNING THE SOIL

Chavie Sobel for Jewish Girls Retreat ©
To the tune of Ekra L'Elokim

Turning the soil, preparing yourself
For the seeds of your *Mitzvos* to grow
Torah our water, the life of it all
To bear fruit, *Shlichus* changing the world

To ensure the success of our garden of life
Pulling weeds, making this world more bright
Maintaining the plants, caring for its needs
Enhancing it, adding in good deeds

Chorus
[CAMP NAME] planted seeds in me, changing my life
Bringing me closer to *Yiddishkeit*
Rebbe Time and Grow Workshops, *Davening* too
What I've learned here forever I'll do

[CAMP NAME] planted seeds in me, changing my life
Bringing me closer to *Yiddishkeit*
Rebbe Time and Grow Workshops, *Davening* too
Rebbe, now I'm proud to be a Jew!

DREAMING OF SPARKLES

Recording by JGR Staff

Dreaming of sparkles, of stars in the night
Twinkling stars dancing, friends holding tight
The moonbeams lovingly, soothing our souls
Uniting us all to *Borei Ha'olam*

Even though the sun has gone away
The moon has come 'til tomorrow's day
So reach and touch upon a falling star
Dream of other worlds, but don't go too far

Shlaf Mein Kind, Hab A Zisse Shlaf
Shema Yisrael, A Gutte Nacht

[שלאָף מיין קינד, האָב אַ זיס שלאָף
[שמע ישראל, אַ גוטע נאַכט*

Each time that you smile, each thing that you share
You're changing the world 'cause you took time to care
You're giving us *Nachas*, each *Mitzvah* you do
Remember, dear campers; it's all up to you
Remember, dear campers; we really love you

Sleep, my child, have a sweet sleep. "Hear O Israel…" A good night!

🎧 I FLIP THROUGH THE ALBUM

Chavie Sobel for Jewish Girls Retreat ©
To the tune of Two Brothers Together

I flip through the album of memories so dear
I remember all the fun we had, so perfect and so clear
These pictures are so precious and I hold them near my heart
I remember all the friends I made; how hard it was to part

[CAMP NAME], when the summer ends, I can't bear to go home
I want to stay in [CAMP NAME], where the sun shines and it's warm
Where the air is full of laughter and I know that I belong
Where the atmosphere is bright and girls burst into song

Those few days in the summer recharge my batteries
They hold me 'til the next time I am back and I can see
That every part of camp is back exactly where it goes
I look around and smile - see how everybody glows

[CAMP NAME], when the summer ends, I can't bear to go home
I want to stay in [CAMP NAME] where the sun shines and it's warm
Where girls' faces shine with joy and love
and beam with special pride
'Cause no matter where they come from, they blossom and they thrive

All the counselors love each girl with no strings attached
They accept them so fully and put their hearts into their task
It's a labor of love that they're so dedicated to
They made a difference in my life; if only they really knew

[CAMP NAME], when the summer ends, with regret I say goodbye
I promise to keep in touch, as tears spill out of my eyes
But soon with *Moshiach*, we'll join together once more
And we'll fill *Yerushalayim* with the *Ruach* of [CAMP NAME]

IMAGINE A FAMILY

Chaviva Tarlow
To the Tune of B'Sheim Hashem by Benny Friedman
Edits by Basya Feldman, Recording by Chaviva

Imagine a family so close and warm
Each child's a gift, a kind of their own
From far corners coming, uniting as one
Like harmonies blending in song

[CAMP NAME], you are the family I know
We are empowered to shine on our own
We become leaders discover our inner strength
No one can take that away

Chorus
I'll remember the moments we shared
I'll remember the times that you cared
Inspiring me with meaning
Uplifting me too
I'm grateful to be a Jew

I'll remember the lessons I learned
I will treasure true friendships I've earned
Though we go our own ways now
It's never goodbye
With you, I'll continue to climb

I hold all these memories before we depart
I know my growth will stay in my heart
[CAMP NAME], thank you for showing me my true light
I now know I make the world bright

JGU CONNECTING AS ONE

JGU Online Class Theme Song 2014
Racheli Jacks ©
Recording by Racheli Jacks

Discover each of your talents
Strength, resilience
Respect and patience
Igniting and nurturing your essence
Thoughtful acceptance

Miracles for you to uncover
A world awaits you
There's joy and wonder
Within you is the power
Of helping another

Inspired, reaching new heights
Here, at Jewish Girls Unite
Lots of interesting girls, all over the world
Spreading friendship, warmth, and light
Singing, drawing, writing, acting in front of girls who care
I'm so excited to grow, to learn and to know
All of the *mitzvos* that we share

Chorus
Together, connecting as one
Together, we welcome everyone
Link by link, *Moshiach* will soon come
JGU achieving a ton

Unlocking the hidden treasures
The gems of our past
Women modestly
Throughout history
Bravely molded our ancestry

And as I grow
I'll pass on what I know
And I'll help my friends grow too
A purpose so true
For me to do
Enhancing my life as a proud Jew

Together, connecting as one
Together, we welcome everyone
Link by link, *Moshiach* will soon come
JGU united as one!

🎧 THE PRINCESS

Bat Mitzvah Camp Theme Song 2000
Sorah Leah Eber ©
To the Tune of Nekadesh by the Miami Boys Choir

One small voice in the dark
What difference can I make
Which path do I take
An answer I must find

But wait, there's a voice
That says I should not fear
That voice it sounds so near
It's my *Neshama* that I hear

Chorus
Reach up high
Take a chance
Climb that mountain, here's my hand
Look inside; I'm your guide
To help you learn and understand

Show your face
Know what it takes
To make this world a better place
Your Jewish pride
You can't hide
It's there inside

You're the daughter of a king
A princess to be seen
Stand up tall, be proud and bold
A true *Bas Yisroel* to behold
Of course, I know
That you will win
Yagatee Umatzasi Ta'amin
[*יגעתי ומצאתי תאמין]
Reach for the stars
Know who you are
You'll go far

Chorus

If you try, you will succeed. -Talmud

SHINE YOUR INNER LIGHT

Rivka Leah Popack for JGU Launch 2015 ©

In those times
When you find
That each door that you try
Is locked, yet again
And it won't let you by
In your heart lies the key
Look inside and you'll see
Believe, just believe

In those days
In the haze
When all you see is true
Seems to fall far behind
And you're lost within you
And you try to be strong
But it's hard to hold on
For so long
For so long

Chorus
Trust your inner light
Shadows fall away
Hold your candle high
Night will turn to day (x2)

Moments when you're feeling small
No reason to give in
Don't you know in the greatest darkness
Light will always win

So be the miracle I believe in
Just be the candle burning bright
You can be the flame we're reaching for
Light up, light up the night

Chorus

Don't you know, this place in time
Is waiting just for you?
To learn, to give, to love, to live
There's so much you can do
So be the miracle we believe in
Be the candle burning bright
You can be the flame we're reaching for
Light up, light up the night

Shine your inner light
Shadows fall away
Hold your candle high
Night will turn to day (x2)

Night will turn to
Night will turn to
Night will turn to day

HOW CAN I TELL YOU?

Miriam Leah Shaw ©

How can I tell you what a treasure you are?
How can I show you when you've strayed so far?
From the life of our fathers and the heritage they
earned
How can you cherish what you've never learned?

How can I tell you what it means to be a Jew?
How can I show you when you don't believe it's true
That your life has a purpose higher than you
understand
And you're not like other nations and you're in a
foreign land

You strive and you struggle to be like those you see
But inside your soul is dying
You're not who you should be
Yes it's hard to be different take responsibility
But a life without courage is without integrity

JEWISH CHILD OF HASHEM

To the Tune of B'nei Heichala Niggun
Composed by Kol Neshama Camp
Recording by Chaviva Tarlow

Each blessed Jewish child
Shares a gift and a destiny
She has a sacred cause
To live by Torah wholeheartedly
With simple trust in G-d

True knowledge of His Name
His Providence and Domain
These are the secrets of creation
This is the reason why He created Yisroel

A Jew has one purpose
A Jew has one true claim
We're partners in creation
With His Holy Name

THE WOMAN OF VALOR

Did you know there is an ancient song we dedicate to the Jewish woman, and that it is all about what makes her shine? We sing it every Friday night before Kiddush to praise the women of our homes. It is called "Aishes Chayil." Tradition teaches us that this beautiful song was composed by Avraham Avinu himself, as a eulogy for his great wife Sarah upon her passing. It was reinstituted years later by Shlomo Hamelech in his book of Proverbs.

Each verse of the song, arranged in alphabetical order, is an allusion to one of the great women of our past and the legacies attributed to them. The song opens, "Aishes chayil mi yimtza -- A woman of valor, who can find?" Indeed, where can we find one like her? It often seems so difficult to reach as high as those who came before us and paved the way for their descendants! Always remember: the Aishes Chayil, this incredible woman, is inside every one of us, woven into our "spiritual DNA."

AISHES CHAYIL

Proverbs 31:10-31.

אֵשֶׁת חַיִל מִי יִמְצָא, וְרָחֹק מִפְּנִינִים מִכְרָהּ

בָּטַח בָּהּ לֵב בַּעְלָהּ, וְשָׁלָל לֹא יֶחְסָר

גְּמָלַתְהוּ טוֹב וְלֹא רָע, כֹּל יְמֵי חַיֶּיהָ

דָּרְשָׁה צֶמֶר וּפִשְׁתִּים, וַתַּעַשׂ בְּחֵפֶץ כַּפֶּיהָ

הָיְתָה כָּאֳנִיּוֹת סוֹחֵר, מִמֶּרְחָק תָּבִיא לַחְמָהּ

וַתָּקָם בְּעוֹד לַיְלָה, וַתִּתֵּן טֶרֶף לְבֵיתָהּ, וְחֹק לְנַעֲרֹתֶיהָ

זָמְמָה שָׂדֶה וַתִּקָּחֵהוּ, מִפְּרִי כַפֶּיהָ נָטְעָה כָּרֶם

חָגְרָה בְעוֹז מָתְנֶיהָ, וַתְּאַמֵּץ זְרוֹעֹתֶיהָ

טָעֲמָה כִּי טוֹב סַחְרָהּ, לֹא יִכְבֶּה בַלַּיְלָה נֵרָהּ

יָדֶיהָ שִׁלְּחָה בַכִּישׁוֹר, וְכַפֶּיהָ תָּמְכוּ פָלֶךְ

כַּפָּהּ פָּרְשָׂה לֶעָנִי, וְיָדֶיהָ שִׁלְּחָה לָאֶבְיוֹן

לֹא תִירָא לְבֵיתָהּ מִשָּׁלֶג, כִּי כָל בֵּיתָהּ לָבֻשׁ שָׁנִים

מַרְבַדִּים עָשְׂתָה לָּהּ, שֵׁשׁ וְאַרְגָּמָן לְבוּשָׁהּ

נוֹדָע בַּשְּׁעָרִים בַּעְלָהּ, בְּשִׁבְתּוֹ עִם זִקְנֵי אָרֶץ

סָדִין עָשְׂתָה וַתִּמְכֹּר, וַחֲגוֹר נָתְנָה לַכְּנַעֲנִי

עֹז וְהָדָר לְבוּשָׁהּ, וַתִּשְׂחַק לְיוֹם אַחֲרוֹן

פִּיהָ פָּתְחָה בְחָכְמָה, וְתוֹרַת חֶסֶד עַל לְשׁוֹנָהּ

צוֹפִיָּה הֲלִיכוֹת בֵּיתָהּ, וְלֶחֶם עַצְלוּת לֹא תֹאכֵל

קָמוּ בָנֶיהָ וַיְאַשְּׁרוּהָ, בַּעְלָהּ וַיְהַלְלָהּ

רַבּוֹת בָּנוֹת עָשׂוּ חָיִל, וְאַתְּ עָלִית עַל כֻּלָּנָה

שֶׁקֶר הַחֵן וְהֶבֶל הַיֹּפִי, אִשָּׁה יִרְאַת ה' הִיא תִתְהַלָּל

תְּנוּ לָהּ מִפְּרִי יָדֶיהָ, וִיהַלְלוּהָ בַשְּׁעָרִים מַעֲשֶׂיהָ

Translation:

Who can find a Woman of Valor?
Her value far exceeds that of pearls.
The heart of her husband, he trusts in her; he lacks no gain.
She repays his good, but never his harm, all the days of her life.
She seeks out wool and linen, and her hands work willingly.

She is like a merchant's ships; she brings sustenance from afar.
She rises while it is still night, and gives food to her household and a ration to her maids.
She considers a field and buys it; from the fruit of her handiwork, she plants a vineyard.
She girds her loins with might and strengthens her arms.
She senses that her enterprise is good, so her lamp is not extinguished at night.
She puts her hand to the distaff, and her palms support the spindle.
She spreads out her palm to the poor and extends her hands to the destitute.
She fears not snow for her household, for her entire household is clothed with scarlet wool.
Bedspreads she makes herself; linen and purple wool are her clothing.
Well-known at the gates is her husband as he sits with the elders of the land.
Garments she makes and sells, and she delivers a belt to the peddler.
Strength and splendor are her clothing, and smilingly she awaits her last day.
She opens her mouth with wisdom, and the teaching of kindness is on her tongue.
She anticipates the needs of her household, and the bread of idleness, she does not eat.
Her children rise and celebrate her; and her husband, he praises her:
"Many daughters have attained valor, but you have surpassed them all."
False is grace, and vain is beauty; a G-d-fearing woman, she should be praised.
Give her the fruit of her hands, and she will be praised at the gates by her very own deeds.

IN LOVING MEMORY OF

Sara Nechama Yarmush

A TRUE AISHES CHAYIL

Bubby truly listened to us with her full heart
She was so proud when in Torah learning we took part
She appreciated all that *Hashem* did for her
She saw *Hashgocha Protis* in everything that did occur

She was constantly praising *Hashem* everyday
For all the *Chesed* and *Rachamim* that came her way
Her *tznius* was refined and exemplary
Even when it was the opposite of society

She was so proud to be a *Yid*
It showed in everything she did
Bubby always encouraged us to do what's right
Her wise advice had much insight

Her *nachas* and joy was her family
Baruch Hashem, she built a Torah dynasty

"You have so much to do, because you have so much!"

WOMEN OF THE FUTURE

Mali New for Jewish Girls Retreat ©
Recording by Chaviva Tarlow

Here I stand today
Paving my own way
Just like Sarah, I will too
Touch the soul of every Jew

Leah changed the norm
Went out to transform
How, *Hashem*, can I be like them?

There's more there than it seems
Take Esther, who was queen
Devorah judged beneath a tree
Left her home so modestly

I'll run that extra mile
Show the world my style
I yearn to be a true *Aishes Chayil*

Time and time again
The power of us women
We can shine our inner light
It's in our hands today
Spread forth the holy way
How can I be a *Shlucha*?
How can I be a leader?

Women of the future
Now is your chance to

See your greater strength unfurl
Shove away the darkness
You have the power to
Bring day to the world

I AM A JEWISH GIRL

Jewish Girls Retreat Staff ©

Every Jewish woman has something deep inside
That can illuminate her beauty, her talents, and her pride
She's different; she's special
She is the cornerstone who creates a loving family, a warm and Jewish home

Chorus
I am a Jewish girl, an *Aishes Chayil*
I can determine my future at will
Uncover to discover
That no goal is too far
With joy in every step
Expressing who we are

Each and every girl is one of a kind,
So do what you can
Search and you will find,
The further you go, the more you will see
We each are unique yet
We can join in unity
In [JGU] we are one family

Who we are and what we can do
Is greater in unity, so see right through
Sheker Hachein [שקר החן*]

What's beautiful is deep within
Bring it to the fore
United from our core
In JGU, we are one family

Charm is false. -Proverbs 31:30

DEEP IN THE GROUND

Racheli Jacks for Jewish Girls Retreat ©
To the Tune of Hu Yiftach Libeinu
Recording by Chaviva Tarlow

Deep in the ground
Yet to be found
A gemstone concealed
Waiting to be revealed
A polish, a shine
And before our eyes
A glittering diamond
In majesty, it lies (x2)

Aishes, Aishes Chayil
A precious woman who can find?
Gleaming in every facet
Revealing she's one of a kind

Through *Challah*, lighting candles
And raising her family
Sheker Hachein [שקר החן*]
It's not appearance or fame
Unlocking her inner beauty (x3)

Charm is false. -Proverbs 31:30

Rebbetzin Chana, wife of Rabbi Levi Yitzchok Schneerson and mother of the Lubavitcher Rebbe, embodied pure devotion and self-sacrifice for her family and Torah. When her husband was exiled for vitalizing Yiddishkeit under Soviet reign, she faithfully joined him notwithstanding the cruel challenges ahead. When her husband, a masterful scholar and author, conceived Torah insights but lacked resources to preserve them, Chana gathered roots and berries and stewed ink herself, with which he penned his thoughts in his books' margins. A beacon of warmth and love in a cold and chaotic country, Rebbetzin Chana was there for all Jews, and continues to inspire us soul-to-soul with her noble legacy.

REBBETZIN CHANA

Recording by Chaviva Tarlow

A precious *Neshama*
Came down to this world
A woman so pious
Hashem she did serve
Dedication so deep
To her husband's needs
Followed him to *Golus* without a complaint

Chorus
Oh *Rebbetzin* Chana, your flame carries on
It ignites the spark in us all
Your *Mesiras Nefesh* we'll never forget
Isha Yirat Hashem He Tit'halal
[אשה יראת ה' היא תתהלל*]

She picked in the fields some grass and herbs
And ink she did make for her husband's sake
Writing along the side of the page
Reb Levi Yitzchok wrote *Peirushim*

Chorus

Later these *Seforim* were brought
Across the sea to her son, our *Rebbe* in 770
Now we study the books which are so dear
If not for her we wouldn't have them here

*A G-d-fearing woman is the one to be praised. -Proverbs 31:30

THE CROWN OF CREATION

Chanale
Composed by Dina Rosenfeld ©
Album: The Crown of Creation

The crown of creation lay broken and bent
What once could have been is all gone
But it is in our power to build and carry on (x2)

Oh, Mother of royalty
Woman of strength
The message alive in your name
Revealing dimensions so hidden within
Restoring the crown to women again

Mother of royalty
Woman of strength
You carry the promise, *Hachein*
The name that you bore
Will yet shine ever more
Restoring the crown to us again

BRICK BY BRICK

Racheli Jacks for Jewish Girls Retreat ©
To the Tune of Adon Olam by the Miami Boys Choir
Recording by JGR choir

Brick by brick and with loving care
With devotion to which nothing can compare
A woman builds her home, her family
Guiding them to be all they can be

So many talents that are necessary
For a mother to fill her role properly
Her expertise and caring, thoughtful deeds
With every action, she's planting seeds

Chochmas Noshim Bansa Baisa
[*חכמות נשים בנתה ביתה]
Starting from our *Bas Mitzvah*
With a woman's wisdom, she's the foundation
Of the Jewish Nation (x2)

Learning from the "Women of Worth"
We contribute to this earth,
As we build our home
We build a home for *Hashem*
And the *Mikdash Hashlishi*, Amen

*The wisest of women each built her house. -Proverbs 14:1

THE ROSE

Recording by Chaviva Tarlow

The radiant sun shines down upon a solitary rose
With soft, red velvet petals she strikes a noble pose
She sets herself apart so that her beauty will endure
Her thorns protect her virtues, safe and pure

A butterfly emerges, spreading her vivid wings
And flies across the world as all of nature sings
It was her warm cocoon that kept her safe until that day
When at that moment she could fly away

Chorus

And so I tell you my child, my beautiful girl
That you hold something special, 'cause you hold up the world

You ask me why, for inside, from there your truth shines
Listen close, *Vehaya Machanecha Kadosh*
[*והיה מחניך קדוש]

A million gems glisten, royal treasures gleam
A lifetime fortune a mass, it's a man's ultimate dream
Where are these riches kept but locked up in a chest
Valued gifts are hidden from the rest

Chorus

And your camp shall be holy. -Deuteronomy 23:15

Dearest Raizel,

'An evening of roses' sets the Song of Shlomo and we think of the roses in Gan Eden. Raizel, you are such a beautiful rose and do so many beautiful Mitzvos: Shabbat programs for the younger children at Shul, Holiday events with college students, discussions with women in the community, visiting the elderly and more. Whatever the circumstance or the setting, you are a 'Rose among the Thorns' of a secular and challenging world and we marvel at your patience, intelligence, creativity, and devotion.

The Hebrew word Shoshanna, or rose, comes from the root word Shosh-or rejoice and can be found in Tehillim 70.4 (Rejoice over Hashem). Raizel, you do everything with dedication and with joy, just as Miriam sang by the sea and rejoiced over that wonder. It is your joy and commitment to Torah and Chassidishkeit that will help to bring about the redemption, speedily and in our day.

May you continue to give naches to the Rebbe, your parents, family, teachers and friends!

Mommy & Tatty

Hinda Sheina Kollin

She taught and endlessly studied. She encouraged and inspired. She gratefully served. Her mind was sharp and broad. Her heart was wide. She radiated warmth. Professionally, she taught cooking and sewing in public school. She loved to cook for others.

Her being was an example of Ahavas Yisroel. She was passionate about her people. Tirelessly, she created synagogue programs, which included lifelong learning for women. She served as president of both Sisterhood and Hadassah. Our lives revolved around our shul and beloved rabbi. She made sure we were in shul every Shabbos.

Yes, she taught us to love Yiddishkeit. She lived to help others. Whatever situation we were in, she was always there, always our Rock. She was the epitome of a mother in Israel. I miss her very, very much.

Chaya Pellin

MY CHILDREN

Leah Namdar ©
Recording by Chaviva Tarlow

*Adar 25 is the Hebrew birthday of Rebbetzin
Chaya Mushka of righteous memory, a woman who
exemplified modesty, kindness, and total selflessness.
Both a scion of the Chabad dynasty and wife of a
Rebbe, yet always unassuming, she dedicated all she
had and was to the mission of Chabad, by giving the
world the seventh Lubavitcher Rebbe. She famously
declared, "A Rebbe belongs to his Chassidim,"
and stood staunchly by his side in both times of
celebration and difficulty. Though they did not have
children of their own, we are all their children. This
song is a tribute to the Rebbetzin.*

A child I was all of four
With my parents through the palace door
She spoke to them in a special way
While I looked for children to play

There were no children to be seen
So I turned to the *Rebbetzin*, our queen
I looked into her beautiful eyes
"Where are your children?" I asked in surprise

Eyes filled with love
Brimmed over with tears
A look I'll remember all my years
Her face shone with pride as she replied to me
My children are in 770

BUILDING THE FUTURE

Sorah Leah Eber ©
Edits by Racheli Jacks
Recording by JGR choir

From the very start of time
Women held a special place
Guiding, nurturing, leading on
Through history leaving a trace

From Sarah's modesty
Rivkah's kindness
Rochel's generosity
Leah's gratefulness

Our foremothers sparkled
With personality
Showing the pathway
For eternity

Chorus
Jewish women, search deep within
You have what it takes
Building the future
Changing the world
Making it a better place

Using our power given from above
You can accomplish anything with love
Inspired by women
Through history
We're doing our mission
To bring eternal peace

Look through the Torah you will see
Women held in high esteem
They did what they must, in *Hashem* they did trust
Even when things tough did seem

From Devorah's wisdom
To Chana's plea
Esther's self-sacrifice
Yael's bravery

Women of the past
Held strong and true
Now dear Jewish women
It's all up to you

Chorus

Women of the past
Held strong and true
Now dear Jewish women
It's all up to you

🎧 BE A STAR
Racheli Jacks for Jewish Girls Retreat ©

As we grow
Each day advancing a new step
We know
A Jew is always moving ahead

Like the stars
Twinkling and brightening the night
We're spreading light, learning what's right
Dispelling shadows, shattering the night

Chorus
Matzdikei Harabim Kekochavim
[מצדיקי הרבים ככוכבים*]
I can be a star
By helping others shine through
Yisroel as a nation as stars we are
Shining across the darkened sky

Glimmering and glowing, showing the way
I have the strength
to sparkle brighter every day

A true example
Through darkness, we'll shine
Let's help to reveal *Moshiach's* time

Chorus

Guiding my friends by doing what's right
I can be a star
By helping others shine through
Yisroel as a nation as stars we are
Shining across the darkened sky

Those who bring the multitudes to righteousness [will shine] like the stars. -Daniel 12:3

🎧 A TEARFUL LESSON

Recording by CGI Detroit

Once when the Mitteler Rebbe DovBer
Was learning late in the night
Torah and holiness sang in his heart
Filling his eyes with their light

Once when the Mitteler Rebbe DovBer
Was learning late in the night
Torah and holiness sang in his heart
Echoing power and might

Nearby his baby was sleeping
It woke up suddenly weeping
And crying aloud for his father
But nobody answered its call

The Rebbe Reb Berl was learning
The Torah within him was burning
The whole world and all of its treasures
Worth less than a dream in the night

Above Reb Berl, his father was up
Learning late in the night
The Alter Rebbe, the *Manhig Hador*
Heard it cry out in fright

Down, down to the baby, he went
And lifted it up in his arms
He dried its tears and sang it a song
Guarding the child from harm

The Alter Rebbe stayed near him
For he knew his son would not hear him
Until he had finished his learning
And then he told him these words

Berl, my son, let me teach you
The cries of a child must reach you
No matter how deep your devotion
No matter how high you may rise

The Alter Rebbe was teaching his son
And every single Jew
To help children cry out in need
This is the task we must do

🎧 TO LOVE A FELLOW JEW

Mayer Rivkin ©
Album: Redemption

To love a fellow Jew
Just the same as you
Is the basis of our holy Torah
He may be far from me
Across the widest sea
But still, I'll always love him just the same

For 70 or 80 years a *Neshama* wears and tears
Just to do a favor for another
Love him with all your heart
The heavens spread apart
For every Jew is really our brother and sister

🎧 GLOW

Chavie Sobel and Racheli Jacks for JGR 2009 ©

Let's get glowing
Let's illuminate the night
Light a spark that always stays
Warm and lit and bright

Today let's light a flame
With actions that carry on
Legacies left behind
Outlines that were drawn

[JGU] it's in our hands
Together, as one we stand

Learning Torah, sharing what we know
Flames that they have lit
We have the power to transmit
For eternity they will glow

Though the night is cold and dark
In our soul, there lies a spark
Girls Light up Our World!
Let's get glowing now! (x2)

IN MEMORY OF
Thalia Hakin A"H
שרה בת מזל ⟶ YARTZEIT 22 TEVES

On January 20, 2017 - Teves 22, 5777 - at the bustling vista of Melbourne's Bourke Street Mall, only G-d could foresee the abrupt shattering to come. At the hands of a sadistic motorist barreling down the walkway, numerous were injured and five were slain. Among the five was ten-year-old Thalia Hakin from Beth Rivkah Ladies' College, a precious candle who touched all whom she knew with her spirit, sweetness, intelligence, and passion for Judaism. Her community - and essentially the entire Jewish People - was devastated, reeling from shock in face of the tragedy as little Thalia's pure soul was called home to her Source.

At this time, halfway across the globe, the One More Light anthology was near to be published. JGU Global Director Nechama Laber chose to scroll through her emails from the previous two years, in a final check to catch any submissions from girls that may have been overlooked. With shock and wonder she discovered - only two days after the girl's untimely passing - an attached poem in Thalia's original handwriting. Thalia had submitted it to the One More Light Writing Contest two years before, but it was Divinely ordained not to be seen until just then.

Thalia's poem had been circulated as well in local publications, a whisper from Heaven sparking hope and strength in broken hearts. Another member of the Melbourne Jewish community, songwriter Rivka Leah Popack, composed a vibrant melody to which she set the verses of Thalia's poem, in her everlasting memory. Thalia's legacy reaches further every day, and her soulful words continue to inspire us to greater faith, and remind us that every single candle we ignite illuminates the world at large, bringing it one step closer to Redemption.

We are taught that the life and merits of one who has passed on uplift the world on a greater level than ever possible to achieve in this world. Together, let's heed Thalia's call, internalize her vision... and sing her song.

🎧 LIGHT UP A CANDLE

Lyrics by Thalia Hakin ob"m
Melody composed by Rivka Leah Popack
Sung and arranged by Sam Glaser for JGU 2017 ©

The production of this song based on Thalia's words
was sponsored by the Seymour Fox Foundation

When you light up a candle
You light up your Neshama
And you light up the world
And when you light up the world
You make it a better place
Like for you, me and everybody

Now the world, the world is dark
But soon it will be bright for us
Im Yirtzeh Hashem Moshiach will come (x2)

When you light up a candle
You light up your *Neshama*
And you light up the world
And when you light up the world
You make it a better place
Like for you, me and everybody

Now the world, the world is dark
But soon it will be bright for us
Im Yirtzeh Hashem, Moshiach will come (x2)

Chorus
Light, light up, light up a candle

Light, light up, light up the world
Light, light up, light up a candle
Light, light up, light up the world (x3)

We're lighting a candle
We're lighting our *Neshamos*
And we're lighting up the world
And when we light up the world
We make it a better place
For you, me and everybody (x2)

Light, light up, light up a candle
Light, light up, light up the world
Light, light up, light up a candle
Light, light up, light up the world

We're lighting a candle
We're lighting our *Neshamos*
And we're light-
ing up the world
And when we
light up the
world
We make it a
better place
For you, me and
everybody

Chorus

When you light up a candle you light up your neshema. And you light up the world And when you light up the world you make it a better place. like for you me and evrybody. Now the world is dark but soon to be bright for us. And mir Hashem mashiach will come.

By Thalia hakin 3Bk

SEE THE GOOD

Composed by Nechama Laber
To the Tune of Ladino Song
Abraham Avinu

For so many years
Tatty I missed you
I never knew
I could see you

Oh Tatty, I longed for you
With my heart and soul
I yearned to be with you
and hear you sing this song

Chorus
"*Kuk Nisht Oif Der Vei*
Kuf Oif Dee Gezunt"
[קוק נישט אויף דער ויי
קוף אויף די געזונט*]
See the good, my Love
And trust the One above

Tatty, you never left me
You were just concealed
Until the day I realized
To open up my eyes

I can truly feel you
I can truly hear you
I can truly love you
I can learn from you

For you are really with me
Each and every moment
You are my guiding light
In the darkest night

Today, we celebrate
Tatty's shining legacy
With our precious family
In total harmony

With your first great-grandson
Your light shines through and
through

From generation to generation
He's your continuation

Chorus

We're singing your song
And we know it won't be long
When we'll sing our song
together
In the Holy Land

Chorus

Tatty, you never left us
You were just concealed
Until the day WE realized
To open up OUR eyes!

*"Don't focus on the pain, focus on the
health!"*

IN MEMORY OF
Tsofia Mesica and Saar Harel

Tsofia Mesica was such a wonderful person. She was so happy and energetic and really cared about everyone. Aside from that she made everyone feel like she was her friend. Her bright smile and bubbly personality made this world a brighter place. She was unfortunately taken from us on September 21, 2015.

Saar Harel was so warm and just the best friend anyone could have. She and I were the best of friends. She made me feel like we were sisters. She was always happy and everyone who knew her was instantly close to her. She was the brightest friendliest person I ever knew. She was unfortunately taken from the world on October 31, 2016.

LIGHT FROM DARK

By Rachael Hannah Tahir
Age 16, Simi Valley, California

Days go by and by
The dark fades to light
Though a hole is made
Their light lives on

Chorus:
Who is there? All those gone
Are not really gone
Their light is still burning
This takes light from dark

The *Shabbos* candles burn, burn
Bright with the past and the future
We end one week but another

Weeks to come and
We still go on

Chorus

We learn from our mistakes
But we also remember the good
and emulate the ways of the
cherished souls in our hearts
Like the words of a friend
You only live once -
So, make the most of your days
while you can

Chorus

My dear friends, the world's
different without you
You will live on
We remember you on *Shabbos*

and always, your beautiful souls
And how you lit up the world
On your *Yartzeit* and on *Shabbos*,
we light up
Candles and bring down the light
of your souls
To the world

Chorus

You are always remembered
And your light is very bright
made
Brighter through the *Mitzvot* we do
And *Moshiach* will come for me
and you

Chorus

Light from dark (x3)

THREE MALACHIM CAME

Racheli Jacks and Ziva Katzenberg ©
Recording by Chaviva Tarlow

Racheli Jacks and Ziva Katzenberg composed this song to present at a High School Convention in New York in 1992. Their mother, Mrs. Bracha Chaya Katzenberg ob"m, helped them find a theme for the song, but unfortunately, she passed away before the Bais Rivkah Montreal choir presented it at the convention and dedicated it to her name. It is still sung world-wide today. Ziva's daughter sang it to her after she had learned it at the Beth Rivkah of Melbourne, Australia and Ziva exclaimed, "That's the song I wrote!"

Three *Malachim* came
When Avraham was in pain
Each one on a *Shlichus* of his own
Fulfilling their task
"Where's Sarah?" they asked
Modestly she remained in the tent

On a camel, she rode
Rivkah left her abode
Yitzchak she saw from afar
She covered her face
Her veil fell in place
Now each Jewish bride does the same

Chorus
Oh, *Bnos Yisroel*, look back and see
The women of our ancestry
They lived modestly, and we can do the same
Oh, *Am Levadad Yishkon* [עם לבדד ישכן*]

Styles may come and styles may go
But as Jewish daughters, we know
Tznius in thought, in action and speech
With bring the *Geulah* with speed

...a nation that will dwell alone... -Numbers 23:9

LOOKING BACK

Racheli Jacks for Jewish Girls Retreat ©
Recording by Chaviva Tarlow

Looking back over so many years
Generations survived through hardships and tears
And yet there remained a spark of hope
Ignited by Jewish women throughout times

Chorus
In the past, they pulled us through
In the future, we will too
Bizchus Noshim Asidin Lehiga'el
[בזכות נשים עתידין להיגאל*]

We eagerly await the eternal *Geulah*
Please *Hashem*, hear our cry; *Ad Mosai?*

Founding a home is her primary role
With devotion, she instills a love for *Yiddishkeit*
In so many ways, she gives of her life
To ensure that *Klal Yisroel* stays alive

Chorus

In the merit of women, in the future we'll be redeemed. -Talmud

RUTH
To the tune of Shir, Shir

Ruth was forty years old
She decided that she'd be a Jew
In the *Megillah* we are told
She knew the Torah was true

From Ruth we can all learn
That a person's not locked in their fate
We can always return
We know it's never too late

Good times, bad times
Come what may
Our *Emunah* will never stray
Ruth was poor, sad, and alone
Her *Neshama* still shone
Her *Neshama* still shone
Her *Neshama* still shone

I WILL GO WHERE YOU WILL GO
Rivky Feld for JGR Movie Ruth's Vision 2008 ©

I will go where you will go
And that is where I'll stay
I want to lead a holy life
Not one of glitter and fame

To be a princess, Moabite
Is not my kind of life
I'd rather stay with you always
In pain, hunger, or strife

Shabbos Kodesh that is what I'll keep
I will go where you will go and that is where I'll sleep
Your people are my people now
Your G-d is my G-d
Amech Ami, V'Elokayich Elokai
[*עמך עמי ואלוקיך אלוקי]

Eretz Yisroel, the focus of G-d's eye
If death will make us separate
That is where I'll lie

I will go where you will go
And that is where I'll stay
I want to live a Jewish life
To be with you always
Please don't push me away
Away

Your people are my people; your G-d is my G-d. -Ruth 1:16

RABBI AKIVAH'S WIFE

A Greater Life JGR Movie
2010 ©
To the Tune of Mi Ha'ish

This is the day I prayed
for
Would have paid for
Laid in wait for

Chorus
While others see a
shepherd
I see only a Torah sage
My life, it is so sweet now
So complete now
I'm at peace now
While others see a
shepherd
I see only a Torah sage

Though I come from great money
The wealth it did abound,
I have never been richer
Then I am with him right now

This is the day she prayed for
Would have paid for
Laid in wait for

Chorus

Akiva, my dear husband
Though you'll be far away
You'll be home in our hearts here
And our prayers every day

This is the day I prayed for
Would have paid for
Laid in wait for
While others see a shepherd
Only I see a Torah sage

THE WORLD WOULD BE NOTHING WITHOUT WOMEN

A Greater Life JGR Movie 2010 ©

You took me when others found me lowly
You saw something holy in my soul
You made me discover what was hidden
You took but a part and made a whole

I've finally become what you have wished for
And now I've come home to you for good
Don't think I don't know all that its cost you
And that I would change it if I could

Chorus (x2)
The world would be nothing without women
And I would be nothing without you
Your strength and your beauty flow endlessly
As pure as the early morning dew

I rose every morning feeling lonely,
Yet each time I tired, I'd see your face
Your words and your trust were all that kept me there
The gentle reminder of your grace

Whenever I think of how you've suffered
No husband at home, the cupboards bare
You gave up a lifestyle dipped in gold for me
You traded it in for one of care

Chorus
The world would be nothing without women

The pillar on which the word survives
With purest devotion to the Torah
We can all live your greater life

JOURNEY TO FREEDOM

Racheli Jacks for JGR 2006 ©

Journey, journey to freedom
Yatza, Yatza Mimitzrayim
[*יצא, יצא ממצרים]
In every generation, experience it again
Embarking on a journey within

Go out – rise above the challenge
See how – *Hashem* leads the way
When the fight gets tough
Just keep your goal in sight
A new step day by day

Chorus
Don't give up – keep on going
Faith and courage always showing
Help a friend – you're not alone
Traveling to *Yisrael*, our home

Travel – travel through the desert
Torah – leads us right along
All our needs provided, we'll journey to our land
United, hand in hand

Chorus

In every generation one must look upon himself as if he had gone out from Egypt. -Mishna

Three months into the Jewish People's transformative journey from the Exodus from Egypt through the wilderness, they arrived at Mount Sinai, camping near the mountain "like one man with one heart." Preceding Israel's acceptance of the Torah there, G-d instructed Moshe, "Koh Tomar L'Veit Yaakov V'Tageid Li'Vnei Yisrael... — So shall you say to the House of Jacob and tell the Sons of Israel..." [Exodus 19:3] The commentator Rashi clarifies that the expression "House of Jacob" alludes to the women, while "Children of Israel" refers to the men. The women were to be addressed first to affirm their unique role in transmitting Torah and instilling it within the next generation, as the primary nurturers and "Akeres Habayis — Foundation of the Home." Indeed, this very instance of "Ladies First" is one powerful reason why Jewish identity is defined via matrilineal descent. Jewish women and girls have the sacred privilege and responsibility to pass on the tradition, the ultimate Song of our people, with insight and joy, dedication and love.

🎧 P'TACH LIBI, I WANT TO GROW

Recording by Chaviva Tarlow for JGR ©

P'tach Libi [פתח לבי], I want to grow
So much that there is to know
Questions waiting to be asked
My thoughts begin to flow

Wider than the greatest sea
Torah is infinity
So how is it that I can grasp
And touch divinity?

A present, an inheritance
To each and every Jew
I can learn and comprehend
Go out and teach it too
If you know aleph pass it on
Reach out apply it too
Never underestimate
The power within you

Tune in Time in JGU
With a special touch
Filled with love I'd never dream
That I would learn so much

Learn it, love it
Live it, teach it
Torah never ends
I'll take the knowledge that I've gained
And pass it on to friends

WE DEDICATE THIS SONG WRITTEN BY

Chana Ahuva Mandella

IN HONOR OF HER BECOMING A

Bas Mitzvah

ON MARCH 22, 2018 - NISAN 6, 5778

FROM HER LOVING PARENTS, ARYEH NACHUM AND ESTHER MANDELLA

"Chana, you are our light!"

COME SING ALONG
Composed by Chana Ahuva Mandella

Everyone can wake up with a tear
But not everyone can fight off all their fear
It takes a hero, takes a friend
To make the whole world understand
That this is a fight worth fighting for

It is a life worth living for
So we will fight it to the end
When *Golus* dies, and we all win

When *Moshiach* is here, and we are in the *Beis Hamikdash!*
Come on sing, come on dance, we will win!
Come sing along, to the song!
We will win, we will win!
Golus say goodbye, we will win, we will win!

Come sing along, to the song!
Come on old and come on young
Here is a song that's not been sung
We will sing it in harmony together
Forever more

QUENCH YOUR THIRST

Racheli Jacks for JGR 2007 ©
Recording by Chaviva Tarlow

In a barren desert, thirsty and dry
A basic essential, even money can't buy
Fresh sparkling water, pouring from on high
Let's go and get some, you and I

Chorus
Quench your thirst
Take it drop by drop
Quench your thirst
Make sure not to stop

Water is Torah
Sparkling and true
Helping us to lead our life as a Jew

Na-na-na-na… *Eimasai*
Na-na-na-na… *Kossi Mar*
Sharing the wellsprings with everyone
Then *Moshiach* will surely come

Chorus

CREATING CONNECTION

Racheli Jacks for JGR Summer 2010 ©
Recording by JGR Staff

Infinite connections, wiring to our soul
Linking our network, one nation as a whole

Texting to all who are out there
What a plan – you can purify the air

Torah is unique
Of *Emes*, it does speak
With letters that get better
When their meaning you do seek

Just look at the design
There's a reason for each line
Reflecting a wisdom divine
Histakel Be'Oraissa Uvara Alma
[*הסתכל באורייתא וברא עלמא]

With letters, He created the whole world
A universe so intricate
We're elevating bit by bit
We are the builders – leading the way

Creating connections
Revealing the "Aleph" ["א"]
From "*Golah*" to "*Geulah*"

*G-d looked into the Torah and created the world. -Midrash

STRETCH OUT YOUR HAND

Racheli Jacks for Jewish Girls Retreat ©

As baby Moshe floated in a basket down the Nile, Hashem delivered him to safety at the shore. While Miriam watched over her brother from afar, Batya — the daughter of Pharaoh — drew the child from the water, as the name she gave him — Moshe — indicates.

When Batya descended to the water's edge to bathe (or according to another opinion, to immerse for conversion to the Jewish faith), the baby's cries evoked her maternal compassion.

Although Moshe floated at a distance beyond the limited reach of mortal limbs, Batya stretched forth her hand in an attempt to accomplish the impossible. Hashem thereupon effected a miracle: Batya's arm extended so she could draw the child close. She demonstrates for all future generations the power and value of a person's effort. We need only try our best, stretch out our hand, and Hashem will take care of the rest.

Stretch out your hand
'Cause all it takes is one good deed
Stretch out your hand

And try to think what others need

An action so small
Seems like nothing at all
Yet it's the pivotal turn
That makes a difference to the world

Chorus
Oh-oh-oh
Reach out, and lend a hand
Compromise and understand
Remember to try your best
And know that *Hashem* will do the rest

There's nothing that you cannot do
Ask – your friends have ideas too
Negotiate and delegate
Hashem will help – do it all the way!

🎧 SPREAD YOUR WINGS

Racheli Jacks for Jewish Girls Retreat ©
Recording by Chaviva Tarlow
To the tune of Ve'haya Machanecha Kadosh by the
Miami Boys Choir

Flustered, ashamed
Oh, what could she gain
Her wings weigh heavily behind her
But on second thought
She's no longer distraught
Discovering that she has the power to fly

And her wings help her soar higher
As she rises ever higher
Not a burden but a gift from above
Telchi Mechoyil El Choyil
[*תלכי מחיל אל חיל]

For us too
Each and every Jew
Hashem gave us a special connection
Torah and *Mitzvos* done with love
Help us rise to our Father Above

And our wings help us soar higher
As we rise ever higher
Not a burden but a gift from above
תלכי מחיל אל חיל

And our wings help us soar higher
As we rise ever higher
Al *Kanfei Nesharim* [על כנפי נשרים]
On eagle's wings, we'll fly straight to *Yerushalayim*

*Go from strength to strength.

🎧 WARMING OUR WORLD

Racheli Jacks for JGR 2010 ©
Recording by Chaviva Tarlow

Warming the whole world
With a meaningful thought
Each Jew is a land of treasures
The Baal Shem Tov taught (x2)

Discover, reveal
Where the beauty lies
Warmth melts down the ice
Hidden talents rise

Chorus
Find your passion – keep it lit
In Torah, all good things do fit
With joy and love, enthusiasm too
There's no limit to what you can do

The fire of Torah keeps us warm
Its strength can conquer every storm
Let's unite
Warm up the night
Our Holy Land is now in sight

Neshama Raquel Sari

We are so proud of you and all that you have accomplished. You are our Light and our Song of Inspiration!

Neshama'le,

The day I dreamed about you, I knew within my *Neshama*, that in my mind I was in the *Shamayim* and I reached out for you and you chose to go with me. I am so grateful for the wisdom of *Hakadosh Baruch Hu*, our holy Creator, for the matchmaking he does between children and parents. A child chooses their parent before coming into this world I am so glad you chose me to be your *Emah*. I remember the first time you called me *Emah* and I never taught you to say it.

I still walk around every day feeling the weight of your adorable little body clinging to my shoulders, sitting in my lap, and holding my hand because to me it was just a moment ago. But at this moment you are no longer a small child you have become an incredible young woman. A daughter for whom any mother would be proud. You are my gift whom I am so thankful to parent.

Each person is sent down to this world in order to fulfill a specific Divine task, to carry out on Earth a lofty, heavenly purpose. *Hashem* endows each person with unique talents and attributes necessary to fulfill this task. These talents cry out within each person, demanding to be expressed and to fulfill the mission for which they were sent to this world.

From a small child you were singing, dancing, and making art and music. You would read for hours when you were still in a highchair and in these books a journey into the imagination would begin. A sparking of your intellect while satisfying your adventurous spirit is the real reason you still sit with books for hours, and up you go, suddenly drawing and creating music from the words you read, telling the stories of *Hashem's* goodness and light.

You were finding your voice, your song, your expression and your light to shine. Here you are a extremely talented girl, singing and dancing the at the sea like Miriam, shining your light like Sarah *Imeinu*, and expressing yourself like Devorah sitting under the tree, because you like doing things by the rules to bring only *kedusha* of *Hashem* into this world. You are already making a huge influence on the world and those around you. You are my teacher and I am so very proud of you. May you always be in harmony, a blessing and a light.

Love, Emah

🎧 YOU ARE THE LIGHT

Written and composed by Neshama R. Sari

The dark is more than dark
The light is more than light
When together
The light shines brighter than the eyes
can see

You are the light
The darkness seems very strong
But you are stronger!

In a room, darkened with unkind
You walk in shining bright
And you make the change

Chorus
'Cause the forces surrounding you
Trying to push away the light
Yet you stand there
With a bright smile on your face
Leading someone's hardships out of
the dark
You are the light

You are more than a girl
A girl's soul is more than a soul
It is a piece of *Hashem* our Creator

You are the candle
But the burn doesn't hurt
It warms up the heart

In a room, darkened with unkind
You walk in shining bright
And you make the change

Chorus

🎧 THE DAY OF MOSHIACH

Written and composed by Neshama R. Sari

Chorus
This is the day of *Moshiach*
Nations united

For all the days to come
Remember the day of *Moshiach*
We're coming to go home
Not gonna go away

Nightfall of song and joy
All of the world is out celebrating
Communicating with those we've lost
So send the joy at last
And the moon is, so telling
Jewish history overwhelming
It's a special time for all
A special time to call

And the day we've all been
Waiting for is finally here
There's a fragrance in the air
Try not to disappear

Chorus

Meanwhile at the *Beis Hamikdash*
Jews in line with the their hopes unsettled
They're rejoining those we've lost
To turn us sad to joy
The mood is so happy
Its extraordinary
Until our missing friends appears
We're not quite in the clear
We're coming to go home, try not to disappear

Chorus (2x)

Bechol Derochecho De'eihu

[*בכל דרכיך דעהו]

Yes there really exists a place
Where heaven and earth meet
It's here, and now, we'll show you how
This oasis you can achieve
This oasis you can achieve

Chorus

*Know G-d in all your ways. -Proverbs 3:6

HEAVEN ON EARTH

Racheli Jacks for JGR 2007 ©
Recording by JGR Choir

Does there really exist a place
Where heaven and earth meet?
It's here and now, we'll show you how
This oasis you can achieve

Each *Mitzvah* – good deed – is a piece from above
Which we do down here below
Revealing G-dliness hidden within
The earth will sparkle and glow
The earth will sparkle and glow

Chorus
We can bring down heaven
Heaven on earth
Through our actions, our *Mitzvos*
Everywhere we go, everything we do

WELCOME TO OUR GARDEN

Racheli Jacks for JGR 2008 ©
Recording by JGR Staff

Welcome to our garden
Its beauty so divine
The grass is green, the flowers thrive
Each plant its own design

Come and join our team
Where we each do our part
Bringing heaven down to earth
A stunning piece of art

To make this happen
We must have a plan
With each of our good deeds
We're planting little seeds

Our souls we are nurturing

Making this world evergreen
Where G-dliness is seen

Now look, the trees are starting to bear fruit
With each of our good deeds
Removing all the weeds
Our world we're nurturing

Geulah revealed soon
Our garden in full bloom
With *Hashem's* help, reap and sow
Ready, set, grow!

LIGHTS, CAMERA, ACTION

Racheli Jacks for JGR 2009 ©

Lights, Camera, Action
What an attraction
[CAMP NAME] -- We're in for a blast

A summer vacation
What a sensation
Design with vision
That's our task

Hashem's holy light does shine
It's our mission to reveal and refine
Working as a [CAMP NAME] team
Let's develop our dream

[BUNK NAME] focus and zoom
We'll see the *Mikdash* real soon
Snap into action high speed
It's time for *Moshiach* to lead

FINDING DIRECTION

Racheli Jacks for JGR 2015 ©

Finding direction
GPS* points out the way
Avodah Shebalev
Each and every day
Words mapped out
To polish our heart and mind
Forming connections
One of a kind

Chorus
Live the message
Journey and reach the goal
Prayer - stems from our soul

Throughout history
Our nation knew we'd always be

Safe with – "*Shema*" at our side
Take each word along with you
Make it part of all you do
You'll be happy
Shining from inside

Let us grow and connect
Recognize and reflect
Tefillah will at last
Unite us worldwide!

Here GPS stands for Global Prayer System

TATTY

To the tune of With a Tehillim
Composed by Miriam Rav-Noy & her
daughter Chani Rav-Noy

Dedicated in memory of our dear
Tatty, Rabbi Ariel Rav-Noy ben
Shaaltiel Zeev
Yartzeit: 8 Shevat

A special *Shliach* our Tatty was
So very caring and full of love
A sensitive *Neshama*, he felt others pain
Everyone turned to him without shame

A devoted husband and father too
He loved his children, he loved every Jew
He knew so much Torah and *Chassidus* by heart
Oy *Hashem*, how did You pull us apart?

Chorus #1
Tatty, oy Tatty we miss you!
How are we to continue?
To guide us, to learn with us, and pull us through
Oy Tatty, we really need you!

We miss your smiles, we miss your embrace
We miss father learning
And slurpees to taste
Your trips and your pranks made life so much fun
Oy Tatty, you're second to none!

Chorus #2
Tatty, oy Tatty we miss you
How long can this *Golus* continue?
We're doing lots of *Mitzvos*
We're making you proud
"*Ad Mosai*" we're shouting out loud!

We know any moment we'll see you again
The *Beis Hamikdash, Hashem* will descend
We'll cry from joy, reuniting with you
במהרה בימינו

MOMMA

by Malkie Peiser, a JGU Member
This is dedicated to my mother and other
hard working mothers around the world.

Momma, you are wisdom of light
You help brighten the night
You took away my fears
You always wiped away my tears

CHORUS
"Momma, Momma, you taught me what I need to do
Momma, Momma, don't leave because I love you, oooh

Oh Momma, you showed me the path I need to know
You are the heart that's shining brightly through my soul
Hug me close, hold me tight, and don't you cry
I'll forever cherish you, dear Momma of mine

CHORUS

My child, you define me by my true essence
You give me the strength to leap through challenges
You give me hope, give me laughter, give me life
You give me the chance to blossom and shine

CHORUS

Forever you will be my child
Even though you are sometimes wild
Like flowers dancing - like lilies
Laughing tons - as much as daisies

CHORUS

Momma, thank you for your true words
I will cherish this all my years
We're the spark to illuminate and bring *Geulah*
We conquer and break away all bad
To bring *Moshiach Tzidkeinu*, at last"

CHORUS

Momma, Momma, Momma, Momma (x2)

CHAPTER 2:
Shabbos

It's Friday afternoon; the sun begins its golden descent, ushering an unparalleled serenity into the chaotic world, elevating the cosmos to a dimension of holiness, renewal, and healing. The weekly redemption of *Shabbos Kodesh* has arrived. It's the coveted privilege of the Jewish woman, in fact, one of her three special *Mitzvos*, to herald it in with her candlelight. She thereby illuminates her home, the nucleus of Jewish life, and furthermore dispels the spiritual darkness in the world as a whole.

The Lubavitcher Rebbe, of righteous memory, encouraged young ladies from the age of three and up to kindle a *Shabbos* candle every week, for every single one of us has an integral role to play in lighting up our corner of the world. With each Friday light, a Jewish woman or girl connects as another link in the golden chain of our heritage, stretching back to our first Matriarch, Sarah, whose "Sabbath lamps" miraculously "were never extinguished."

Allow your senses to be immersed in every detail of the rich experience: the enticing scent of the candle, the feel of the slender matchstick, the alluring glow of the flame and the whisper of your blessing. Use your intimate time secluded with your Creator, to reflect and praise, to dream and pray for any of your needs and others.

QUESTIONS TO CONSIDER:

What is your favorite Shabbos song and why? How does song enhance your Shabbos?

ONE MORE LIGHT

Rivka Leah Popack for JGU One More Light Launch 2016 ©

**Dedicated to every girl and woman
and each one's ONE MORE LIGHT**

Did you hear the story told?
As each soul comes to this world
It answers the purpose of creation

Do you believe that it could be
A single soul, like you or me
Could change the world and all we see forever?

Plant a seed and watch it grow
Drop a stone, the ripples flow
Farther than you'd ever know

The sea is vast, the ocean's wide
But greater is your will inside
A simple act can change the tide

Chorus
Yes, I believe like the sunrise each day
You light up the world each time that you pray
I believe like a flame burning bright
You shine through the darkness with each Friday light
A moment the world is waiting for
For you and your one more
Your one more light, your one more light (x2)

Reach within to find your art
The colors that define your heart
Each of us can paint our part

Inspire me; I'll inspire you
You'll hit a wall; I'll pull you through
Heart and soul in everything we do

A million beats of a million hearts
Flames collide and outshine the stars
One melody with a thousand parts

Chorus
*Sheker Hachein Vehevel Hayofi
Isha Yirat Hashem He Tit'halal
T'nu La Mipri Yadeha
Vi'yhaleluha Beshe'arim Maseha*

שֶׁקֶר הַחֵן וְהֶבֶל הַיֹּפִי]
אִשָּׁה יִרְאַת־ה׳ הִיא תִתְהַלָּל
תְּנוּ־לָהּ מִפְּרִי יָדֶיהָ
[*וִיהַלְלוּהָ בַשְּׁעָרִים מַעֲשֶׂיהָ

Yes, I believe like the sunrise each day
We'll light up the world each time that we pray
I believe like a flame burning bright
We shine through the darkness with each Friday light

A moment the world is waiting for
Let us light just one more
Just one more light, just one more light
Just one more light, just one more light

I believe, like the sunrise each day
We'll light up the world

*Charm is false and beauty is futile; a G-d-fearing woman is to be praised. Give her of the fruit of her hands, and her deeds will praise her in the gates. -Proverbs 31:30-31

🎧 A YOUNG BOY

Chaya Aydel Lebovics ob"m
To the Tune of Keili Atah
Recording by Chaviva Tarlow

A young boy holds a full cup in his hand
Reciting words he can barely understand
But on his face there shines a joyful light
He is making *Kiddush* Friday night

"Father, Father, please join in with me
Father, Father, I'm lonely, can't you see?
Let's *Daven* together, that is my dream"
Veheisheiv Leiv Avos Al Banim
[*והשיב לב אבות על בנים]

A young girl holds a candlestick so bright
Preparing to light
Her candle Friday night
Her mother is watching with tears in her eyes
Her daughter turns to her and cries

"Mother, Mother, please join in with me
Mother, Mother, I'm lonely, can't you see?
Let's light together, that is my dream"
והשיב לב אבות על בנים

Throughout the world, children pure and true
Are teaching *Mitzvos* to every single Jew
Their parents are learning, and they are so proud
Then together we will all cry out loud
"Father, Father, when will the *Geulah* be?
Father, Father, we're lonely, can't you see?

Please send *Moshiach* and fulfill our dream"
והשיב לב אבות על בנים

*He will return the hearts of the fathers through the children.
-Malachi 3:24

🎧 AS THE SUN IS SETTING LOW

Melody composed by Robin Garbose ©
Lyrics by Chaviva Tarlow and Menucha Levin
Recording by Chaviva Tarlow

As the sun is setting low
The *Shabbos* candles light aglow
I welcome in the *Shabbos* Queen
And with her, a feeling serene

Chorus
Lighting the candles so bright
It has so much power in this dark night
Touching my soul down deep within
What a special gift G-d has given

Connecting a nation so vast
One family united at last
A bond that can never break
The power that one small candle can make

Shabbos candles' special light
I'll kindle them each Friday night
The blessing I'll thank You above
For giving this *Mitzvah* with love

Chorus

DEDICATED TO OUR BELOVED EMA

Mrs. Gittel Laber שתחי'

Dear Ema,

Although we didn't hear you sing that much growing up, we know how much you loved listening to our singing and the singing in *shul* on *Shabbos* and *Yom Tov*. Your speaking voice was always and still is soothing to listen to and we benefit from your wisdom and advice all the time. Your voice brings harmony to the home.

We love you!

Love,

Moshe & Esther, Avraham & Nechama Dina, Uri & Bassie, Yossi & Malkie, Shmuli & Sorah Leah, Moishe & Dena, Shimon & Chanie, Menachem & Nechama, Rochel & Eli

How soothing is your voice

A loving and kind word always on your tongue

Reacting calmly to stressful situations

Moving mountains, having an impact on another

Opening your heart

Never expecting any honor

You are truly special!

FROM MY HEART

By Sorah Leah Eber

As I watch you light
The candles Friday night
With covered eyes you begin to pray
I wonder what you say

Another busy week's gone by
You handled it with grace
Although your day so busy
You always give your children space

You may not always see the results
Or hear my voice of thanks
But I'm forever grateful
You instilled within me honesty, respect, and faith

Chorus:
You laugh with me, you cry with me
You share in all my smiles
Through dirty dishes stacked so high
And laundry waiting in piles

At times I'm sad
But your words make me glad
You know what life is all about
I sing with thanks to you from my heart.

Lighting my own candle
I thank *Hashem* for all you do
I pray that I'll be a source of *Yiddishe Nachas* to you

Welcoming the *Shabbos* Queen
The home is warm and snug
Your eyes twinkle proudly
As we share our *Shabbos* kiss and hug

Chorus

ONE PEACEFUL FRIDAY NIGHT

To the Tune of Mikolos Mayim Rabim
Recording by Chaviva Tarlow

One peaceful Friday night
The table decked in white
The gloom and darkness of *Golus*
Seemed lost in the candlelight

Entranced by the brilliant glare
The young boy pondered and stared
He dreamed of a world of *Kedushah*
Where *Shabbos* is kept everywhere

Chorus
With *Zemiros* and learning, and bright candles burning
My weekly *Nechama* lifts up my *Neshama*
For *Shabbos Hayom LaHashem* [*שבת היום לה']
We are so different from them

We raise up our voices, the whole world rejoices
Shema Koleinu, Hashem Elokeinu
[**שמע קולנו, ה' אלוקינו]

With zeal and desire, each week we strive
To keep this tradition alive
Because we're the *Am Segulah*
An *Am* of Torah and *Kedusha*
If only we'd all keep the *Shabbos*
We'd surely bring the *Geulah*

As the candles dwindle in size
Tear drops form in my eyes
A feeling of sadness surrounds me
As the flame flickers and dies

Chorus

A ray of hope still remains
In a world filled with darkness and pain
Each week light will shine through the darkness
And Shabbos Hamalka will reign

*Today is a Sabbath to G-d.
**Lord, our G-d, hear our voice.

🎧 AVENGE OUR BOYS

Lyrics by Saralaya Perl for JGR's Follow the Flame ©
To the tune of Believers by Moshe Hecht
Recording by JGR campers

In memory of Naftali Frenkel, Gilad Shaer, and Eyal Yifrah, HY"D.

What can we do? What can we say?
Our hearts bleed as one; our hearts cry as one
What should we do? What should we say?
The battle ended, the storm has started

This pain does not bring on uncertainty
Doesn't halt our resolution
Seeped in our souls, now bursting forth
A flood of sorrow, a flooding River
Why?

A pain so real, the answer so a part of me
The light they held will burn for all eternity
We will light our candles to guide *Moshiach* here
To guide our boys, to bring our boys home once more

Chorus
A task so real, the mission so a part of me
Our Shabbos lights will burn for all eternity
Then today we'll see them marching proud and tall
When Gilad, Eyal, and Naftali will greet us all

What can we do? What can we say?
Do we forsake our unity?
What should we do? What should we say?
Cast aside our eternal faith?
Three boys sewed a nation into a whole
Linked together, tied together
In memory, we will beat defeat
When we stand as one, united as one

A pain so real, the answer so part of me
The light they held will burn for all eternity
We will light our candles to guide *Moshiach* here
To guide our boys, to bring our boys home once more

Chorus

Sing with me, join our vow in the melody

The light they held will burn for all eternity
We will light our candles to guide *Moshiach* here
To guide our boys, to bring our boys home once more

🎧 GUIDING LIGHT

Lyrics by Saralaya Perl for the JGR Movie Follow the Flame ©
Music by Shimon Biton
To the tune of Mitzvah Haba'ah by Tmimim Boys Choir

Dear guest, come inside, enjoy this *Shabbos* night,
Here you are welcomed by the candle light
We're honored you are here, to beckon *Shabbos* near
Our shadows now we'll ignite (x2)

Shabbos night, the flame burns so bright, candle light,
to greet you to our home tonight (x2)

Burning, for the light, for the light
Our yearning, for the light, for the light (x2)

Take it in now, feel the warmth surround you

Shabbos night, the flame burns so bright, candle light,
to greet you to our home tonight (x2)

One flame stands alone, it's magnetic light aglow
It speaks to our soul, guiding is it's goal
The pull is so strong, a lamp to lead us on
The darkness turned into dawn

One flame stands alone, it's magnetic light aglow
It speaks to our soul, guiding is it's goal
The pull is so strong, a lamp to lead us on

The darkness turned into dawn

Shabbos night, the flame burns so bright, candle light,
to lead you to your home tonight (x2)

Burning for the light, for the light
Our yearning for the light, for the light (x2)

Take it in now, feel the warmth surround you

Shabbos night, the flame burns so bright, candle light,
to lead you to your home tonight (x2)

🎧 SHLOIME'LE

Composed by CGI Detroit Staff
Recording by Chaviva Tarlow

It was after the meal on Friday night
The house was filled with *Shabbos* light
At the candles stare a boy of three
He watches the *Lichtelach* lovingly

Suddenly a cry was heard
The candles tipped, his hand was burned
It left on him a scar so deep
A memory he knew he'd always keep

At five years old he was taken away
From the *Derech* of Torah he did stray
Taken to the army as captive
As a Jew, he could not live

His parents *Davened* for him each night

That the KGB he'd be able to fight
Their *Mesiras Nefesh* was burning strong
How long will it last, *Hashem* how long?
His father's *Emunah* would never dim
He continued teaching his *Talmidim*
Spreading the warmth of *Yiddishkeit*
Till the ominous sound of a knock one night

To Siberia, he was forced to go
But still in the icy winds and snow
He continued his work that was forbidden
In a small, cold shack that was much hidden

He gathered men, they sat and learned
In each, the flame of *Bitachon* burned
One Friday night, there deep in thought
A soldier barged in; the *Chossid* was caught

In a rage, the soldier lifts his arm
He's stopped by the *Chossid's* cry of alarm
The *Chossid* sees the scar within
Memories flash before him

He starts to hope, "How could it be
My only son returning to me?
Oy vey, *Hashem*, what have they done?
Shloimele, Shloimele, you are my son."

IF I WOULD HAVE THE MIGHT
To the tune of Mikolos Mayim Rabim
Recording by Chaviva Tarlow

If I would have the might

I would run into the night
And I would scream
"*Shabbos, Shabbos, Shabbos, Shabbos!*"
Shabbos, Shabbos, Shabbos, Shabbos
Shabbos, Shabbos, Shabbos, Shabbos
Shabbos Hayom LaHashem
[*שבת היום לה']

*Today is a Sabbath to G-d.

JUST ONE SHABBOS
Mordechai Ben David ©
Album: The English Collection

The Western Wall on Friday night
His first time ever there
Strapped into his knapsack
With his long and curly hair
He stood there for a while, broke out with a smile
Emotion, overwhelming joy, with tears

The men were dancing there
Their hearts so full of love
They sang such happy tunes, to thank the One Above
For showing them the way, for giving them a day
Rest, rejoice, with peace of mind, to pray

Chorus
Just one *Shabbos*, and we'll all be free
Just one *Shabbos*, come and join with me
Let's sing and dance to the sky
With our spirits so high
We will show them all, it's true
Let them come and join us, too (x2)

I said, "Hello, my friend; you seem to be amused"
He said, much more than that, "I am a bit confused
I know I am a Jew, I was *Bar Mitzvah* too
But *Shabbos*, in our home, who ever knew?"

He asked to join with us, to understand and see
He spent some time with us, in total ecstasy
Next *Shabbos* came along; his feelings grew so strong
He first began to feel that he belonged

Chorus

He found his treasure, made some changes in his life
A brand-new family, his children and his wife
They learn new things each day, to live the Torah way
The message of the *Shabbos* they will relay

Now, every Friday night, they go down to the Wall
Invite some people home, and they will tell them all
We'll teach you this new song, so join and sing along
Soon we'll all be free, it won't be long

Chorus

🎧 I'M BIG GEDALIAH GOOMBER

Suki & Ding ©
Album: I Remember That!

I'm big Gedaliah Goomber
I'm not exactly small
But really, not so very big
Just seventeen feet tall
I'm rigged for working

CONGRATULATIONS ON THE WONDERFUL WORK.

MAY IT BRING US TO THE ULTIMATE LIGHT OF MOSHIACH!

Leah & Yitzchok Gniwisch

For that, I'm very fit
Six days a week, I'm at it
On the seventh day, I quit

Chorus
Ain't gonna work on Saturday
Ain't gonna work on Saturday
Even double, triple pay
Won't make me work on Saturday
Ain't gonna work on Saturday
It's *Shabbos Kodesh*

I turned to deep-sea diving
And took an awful chance
On a sunken steamer's deck
I got caught by my pants
And trapped beneath the ocean, I couldn't set me free
But, I got home for *Shabbos*
And I dragged the ship with me

Chorus

I once was an explorer
To Africa, I went
One *Shabbos*, hungry lions
Came roaring 'round my tent
My assistant grabbed my rifle
"Go Goomber, shoot those pests"
Instead, they were invited
To be my *Shabbos* guests

Chorus

I once helped raise a building

And on the hundredth floor
I was carrying a load of bricks
An easy ton or more
And here, it's late on Friday
I knew I'd have to stop
So I yelled, "Watch out below!"
And I let the whole thing drop

Chorus

At driving a locomotive
I thought I'd take a crack
I had the throttle out
Just zooming down the track
And suddenly, it's *Shabbos*
The sun's about to set
So, I dived into a mud hole
And the train is running yet

Chorus

I worked down in a coal mine
And lost myself alright
I couldn't tell the days
Because there was no light
So I set myself to digging
As fast as you may please
And, I popped up in an hour
Where the people speak Chinese

Chorus

I dress my best on *Shabbos*
Three meals, I feast me fine

I make a royal *Kiddush*
On a barrel full of wine
And when I sing my *Zemiros*
For a thousand miles, they know
I'm gonna enjoy my *Shabbos*
'Cause *Hashem* has told me so

🎧 BLESS US ALL

Tzivia Kay ©
Arranged by Igor Mescoi
Album: Tell Me Why?

Chorus
Hashem bless us all
Dear G-d, bless the world
So we should find our home
Bless our souls (x2)

I'm sipping my coffee; it's 7 AM
It's Friday morning,
Thank you, *Hashem*
The kids are still sleeping
And there is no school
Mid-winter vacation
And the men are at *Shul*

Chorus

Shabbos is coming at 4 PM
TGIF*, I'm not a man
There's lots of work around the house
Hashem give me strength
Before I'm knocked out

Chorus

I'm sipping my coffee; it's 7 AM
Don't know where to start
But I'm thankful I am
I hear the clock ticking
It's calling my name
But I turn to You
And continue to pray

Chorus
Hashem bless us all
Dear Father, bless the world
So we should find our home
Bless our souls (x2)

*TGIF stands for "Thank G-d It's Friday."

🎧 SHABBOS IS COMING

Suki & Ding ©
Album: Uncle Moishy and the Mitzvah Men, Volume 5

Shabbos is coming; we're so happy
We're gonna sing and shout out loud
Six days a week we wait for *Shabbos*
A gift from *Hashem*, and we're so proud

So, let's shout together, "*Shabbos!*"
Whisper together, "*Shabbos!*"
Let's sing together, "*Shabbos!*"
Tell it to the world, "*Shabbos!*"

SHABBOS IS ALMOST HERE

Rebbetzin Tap ©
Album: Shabbos & Holiday Collection

You don't have the time to doze
When you're folding all the clothes
Shabbos is almost here
This is not the time to *Plotz*
When you're scrubbing out the pots
Shabbos is almost here

Chorus
Gotta clean, gotta clean
Gotta clean gotta get ready
Shabbos is almost here (x2)

No delaying anymore
When you're mopping up the floor
Shabbos is almost here
Got to go out in a flash
When you're taking out the trash
Shabbos is almost here

Chorus

There's no saying you're not able
When you're setting up the table
Shabbos is almost here
It is not the time to rest
While you finish getting dressed
Shabbos is almost here
Chorus

Gotta sing, gotta sing
Gotta sing, gotta get ready
Shabbos is almost here (x2)

Gotta shout, gotta shout
Gotta shout, gotta get ready
Shabbos is almost here
Gotta clap, gotta clap
Gotta clap, gotta get ready
Shabbos is almost here

Gotta dance, gotta dance
Gotta dance, gotta get ready
Shabbos is almost here
Gotta spin, gotta spin
Gotta spin, gotta get ready
Shabbos is almost here

Gotta run, gotta run
Gotta run, gotta get ready
Shabbos is almost here
Gotta jump, gotta jump
Gotta jump, gotta get ready
Shabbos is almost here

Gotta go, gotta go
Gotta go, gotta get ready
Shabbos is almost here
See you soon, see you soon
See you soon, see you next time
'Cause *Shabbos* is almost here

🎧 I FEEL SHABBOS

Rebbetzin Tap ©
Album: Shabbos & Holiday Collection

I feel *Shabbos*, almost *Shabbos*
And the whole world is coming alive
Erev *Shabbos*, my *Neshama* is ready to revive

Cooking chicken, time is tickin'
Smells of *Shabbos* are filling the air
Making *Shabbos*, I am practically without a care

See the *Imas* taking their kids to *Gan*
See the *Abbas* heading off to work

Ironing the shirts
Whipping up desserts
Pruning the bouquet
Such a holy day

I love *Shabbos*, almost *Shabbos*
I can work on my scrubbing technique
Erev *Shabbos*, the most wonderful time of the week

I hear *Shabbos*, sounds of *Shabbos*
Checking lettuce will get us to sing
Erev *Shabbos*, making music out of everything

Table setting, potatoes shredding
As we're helping our *Imas* prepare
Erev *Shabbos*, I can hear the toilet paper tear

See the people putting their *Cholent* on
What *Cholent*, where?
Who can that *Shabbos* queen be?
Which, what, where, who?

Mopping all the floors
Muktzeh in the drawers
Taking out the trash
Think I'm gonna crash

I love *Shabbos*, nearly *Shabbos*
It's a sweetly, completely unique
Erev *Shabbos*, the most wonderful time of the week

🎧 CHALLAH, CHALLAH!

Rebbetzin Tap ©
Album: Shabbos & Holiday Collection

What is that delicious smell?
Something baking I can tell
Could it be our favorite treat?
Homemade *Challah*, love to eat

Chorus
Challah, Challah, sing it with me la, la, la
Challah, Challah, takes us through *Havdala*

Raisin, poppy, sesame
Every kind tastes good to me
White wheat, whole wheat, even spelt
Put it in your mouth and watch it melt

Chorus

Rounded, braided, make a heart
Any shape you can impart
As long as it's not made of clay
Tastes like *Challah* anyway

Chorus

Shabbos table is all set
Is the *Challah* ready yet?
Daven, Kiddush, could it be?
Wash and make "*Hamotzi*"

Chorus

Challah ,Challah, one more time... la, la, la
Challah ,Challah, for Melava Malka

THE CHALLAH LADY

Yitzy Erps ©
Album: Yanky and Shabbos

There's a wealthy lady
Who lives in my neighborhood
She has a cook to stock every shelf
But Wednesday night she yells "Hooray!"
And shoos the cooks away
Because she wants to bake the *Challah* herself

You can tell that baking *Challah* is her pride and joy
It's a *Mitzvah* she won't ever shirk
Smells so good that I suppose
That if you follow your nose
You will find the *Challah* Lady at work

And she kneads, kneads, kneads her *Challah* dough
The only thing she needs is *Challah* dough

Now this *Challah* Lady had a dinner to attend
With the wealthiest people in town
"Well if you want to attend,"
Said her fine and fancy friend
"Then you need, you need, you need a new gown"

But the store would only sell the gowns on Wednesday
night
The *Challah* Lady said, "I cannot go
I'll put some new lace on my wrist
To give the old gown a new twist
Like the twist I give to my *Challah* dough"

Now the *Challah* Lady went to visit Dr. Smith
And he told her she had to lose weight
He said, "Here's a nice surprise
There's a class in exercise
For the ladies every Wednesday at eight"

Now the *Challah* Lady said, "I just cannot come
But you say I am heavy so
I'll just have to put more might
Into kneading Wednesday night
So that I'll be as light as my dough"

It was summer, and the air conditioner broke down
It was a hundred degrees in daylight
Said repairman Yerachmiel
"I've begun a great new deal
I'll be selling my tools Wednesday night

"It's the only night I'll fix the air conditioning
Or you'll wait till I buy new supplies"
The *Challah* Lady then did speak
And she said, "I'll wait a week
While the heat will help my *Challah* dough rise"

Now the *Challah* Lady had a wig of lovely hair
And she wanted it handsomely brushed
But the stylist said she might
Only do it Wednesday night
But at any other time, she'd be rushed

Now the *Challah* Lady said, "I just cannot go
But my *Sheitel* needs setting, I know
So I'll just dye my wig a shade
And I'll give it a new braid
Like the braid, I give to my *Challah* dough"

Now the *Challah* Lady told me why her baking is
More important than all of these things
It's because ladies have alone
This *Mitzvah* as their own
And so when she bakes the Challah, she sings

WHEN ZAIDY WAS YOUNG

Shmuel Kunda ob"m ©

When *Zaidy* was young, he would take a ride
To visit his *Bubby* on the East Side
Each Friday morning, he traveled by trolley
To bring back some of his *Bubby's* fresh *Challah*

Chorus

She said, "Eat my *Challos; es iz gut far ahlles**
You'll feel so good if you just eat my *Challos*
If you'll eat *meiyn Challos far a hundret yor****
You will live very long, that is for sure!"

When *Zaidy* grew up and was ready to marry
He thought of those *Challos* that he used to carry
He said, "I will only take for a *Kallah*
A girl who, like *Bubby*, knows how to bake *Challah*

Chorus

It's many years later; there's no more trolley
But *Zaidy* still brings *Bubby's* freshly baked *Challah*
Each *Erev Shabbos* he takes great pride
And brings us those warm *Challos* from the East Side

Chorus

And he says, "*Essen meiyn Challos*, please eat my *Challos*
Then when you're finished, just sing '*Shir Hama'alos*'
If I bring you *Challos* far a *hundret yor*
We will both live long, and that's for sure!"

Then after *Shul*, he'd take off his *Tallis*
First, he'd say *Kiddush*, then slice the *Challos*
We each ate five pieces, and when we were done
He told us these *Challos* are just like the *Mun*

Chorus

The *Mun* had a cover, just like these *Challos*
And it was white like a new *Shabbos Tallis*
The *Yidden* ate *Mun* for just *Fartzik Yor*
But we'll eat our *Challos* a hundred or more

It is good for all.
**If you'll eat my challah for a hundred years...*

MY LIGHTS

Rivkah Krinsky ©
Composition and lyrics by Shmuel and Bentzy
Marcus

Dedicated to Chaya Pellin
May your light always shine!
Love, Devorah Barnett

I've seen my lights in a place called California
I've seen my lights down under in Australia
I've seen my lights around the world dancing
pretty
I've seen my lights crying out through your history

There's a light so pure and so golden
You know the flame in your heart that you're holdin'
Yeah, that flame can burn away the darkness
Shinin' like souls of the righteous

Chorus
Im Atem Meshamrim Neiros Shel Shabbos
Ani Mareh Lachem Neiros Shel Tziyon
[*אם אתם משמרים נרות של שבת]
[אני מראה לכם נרות של ציון]
Im Atem Meshamrim Neiros Shel Shabbos
I will show you the lights of Zion

I've seen my lights from Beijing to Cincinnati
From London to Brazil and Kentucky

From the streets of Russia cold and wintry
But I want to see the lights of my Holy City

At dawn, Jerusalem she cries
Just waiting for the sun to rise
Millions of flames now dancing all together
Let's brighten up this dark world forever

Before the sun sets on your Friday night
Let your light shine onto me
Before the sun sets on your Friday night
Come and share your flame with me

Will you let your light shine down on me?
Will you let your love shine down on me?

אם אתם משמרים נרות של שבת

אני מראה לכם נרות של ציון

If you will observe the kindling of the Shabbat lights
You will merit to see the lights of Zion

*If you keep the Sabbath lights, I will show you the lights of Zion.
-Midrash*

🎧 IM ATEM MESHAMRIM

Dovid Pearlman
Composed by Chayala Neuhaus ©
Album: Miracles

The sun sets over the clouds
As the world stands so still, not a sound
But listen carefully
You can hear the whispering
Announcing the arrival of the *Shabbos* Queen

The candles reflecting the joy
On the faces of every girl and boy
Mother prays there silently
Children sing *Lecha Dodi*
As the *Shechina* descends to fill the world with peace

Chorus
Suddenly from the dark
Comes my *Shabbos*, my spark
And its holiness lights up my soul
It's a treasure that makes me feel whole
And my spirit soars 'cause my heart feels at home

And on each Friday night
I can close my eyes tight
I can picture it so vividly

I can taste the *Geulah* so sweet
It's my time in Gan Eden my *Neshama* seeks

And as long as *Klal Yisroel* keeps the *Shabbos*
Very soon *Hashem* will also keep His promise
And on that day His candles cast their glow
We'll be on our way back home to *Yerushalayim*
Im Atem Meshamrim Neiros Shel Shabbos
Ani Mareh Lachem Neiros Shel Tziyon
[*אם אתם משמרים נרות של שבת
אני מראה לכם נרות של ציון]

The sun sets over the clouds
The world is alive, joy abounds
Listen carefully, you can hear the calling
Announcing the arrival of *Moshiach ben Dovid*

The candles are brighter than before
They will light up the world forevermore
Oh, the *Golus* has been long
But *Klal Yisroel* remains so strong
אני מראה לכם נרות של ציון

*If you keep the Sabbath lights, I will show you the lights of Zion.
-Midrash*

🎧 AMONGST THE SMILES

Sung by Chanale ©
Album: The Crown of Creation

Amongst the smiles, amongst the tears
Of my childhood's sweet and bitter years
There's a picture that my memory fondly frames
And through it shine two tiny flames

Chorus
My mother's *Shabbos* candles
They made our home so bright
Which faithfully she kindled
With a prayer on Friday night

And then around the table
We gathered as we heard
My father chant the *Kiddush*
His heart in every word

Our humble home became a mansion
In that mystic glow
Our hearts were filled with hopes and dreams
And thoughts of long ago

Chorus

And yet the tragic stories
Of Israel's darkest nights
Will never dim the glory
Of my mother's *Shabbos* lights

SHABBOS QUEEN

Sung by Chanale ©
Composed by Yocheved Reich
Album: Believer

I used to think my mother was the *Shabbos* Queen
She'd stand so regally with royal grace
And whisper to the King of the universe, *Hashem*
In a very special place behind her covered face

I know that she's not asking Him for diamonds
My noble mother doesn't ask for gold
She's asking Him to help me study in the Torah's ways
And to let her eyes behold
The joy as she grows old

Chorus
When I grow up, no matter what life brings
Hashem will give me the strength I need to handle it
And I will walk by the lights of a thousand Friday
nights
And the *Tefillos* of my mother, who always had her
candles lit

My mother turns our home into a palace
Her wisdom and her warmth both make it so
She *Bentches Licht* and I can hear her tender feelings
speak
Without any voice or words, but the kiss on my cheek

The *Shabbos* candle's light is gentle and so soft
It smooths away her worries every week
And suddenly the troubles of the past week disappear
All our fears and worries cease, in this moment of
peace.

Chorus

I think of how it hurts my mother when I'm doing
wrong,
When I do not let my good side show
But this week I decide I will make my mother proud
Because how else will she know, that I love her so
Each *Mitzvah* that I will do will be a diamond

Each smile of mine will be a precious stone
To put onto the crown she seems to wear each Friday night
And when I am fully grown, I'll wear a crown of my own.

Chorus

GREET THE SHABBOS QUEEN

Chana Yerushalmi ©

Dressed in your best to greet the *Shabbos* Queen
Peacefulness hovering over you
Lighting the *Shabbos* candles, that is so supreme
Beloved how are you to the King
Whispering that hopeful prayer to *Hashem*
Neglecting thoughts unneeded
Figuring a way to make yourself a bond
Breaking all boundaries so you can be fond

Chorus (x2)
Hashem you hear me praying on this holy day
Malachim gathering as I say
I'll devote myself wholly to you
Please accept my *Teshuva*
And I'll be cleansed

Sitting by the meal, surely holy food will heal
Broken wounds opened up during the week
At night as I lay in bed *Tehillim* I will say
Devoting my time to His commandments make me sing

IT'S TIME TO SAY GOOD SHABBOS

Abie Rotenberg ©
Album: Journeys Volume 1

The sun is going down,
It's shining through the trees
Another week's gone bye,
Become a memory
So throw away your hammer,
There's nothing left to do
Go on home and find the gift
That's waiting there for you

Chorus
Oh, it's time to say "Good *Shabbos*"
'Cause all your work is done
Gonna spend the day together with the Holy One
Say a special blessing on a cup that's filled with wine
Man and his Creator, it's a very special sign

Your candles will be burning
They'll fill your home with light
Singing songs of *Shabbos*
Well into the night
So throw away your hammer
There's nothing left to do
Go on home and find the gift
That's waiting there for you

Chorus

You can spend time with your family,

You'll study, and you'll pray,
When not wait till after *Shabbos*,
All those nails won't run away
So throw away your hammer,
There's nothing left to do
Go on home and find the gift
That's waiting there for you

Oh, it's time to say "Good *Shabbos*"
'Cause all your work is done
Gonna spend the day together with the Holy One
Say a special blessing on a cup that's filled with wine
Man and his Creator, it's a very, very, very, very, very,
very, very, very, very special sign

OPEN MY HEART

*Lyrics by Chava Meira Dunn for the 2017 JGR Movie,
At the Breaking Point ©
Music by Mirele Rosenberger
Sung by Rachel Levy*

When I was lost and down
I could not find my way around
I did not make a sound
and still, I wish I had been found

Tears in my eyes and a broken heart
I turned around to start over, over
When my eyes were closed tight
You came around and gave me sight
Your words echo in my head
I'm a Jew, I want nothing instead

Chorus
Shining, I'm shining bright
You helped me find my light
This is who I am
I can feel my soul beaming within
I can see my horizon
You gave me a hand and it opened my heart
Opened my heart

Trying, trying to do what's right
I have the power to win this fight
Nothing's gonna stop me now
I'm leaping forward you showed me how

Chorus
Shining, I'm shining bright
You helped me find my light
Shining, I'm shining bright
You helped me find my light

SHABBOS IS GOING AWAY

Suki & Ding ©
Album: Uncle Moishy and the Mitzvah Men, Volume 1
Recording by Chaviva Tarlow

Shabbos is going away
The sky's getting dark
It's the end of the day
Oh, *Shabbos* you really should know
We're sorry to see you go

But you will come back next week, we know
You will come back for we love you so
So, let us thank *Hashem*
Who will bring *Shabbos* back again

SHAVUA TOV

Shabbat Conclusion Liturgy
Franciska ©
Album: Kol Haolam

אֵלִיָּהוּ הַנָּבִיא
אֵלִיָּהוּ הַתִּשְׁבִּי
אֵלִיָּהוּ הַגִּלְעָדִי
בִּמְהֵרָה יָבוֹא אֵלֵינוּ
עִם מָשִׁיחַ בֶּן דָּוִד
שבוע טוב (x4)

Translation:
Elijah the prophet
Elijah the Tishbite
Elijah the Gileadite
May he soon come to us
with the *Moshiach*, son of David
Good week! (x4)

CHAPTER 3:
Jewish Women

The light of Sarah within you is ready to gleam. The voice of Miriam within you is yearning to sing. The strength of Esther within you is waiting to take action.

You are an invaluable link in the golden chain. Now it is your turn to sing the unique song of your soul, for it is the key to unlocking the treasures and spirits of our majestic matriarchs.

Carry on their legacy with pride. They're waiting for you to continue singing their song!

QUESTIONS TO CONSIDER:

Which Jewish woman inspires you? How can song uplift you each day?

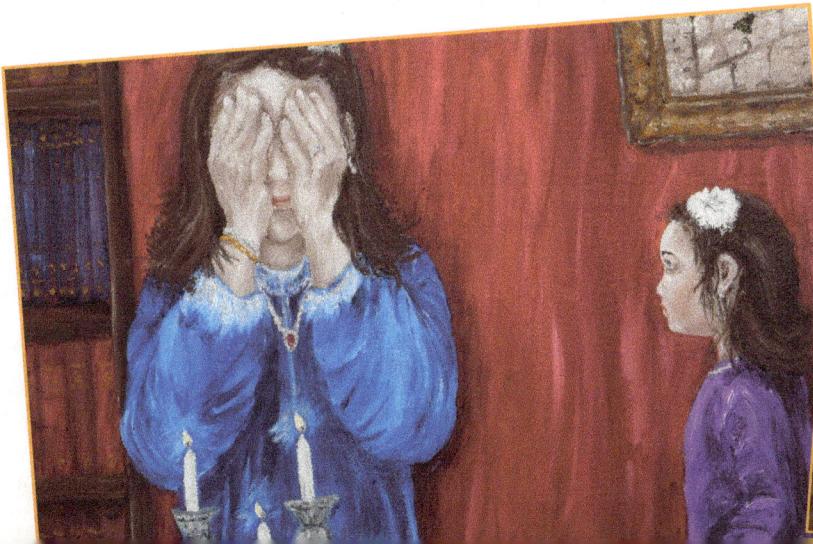

DEDICATED WITH LOVE
TO OUR PRECIOUS DAUGHTERS
Meirah, Sivan, and Lielle Schwartz

MAY YOU ALWAYS SHINE YOUR UNIQUE LIGHT AND
SING WITH GRATITUDE TO HASHEM.

Love, Mom and Dad

🎧 SHIRU L'HASHEM

by Franciska ©, Album: Kol Haolam. For more songs visit www.franciskamusic.com

וַתִּקַּח מִרְיָם הַנְּבִיאָה אֲחוֹת אַהֲרֹן אֶת־הַתֹּף בְּיָדָהּ וַתֵּצֶאןָ כָל־הַנָּשִׁים אַחֲרֶיהָ בְּתֻפִּים וּבִמְחֹלֹת.
וַתַּעַן לָהֶם מִרְיָם שִׁירוּ לַה׳ כִּי־גָאֹה גָּאָה סוּס וְרֹכְבוֹ רָמָה בַיָּם.

Translation:
Miriam, the prophetess, Aaron's sister, took a timbrel in her hand, and all the women came out after her with timbrels and with dances. And Miriam called out to them, Sing to the Lord, for very exalted is He; a horse and its rider He cast into the sea. (Exodus 15:20)

From her earliest youth, Miriam played a crucial role in Jewish history. As a child, she would help her mother Yocheved care for the newborn Jewish children in Mitzrayim. Pharaoh decreed the killing of all Jewish baby boys at birth, but Yocheved and Miriam courageously defied him. The catalyst of the Geulah, Miriam prophesized that her parents would have a baby boy, the future leader, and liberator of the Jewish people. She convinced her parents to remarry, and as a result, her brother Moshe was born.

Miriam watched over her baby brother as he drifted down the river in his mother's makeshift boat. It was Miriam who contrived the idea that her mother, a Jewish woman, would care for the infant on behalf of Batya, Pharaoh's daughter, who retrieved Moshe from the river.

And it was Miriam who encouraged the women to have faith and prepare their tambourines for the redemption. She led the women, with music and tremendous joy and praise to G-d, as they left Egypt onto freedom and experienced the splitting of the sea. On account of her sincere devotion, she became the mother of the royal house of King David, from whence Moshiach will soon come.

MIRIAM
by Leah Wolfe

Miriam, a prophet so real
Miriam, second to none, strong
Miriam cooed babies, a mother so nourishing
and kind
Miriam with faith
Tambourines ready
Miriam, full of hope, love and light
Miriam, a leader

Yes, you can do the same at full length
You have tambourines ready
You coo babies, a mother so nourishing and kind
You with faith
You, second to none, strong
You, full of light, love, and hope
You

🎧 YES, I BELIEVE
Rivka Leah Popack for Jewish Girls Unite ©
Adapted by the Tambourines Academy
Recording by Tambourines Academy

Did you hear the story told?
As each soul comes to this world
It answers the purpose of creation

Do you believe that it could be?
A single soul, like you or me
Could change the world and all we see forever

Plant a seed and watch it grow
Drop a stone, the ripples flow
Farther than you'd ever know

The sea is vast, the ocean's wide
But greater is your will inside
Geulah now, change the tide

Chorus
Yes, I believe like the sunrise each day
Moshiach will come, we'll bring him today
I believe like a flame burning bright
We'll shine through the darkness; we'll light up the
night
A moment the world is waiting for
Celebrate forevermore

Eternal light
Songs through the night
Dancing in sight
Women Unite

Reach within to find your art
The colors that define your heart
Each of us can paint our part

Inspire me; I'll inspire you
You'll hit a wall; I'll pull you through
Heart and soul in everything we do

A million beats of a million hearts
Where's your *"Tof Beyadah"*?
A new melody is about to start

Chorus

Vatikach Miriam Hanavia Et Hatof Beyadah
Vataytzena Kol Hanoshim B'Tupim Uvim'cholos
וַתִּקַּח מִרְיָם הַנְּבִיאָה אֶת־הַתֹּף בְּיָדָהּ [
[*וַתֵּצֶאןָ כָל־הַנָּשִׁים בְּתֻפִּים וּבִמְחֹלֹת:]

Chorus

Eternal light
Songs through the night
Dancing in sight
Women Unite

I believe, with my tambourine, *Bizchus Nashim...*

*Miriam, the prophetess... took a timbrel in her hand, and all the
women came out... with timbrels and with dances. -Exodus 5:20

MIRIAM'S SONG

Debbie Friedman ob"m ©
Album: Songs of the Spirit: The Debbie Friedman
Anthology

Chorus
And the women dancing with their timbrels
Followed Miriam as she sang her song
"Sing a song to the One Whom we've exalted"
Miriam and the women danced and danced the whole
night long

And Miriam was a weaver of unique variety
The tapestry she wove was one which sang our history
With every thread and every strand, she crafted her
delight
A woman touched with spirit; she dances toward the
light

Chorus

As Miriam stood upon the shores and gazed across the
sea
The wonder of this miracle she soon came to believe
Whoever thought the sea would part with an
outstretched hand
And we would pass to freedom and march to the
Promised Land

Chorus

And Miriam the prophet took her timbrel in her hand
And all the women followed her just as she had planned

And Miriam raised her voice in song
She sang with praise and might
We've just lived through a miracle
We're going to dance tonight!

Chorus

COPER MIRRORS

Lyrics by Fruma Schapiro
Produced by Ohel Chana High School, Los Angeles ©

Peer into the copper mirror
Tell me, tell me, what you see
Do you see a slave girl or one who is free?
Am I free to use my mind, follow my heart, do what is right?
Reflected in this mirror's deepest parts

In the copper mirror look into your eyes
Understand the sacred task where my identity lies
A Jewish mother I can be
Generations we will see
Reflected in this mirror's deepest parts

We know we must, with firm belief, sacred trust
A woman uplifts her home with courage and care
Let the mirror play its part
Kindle hope in aching hearts
In the face of darkness and despair

Eilu, Eilu Chavivin Olai Min Hakol
[אלו, אלו חביבין עלי מן הכל*]
I will let my mirror play its G-d-given role
Holy enduring beauty binds us to *Hashem*

Each child born is another precious gem
Our intentions pure, with copper mirrors we secure
The future of our people despite this slavery
Bizchus, Bizchus Noshim, Noshim Tzidkaniyos
[בזכות, בזכות נשים, נשים צדקניות**]
In merit of the women's bravery

Hashem will extol
חביבין עלי מן הכל
Mesiras Nefesh shining in the form of the *Kiyor*
You overcame inflicted pain
To carry on a precious chain
Your mirrors will now shine forever more

אלו, אלו חביבין עלי מן הכל
I will let my mirror play its G-d-given role
Holy enduring beauty binds us to *Hashem*
Each child born is another precious gem

Our intentions pure, with *Mesiras Nefesh* we secure
The *Geulah* of our people as we march to victory
בזכות, בזכות נשים, נשים צדקניות
In merit of the women's bravery

We know we must, with firm belief, sacred trust
A woman uplifts her home with courage and care
Let the mirror play its part
Kindle hope in aching hearts
In the face of darkness and despair

אלו חביבין עלי מן הכל, מן הכל

These are more precious to Me than anything else. -Midrash
 **In the merit of righteous women... -Talmud*

BEZCHUT NASHIM

Rivkah Krinsky ©
Composed by Shmuel Marcus
Lyrics by 8th Day, Yosi Friedman and Rivkah Krinsky

I know you although we've never met
A legacy we will not forget
A common thread since ancient times
Generations you've defined
Your image embedded in my mind

Sarah's candle's still burn bright
Rivkah's kindness brings the light
"Ko Tomar L'Veit Yaakov"
[*כה תאמר לבית יעקב]
Tell them first, they need to know
Rachel and Leah's tears are by our side

Chorus
Mothers and daughters
Who are reaching out to others
Tell them that it's up to you and me
Pharaoh and the others
Couldn't stop our holy mothers
Now we tell them that it's up to you and me

"Bezchut Nashim Tzidkaniyot Nigalu Avoteinu"
[**בזכות נשים צדקניות נגאלו אבותינו]

From old to young your story's told
Your strength and beauty forged a mold
Heroines in daily life
Our anchor in times of strife

Your courage made us who we are
Devorah tell us prophecy
Miriam lead us in melody
Souls of then are souls of now
We are one and we'll witness how
Our faith brings redemption to the world

Chorus

Daughters of Israel, can you hear me?
Esther, go and tell the king
Yehudit, save your Maccabees
Daughters of Israel, can you hear me?
Take this song for all to sing
It's our time in history

*So shall you say to the house of Jacob... -Exodus 19:3
**In the merit of righteous women our forefathers were redeemed
[from Egypt]. -Talmud

TEARS

8th Day ©
Album: Inner Flame

When the world skips a beat
Knocks you gently off your feet
That's not thunder, it's your cries
When the news comes inside
And you just want to run and hide
It's not thunder, it's your cries

Chorus
And your cries were not in vain
Small tears they link into a golden chain

Pulling down the walls that divide us
Al Eileh, Al Eileh Ani Bochiya
[על אלה, על אלה אני בוכיה*]
Sarah, Rivkah, Rochel, and Leah
Now their tears are in your eyes

When the world turns around
No one cares if you're lost or found
It's not thunder, it's your cries
And it seems no one's on your side
Pain so strong that we just can't hide
That's not thunder, it's your cries

Chorus

In your eyes, there's a strength I've never seen
In your eyes, the love is so blinding
In your eyes, the world is one blessing
In your eyes, the lost are returning (x2)
In your eyes

Chorus

Over these things I weep. -Lamentations 1:16

THE LIGHT

Shaindel Antelis ©
Album: Change

There's a song that's inside of my soul
And it follows me wherever I go
And the words, oh the words only I know
In that song, in that song inside my soul
Here's how it goes

Chorus
We are strong, we are wonderful
We can do anything even if we fall
We'll stand together and do what's right

We will spread the light
There's a dream that I have today
Is to make a difference to change the way
That we look at the world
Every woman, every girl
You are beautiful, don't need to change at all

Chorus

One little candle can light up a whole room
So keep being amazing
Oh, you'll never know just what you can do

Chorus

AVADTI

Esther 4:16
Franciska ©
Album: Adon Olam

לֵךְ כְּנוֹס אֶת־כָּל־הַיְּהוּדִים הַנִּמְצְאִים בְּשׁוּשָׁן וְצוּמוּ עָלַי וְאַל־תֹּאכְלוּ וְאַל־
תִּשְׁתּוּ שְׁלֹשֶׁת יָמִים לַיְלָה וָיוֹם גַּם־אֲנִי וְנַעֲרֹתַי אָצוּם כֵּן וּבְכֵן אָבוֹא אֶל־
הַמֶּלֶךְ אֲשֶׁר לֹא־כַדָּת וְכַאֲשֶׁר אָבַדְתִּי אָבָדְתִּי

"Go, assemble all the Jews who are present in Shushan
and fast on my behalf, and neither eat nor drink for
three days, day and night; also I and my maidens will
fast in a like manner; then I will go to the king contrary
to the law, and if I perish, I perish."

For generations, the prophetess Devorah has been an inspiration to women as an influential leader, courageous warrior, and above all, in her own words, "I arose as a mother in Israel." She was the Judge of Israel who brought peace to her people.

DEVORAH'S SONG

Debbie Friedman ob"m ©
Album: Songs of the Spirit: The Debbie Friedman Anthology

Chorus
Arise, arise Devorah
Arise, arise and sing a song
Arise, arise, Devorah

Uri, Uri, Dabri Shir
[עורי, עורי, דברי שיר*]

Devorah the prophet was a judge in Israel
She sat beneath her palm tree on a hill
And people came from everywhere
Just to hear her judgments, honest and fair
Devorah the prophet, Devorah, a mother in Israel

Chorus

Devorah the prophet was courageous, strong and wise
Her people lived in peace for forty years
The twelve tribes lived together as one
For the first time since the world had begun
Devorah the prophet, Devorah, a mother in Israel

Chorus

Arise, Devorah, arise and sing a song
Arise, Devorah, עורי, עורי, דברי שיר
עורי, עורי, דברי שיר

Devorah the prophet, a woman of fire, her torch in hand
She led the Israelites to victory
Barak said, "Devorah, I cannot fight
Unless you are standing right by my side"
Devorah the prophet, Devorah, a mother in Israel

Chorus (x2)

עורי, עורי, דברי שיר...

Praise! Praise! Utter a song. –Judges 5:12

Yaakov Avinu arrived in Charan, where he served his uncle Lavan as a shepherd for seven years, in return for Lavan's regal daughter Rachel in marriage. Rachel had an older sister named Leah, with whom she was very close. It was uncustomary in those days to wed a younger child before her older sister. Yaakov and Rachel were aware of her father's deceitfulness and foresaw his sly switch of the sisters at the wedding; thus, they established a private signal to ensure Yaakov was standing beside the right partner beneath the Chuppah.

At last, the special day arrived after a whirl of preparations and Rachel saw Lavan adorning and veiling Leah to be married. When Yaakov would discover he had the wrong bride, Leah would be humiliated. An inner battle tore Rachel's heart. Should she transmit the password to her sister, sparing her from degradation, and relinquish her own chance to be bound to her love? Compassion triumphed, and she disclosed the signal to her sister.

Generations later, the First Temple in ruins and the evicted Jewish people en route to Babylon, the exiles passed Rachel's roadside grave in tearful prayer. Their voices roused their forebears' souls on High, and each came before G-d on their children's behalf. Each was denied. Rachel stepped forward and challenged, 'Even I, a mere mortal, overcame jealousy of my rival and had compassion on her; then surely You, the ultimate Source of Compassion, can disregard Your idolatrous 'rivals' they served, and have mercy on the children!'

Her plea won Hashem over, and in reward for her superhuman effort, He promised hope for her future: her children would be redeemed and returned home.

The impact of Rachel's Tefillah stretches on and resounds just as poignantly today. "Mama Rochel, we are lost, in pain, and so very weary. You hold the key." Mama Rochel is crying for us again...

🎧 MAMA ROCHEL

Abie Rotenberg ©
Arranged and conducted by Yaakov Leib Rigler
Album: Journeys Volume 4

With the rising sun, on her wedding day
She raised her eyes to the heavens
And she thanked *Hashem*, for the man of truth
With whom she would build a nation

But with nightfall came destiny betrayed
The veil concealing another
Yet a sister's shame, not her shattered dreams
Took hold of her heart and her senses

Chorus
Mama Rochel, cry for us again
Won't you shed a tear for your dear children?
If you raise your sweet voice now as then the day will
come
Mama Rochel, cry for us again
Won't you shed a tear for your dear children?
Bizechutaich Veshavu Vonim Ligvulom
[בזכותך ושבו בנים לגבולם*]

In a roadside grave, she was laid to rest, in solitude
forever
But her voice gave hope to the broken hearts
Of her daughters and sons bound for exile

When her plaintive cry gained Divine consent
A challenge to her Maker
Can the mercy of mere flesh and blood

Run deeper than Yours, our Creator!?

Chorus

Now your voice is still as you heed the call
Of *Mini Koleich Mibechi* [מנעי קולך מבכי**]
It's our Father's will, He who made us all
Dare we ask of you to defy Him?

Yet a frightened child, numb from pain and grief
Remains forlorn and uncertain
Clinging to the faith, that it can be heard
As it cries out to its mother

Mama, Mama, *Vain Nochamol*
Trerren Zolttz Du Gissen Un A Tzohl
Beten Fun Bashefer In Himmel, B'Kol Rom
Mama, Mama, Vain Nochamol
Trerren Zolttz Du Gissen Un A Tzohl
בזכותך ושבו בנים לגבולם

Rachel Imeinu, S'ee Kolaich
Shuv Shifchi Kamayim Dimataich
B'Chi Nah Al Banim Asher Galu V'Al Sivlam
Rachel Imeinu, S'ee Kolaich
Shuv Shifchi Dimah Lifnei Konaich
בזכותך ושבו בנים לגבולם

Chorus

בזכותך ושבו בנים לגבולם...

In your merit, the children will return to their border. -Jeremiah 31:16
Restrain your voice from weeping. –Jeremiah 31:15

MAMAN, MÉMÉ ADORÉE

93 Years from Constantine to Jerusalem

Meme Rachel Allouche Bouskila ז"ל

1 CHESHVAN - 7 SHEVAT

Ma grand-mère Rachel Bouskila Allouche et moi avons partagé tellement de choses depuis ma naissance, que notre complicité était belle et franche.

Certes elle m'a donné une Mère extraordinaire mais elle m'a aussi beaucoup élevé et éduqué je pense.

Je n'ai que des merveilleux souvenirs dans ma tête et dans mon cœur. Je me souviens de sa joie de vivre permanente. Son sourire était contagieux. Son regard était sincère. C'était une personne juste. Sa générosité était sans faille. Sa disponibilité était permanente. Sa patience infaillible. Son dévouement pour autrui était constant. Sa gentillesse n'avait pas de limite. Elle apaisait les gens qui l'entourait et savait les écouter.

Son calme presque irréel parfois. Mais elle était aussi très énergique et rien ne l'arrêtait. Ni la peur, ni les intempéries, ni même les kilomètres, c'était une marcheuse aguerrie. Excellente cuisinière (d'où son surnom de Mémé Gâteau), excellente femme au foyer, excellente confidente, elle contribue encore aujourd'hui dans mes pensées à me guider et à me rendre plus fort.

Aussi je vous livre un de ses secrets: quand elle cherchait une réponse à une question oubien quand elle avait une demande particulière à a faire, elle n'hésitait pas à fermer ses yeux, à penser très fort à Hachem et à Lui parler, comme si c'était la chose la plus simple à faire !

D'après ses dires les portes s'ouvraient, les solutions apparaissaient, les montagnes se déplaçaient car Hachem lui répondait dans son sommeil. Chacun peut, s'il est sincère et bon, essayer au moins pour commencer de demander quelque chose à Hachem; je vous invite donc à en faire autant. Elle a toujours accepté et considéré mon épouse Yael comme sa petite fille, à sa juste valeur et je suis fier d'avoir avec elle quatre enfants magnifiques, que des filles à son image.

Merci Mémé pour tout ce que tu nous as transmis.

J'aimerais que tu puisses continuer encore à veiller sur notre famille. Je t'embrasse de tout mon cœur,

Je t'aime.

Affectueusement.

Ton petit fils Regis Menahem Attuil

Meme was the life of the party as she danced with the Sephardic twist at every family Simcha. She showed us how to give generously to others and would sing "Donnez Donnez - Give, Give, and G-d will give it back!"

Meme is still singing, dancing and praying from heaven for her children. May we all return home to our Holy Land, reunited with our loved ones speedily in our days.

Mémé amenait la joie de vivre avec ses dances à l'orientale dans les fêtes familiales. Elle nous a montré comment donner avec générosité tout en chantant Donnez Donnez, D.ieu vous le rendra.

Mémé est toujours en train de chanter danser et de prier du Gan Éden pour ses enfants et toute sa famille. Que D.ieu fasse que nous soyons tous réunis très bientôt avec nos chers disparus sur notre terre sainte en Israël.

🎧 MOTHER ROCHEL

Mother Rochel, please don't cry
Wipe those tears off from your eyes
Your dear children will return
Back home once again

*Mère Rachel ne pleure pas
Sèche tes larmes
Ne t'en fais pas
Tes enfants ils reviendront bientôt à la maison*

🎧 DONNEZ DONNEZ

*Composed by Enrico Macias,
a family cousin*

Donnez donnez dodo-onnez
Donnez donnez
Donnez donnez dodo-onnez
Dieu vous le rendra

RACHEL'S SONG

Rivka Leah Popack ©
Lead and backing vocals by Laiya Rothberg
Album: Silent Prayer

I sit by the river and weeping willows all alone
Waiting for the day, you'll come and take me home
A stranger in a stranger's land
A language I don't understand
Trying to find direction, where do I turn
Then I hear...

Chorus
Rachel's song
A voice that wills me to go on
Rachel's cries
Teardrops falling from the skies
Rachel's prayer lights my way

Desert winds and sandstorms hide the road beneath
Mountains stand between me and the life I want to lead
The climb's too steep; my strength won't last
I feel it's all beyond my grasp
Although I'm just a heartbeat
From where I'm meant to be
Then I hear

Chorus

I hear your dust and cobblestones calling to my heart
I've lost the voice within me; I'm strings without a harp
Land that fills my waking dreams
I'd fly to you with broken wings

A solitary songbird

Chorus

Mini Koleich Mibechi Ve'einayich Midima
Ki Yesh Sachar Lifulateich N'oom Hashem
Yesh Tikvah Le'achriteich
[מנעי קולך מבכי ועיניך מדמעה
כי יש שכר לפעלתך נאם ה'
יש תקוה לאחריתך*]

"Refrain your voice from weeping and your eyes from tears, for there is reward for your efforts," says the Lord... "and there is hope for your future."– Jeremiah 31:15-16

KOL BERAMA

Franciska ©
Album: Libi Bamizrach
Jeremiah 31:14-16

קוֹל בְּרָמָה נִשְׁמָע נְהִי בְּכִי תַמְרוּרִים
רָחֵל מְבַכָּה עַל־בָּנֶיהָ מֵאֲנָה לְהִנָּחֵם עַל־בָּנֶיהָ כִּי אֵינֶנּוּ
כֹּה אָמַר ה' מִנְעִי קוֹלֵךְ מִבֶּכִי וְעֵינַיִךְ מִדִּמְעָה
כִּי יֵשׁ שָׂכָר לִפְעֻלָּתֵךְ נְאֻם־ה' וְשָׁבוּ מֵאֶרֶץ אוֹיֵב
וְיֵשׁ־תִּקְוָה לְאַחֲרִיתֵךְ נְאֻם־ה' וְשָׁבוּ בָנִים לִגְבוּלָם

A voice is heard on high, lamentation and bitter weeping: Rachel weeps for her children; she refuses to be consoled for her children, for they are gone. So says the Lord: "Restrain your voice from weeping, and your eyes from tears, for there is reward for your efforts," says the Lord, "and they shall return from the land of the enemy. And there is hope for your future," says the Lord, "and the children shall return to their border."

VATISPALEL CHANA

Chanale ©
Album: Vatispalel Chana

On a mountain of Israel, two women are known
One walks with children, while one walks alone
Day after day turns to year after year
The burning inside turns to pain she can't bear

No words can console her; no love can replace
Her arms start to tremble, her whole body shakes
A womb oh so empty, a heart filled with pain
Her grief knows no boundaries and tears pour like rain

Vatispalel Chana [ותתפלל חנה*], she prays all the while
"Have I been forgotten; don't I get a child?
I don't ask for many, just give me one
And in return your maid Chana will give You her son"

Eli *Hakohen* watches from far
"Daughter of Israel, tell me who you are
Your whispers have traveled; your home will be blessed
So now go in peace, for He'll grant your request"

Her *Tefillos* accepted, her prayers are heard
He gives her a child; she gives Him her word
A son only borrowed, a son she won't raise
Her joy knows no boundaries, and G-d she does praise

ותתפלל חנה she turns to the sky
"*Hashem* is my Savior, *Hashem* upon high
Ein Tzur K'Elokeinu [אין צור כא-לוקינו**], Hashem,
You are One

And blessed be Your Name, for You gave me a son
And blessed be Your Name, now I give You my son"

*And Hannah prayed. –II Samuel 2:1
**There is no rock like our G-d. –II Samuel 2:2

IN MEMORY OF MY DEAR MOM,

Priscilla Jacobs OBM

WHOSE FAITH IN HASHEM, LOVE
OF YIDDISHKEIT AND DEVOTION
TO THOSE LESS FORTUNATE
IMPACTED ALL WHO KNEW HER.
MEMORIES OF HER, HER WARMTH,
AND HER KINDNESS, WILL ALWAYS
BE A BLESSING IN OUR LIVES.

BIRTHDAY, APRIL 13, 1910 -
YARTZEIT, JANUARY 9, 2009

-ED AND LAURA JACOBS

A YIDDISHE MAMEH

Melody composed by Lew Pollack ob"m ©
Lyrics by Jack Yellen ob"m

איך וויל ביי אייך א קאשע פֿרעגען, זאגט מיר ווער עס קען
מיט וועלכע טײַערע פֿארמעגען בענטשט ג־ט אלעמען
מ'קויפֿט דאָס נישט פֿאר קיינע געלט, דאָס גיט מען נאָר אומזיסט
און דאָך אז מען פֿארלירט דאָס אוי, ווי טרערן מען פֿארגיסט
א צווייטען גיט מען קיינעם ניט' עס העלפֿט נישט קיין געוויין
אוי, ווער עס האָט פֿארלוירען, דער ווייס שוין וואָס איך מיין

א ייִדישע מאַמע, עס גיבט נישט בעסער אויף דער וועלט
א ייִדישע מאַמע, אוי ווי ווי ווי ביטער ווען זי פֿעלט,
ווי שיין און ליכטיג איז אין הויז ווען די מאַמע איז דאָ,
ווי טרויעריג פֿינסטער ווערט ווען ג-ט, נעמט איר אויף עולם הבא

אין וואַסער אין פֿײַער וואַלט זי געלאָפֿן פֿאר איר קינד
נישט האַלטן איר טײַער, דאָס איז געוויס די גרעסטע זינד,
אוי ווי גליקליך און רייך איז דער מענטש וואָס האָט,
אַזא שײַנע מתנה געשײַנקט פֿון ג־ט,
נאָר איין אַלטישקע ייִדישע מאַמע
אוי מאַמע מײַן

Translation:
I'd like to ask you a question, tell me who knows
With which dear possession does G-d bless
everyone?
It cannot be bought for any money; it's given only
for free
And when it is lost, how many tears are shed
A second is given nobody; no cry can help
Oy, he who has lost it, he already knows what I
mean

A *Yiddishe Mameh*
It doesn't get better on this earth
A *Yiddishe Mameh*
How bitter it is when she is missing.
How nice and bright it is at home
when the Mameh is here
How sad and dark it becomes when G-d takes her to
the World to Come

Through water, through fire,
she would have run for her child
Not to hold her dear is surely the greatest sin
How lucky and rich is the one who has
Such a beautiful gift presented from G-d
Like an old *Yiddishe Mameh,* my *Yiddishe Mameh!*

🎧 SO MUCH TO GIVE

Shoshana Bander ©

The rooster crowed, "It's morning!"
Mommy opened her eyes
The baby started crying
She brought him by her side
Another day was born
The sun would rise and set
She'd work from dawn till dusk
Then get up and do it all again

The kettle whistled, "Coffee!"
No time to sit down for a drink
She pack all the children their lunches
Then wake each one while she'd sing
A smiling "good morning" kiss
Dress the little ones for school

Cook them a nice warm breakfast
Then write her daily list of things to do

Chorus
We want so much to give
So much to love
We want to open up our very heart and souls to you
Like a flower in the morning sun
Spreads her petals for the light
Then shines her beauty throughout the day and night

The telephone was ringing
As she drew up her lesson plan
There was a family of a new Russian immigrants
Could she possibly lend a hand?
She wrapped up some fresh-baked *Challah*
Bundled the baby against the cold
Invited them for *Shabbos*
And told them that her house
Was now their second home

Chorus

A quiet calm descended
As the last child went to sleep
Mommy finally sat down
Put her feet up and sipped a tea
A knock on the old front door
A poor woman walked from town
"Won't you please come in?
I'll make you some supper
Here's a chair, please sit down"

Chorus

🎧 MY DEAR IMA

Suri Berman

My dear *Ima*, I'm sending this letter
To say the things I've never said
Of my impression as your daughter
These thoughts are going through my head

As far back as I can remember
You said *Shema* with me at night
Each week I saw you welcome *Shabbos*
I saw your candles burning bright

You made our home a house of Torah
Encouraged Abba to learn each day
You stood behind him during hard times
You gave him strength in your own way

You taught us all about the *Mitzvos*
Showed us the right way from the start
We always saw your love for Torah
You instilled it in our hearts

Now your children have grown older
Each one has gone their separate ways
But yet we follow in your footsteps
You made us what we are today

Now your daughter is a mother
I do the things you used to do
Not only did you build your own home
But Ima you built my home too

🎧 IMA

Dedi ©
Album: Rotzoh

There is a time I can remember
Days that were spent, just you and me
I shared my childhood dreams and secrets
You told me how they'd come to be
Oh, all the stories that you told me
I was afraid, and you would hold me
Then you were all that I needed
I was your world, and you were mine

Chorus
Ima, Ima don't you know?
For if you don't by now
I will tell you so
My world was made for you
It's there in all I do
For you have taught me
Showed me, helped me grow to who I am
Still, I am your child
What I would give to be the reason for your smile
Be all that I can be
Have your light shine through me
If I could give you, *Ima*, all you've given to me

Now I have grown to understand you
All that you gave with all your heart
How you inspire those around you
You were my guide right from the start

And whatever joy or pain I bring you

These are the words I will sing you
Ima, Ima, you're my *Ima*
No one could ever take your part

Chorus

There is a time I can remember
Days that were spent, just you and me
And when I think about my lifetime
You are the *Ima* that I see

Ima...

A SONG FOR MY DAUGHTER

Sheira Brayer ©
Album: Motiv8: 8 Songs to ROCK Your Own World

Dedicated to my precious daughters, Rebecca and
Sarah, my daughter-in-love Samantha and my
granddaughter, Charlie.
-Julie Hintz

I remember when you were a little girl
Full of wonder at the world
Through those precious years
I tried so hard to
Hold on to all that you'd say and do

Yet here you're standing
I can't believe what I see
A little woman smiling back at me

Chorus

In my dreams, there could never be
A greater daughter than what you are to me
You give me love, laughter, and inspiration
You give me hope for the next generation

The hardest part for me is learning to let go
Though I try not to let it show
So promise me you will
Always make a choice
Listening to your inner voice

Embrace the silence
Your answers will appear
But above all, know that I am here

Chorus

You are my joy, my song, my celebration
You are my hope for the next generation

REBBETZIN CHAYA MUSHKA

Chaya Aydel Lebovics ob"m
To the Tune of Shema Yisrael by Mordechai Ben David
Recording by Rabbi Lebovics

With deep and thoughtful eyes
And a noble face
Radiating warmth and grace
A true king's daughter, avoiding honor
We very rarely saw her face

Chorus
Kol Kevudah Bas Melech

Bas Melech Penima

כל כבודה בת מלך
[בת מלך פנימה*]
Doing her holy work unseen
כל כבודה בת מלך
בת מלך פנימה
She taught us what these words really mean

Her great devotion to her holy grandfather
Sitting saying *Tehillim* by his side
He knew her loyalty, her special qualities
He said that she should be the *Rebbe's* bride

Chorus

Her wisdom matched by few
This her father knew
Into exile he took her along
Through suffering and strife
She risked her health, her life
To protect us all from any wrong

Chorus

The modest mother of our generation
The *Aishes Chayil* of our *Nasi*
Oh, oh *Rebbetzin* Chaya Mushka
Your children we will always be

כל כבודה בת מלך
בת מלך פנימה
Doing your holy work unseen
כל כבודה בת מלך
בת מלך פנימה

You taught us what these words really mean

All the glory of a princess is within. -Psalms 45:14

WALKING DOWN THE HALLWAY

Chaya Aydel Lebovics ob"m
To the Tune of Keil Hahoda'ois
Recording by Rabbi Lebovics

Walking down the hallway for the very first time
For the very first time
Holding mother tightly

A tiny girl of three
She shyly lifts her eyes and sees a smiling face
This is her first [Beis Rivkah or School Name] memory

Chorus
[Beis Rivkah] through the years
Through the laughter and the tears
In our hearts
A flame so bright
Warming us with the Torah's light

Running through the hallway
With dear friends beside her
Full of school spirit
How swiftly time goes past
The *Rebbe* is guiding
Devoted teachers helping
The knowledge she's absorbing will forever last

Chorus

Walking to the *Chuppah*
Holding mother tightly
A prayer in her heart
And happiness so strong
A new life awaits her
She slowly does approach it
And always within her
[Beis Rivkah] walks along

Chorus

Aydel Lebovics

(CHAYA AYDEL BAS R' AVROHOM DOVID) A''H

was a beloved wife, mother, sister, foster mother, grandmother and mentor to many. She was a devoted and creative teacher. She put her entire heart and soul into everything she did. A gifted writer, she wrote poetry, children's books and songs. It is a comfort to us that her songs, which are already sung by many around the world, will now be spread even further through this songbook.

DEDICATED BY
THE LEBOVICS, DWORCAN,
AND ROSENBERG FAMILIES

🎧 LEGACY
By Chana Yerushalmi

Tears have been wept down from my face
Bubby, Bubby where are you now?
I could see your holy face your image in my mind
Come back to me to those *Shabbos* nights

She worked and toiled to fulfill her goal
Let heaven and above bless her soul
A true mother and *Aishes Chayil*
that was what portrayed
Self-sacrifice is what she clearly laid

The woman who fought for what was right
A full time nurse way into the night
She is loving she is caring to this very day
Bubby you always remain in my heart
The thoughtful lessons which you pointed out

I will carry your legacy on!
We will carry your legacy on!

🎧 MEMORIES OF LOVE
By Chana Yerushalmi

Looking back at the memories so sweet
When you'd take me out in the heat
How you love me, how you praise me so
Oh, how I love that precious *Challah* dough
Ima, you have guided me through, and you
know it, it's so very true
Buying presents, singing to me, it just shows
who you really are

Chorus (x2)
Ima, Ima, please stay with me
Your *Chayus* keeps me through those dark
nights
I'm your precious, you're my love

Let's hold each other hand in hand, listening to
every word
Giving advice when it needs to be learned
I hope I will please you all my life
Mother, Mother you are my light

*Miriam's Yerushalmi's books are sold on Amazon.com. Her
classes are available on torahanytime.com, torahcafe.com
and at bit.ly/MriamYoutubeChannel.*

IN MY HEART ALWAYS

Chaya-Bracha Rubin ©

In loving memory of Miriam Bas
Mordechai Benamy.
-Chaya Bracha Rubin

Chorus
A voice of comfort, a voice of strength
A voice of reason, guidance and faith
A voice of unwavering support all my days
And her voice is in my heart always

Every time I reach out for it
I know the softness of her hand
And no matter the distance
She'll listen and understand
 So many look to her for guidance
And yet she always makes the time
And with every conversation
She has my best in mind

If my words were blossoms
And I tried to express
The magnitude of my gratitude
The flowers would be endless

Chorus

Through all my trials and tribulations
She knew what to do or to say
And if it weren't for her love
I wouldn't be here today

If my words were blossoms
And I tried to express
The magnitude of my gratitude
The flowers would be endless

Chorus

Yes, her voice is in my heart always
In all ways, always
In all ways, always

CHAPTER 4:
Friendship & Unity

Songs are compelling, especially because each note is vital in shaping the beauty of the music. A musical note alone may not sound gorgeous, but combined with the others it becomes an uplifting melody. Likewise, when we unite with others, we create a harmonious symphony for *Hashem*. The very fact that we are diverse reveals how important each one of us is to *Hashem*, in making the world a dwelling place for His Presence.

You may be familiar with a highlight in our daily prayers, which opens with the words "*Az Yashir*" when the Jewish people burst into song after they safely crossed the sea. Led by G-d's Hand and mighty Arm, they were redeemed from bondage and witnessed miracles transcending nature. It was only fitting that praise and thanks to *Hashem* would be first in order. The real wonder, we are taught, is that the entire nation erupted into one song, in total harmony. There was no discussion or rehearsal beforehand. The nation was on such a high level at this time, so close to their Maker, that the thread connecting every individual, the unity of all souls to one another, was revealed through their singing to *Hashem*. Even the rest of creation, flora, and fauna joined in! "*Ashira la'Hashem Ki Gamal Alai* — I will sing to *Hashem* for He has dealt kindly with me!" [Psalms 13:6]

What is the difference between noise and song? Noise is fractured, disjointed, and caustic to the ear; whereas in song, there is harmony. Each key and note has a purpose and blends with its neighbor. When we unite with other Jews, we blend in harmony. We may be different, but we can all sing to *Hashem*.

Raising our voices in harmony inspires a warm and moving sensation and mirrors true unity. The words of "the sweet singer of Israel," *Dovid Hamelech*, rang true when he famously stated "*Hinei Ma-tov Umah Na'im Shevet Achim Gam-Yachad!* – How good and pleasant it is for brothers to sit together!" [Psalms 133:1]

QUESTIONS TO CONSIDER:

How can you increase harmony in your environment?

🎧 OUR CIRCLE

Rivka Leah Popack ©
Album: Silent Prayer

There's magic in your smile
The way it fills my heart
And speaks a language
Words will never know

There's wonder in the way
You laugh at each new day
You're teaching me
To let my spirit grow

As sure as all that's true
I've got a friend in you
Whatever comes my way

It'll be okay, 'cause...

Chorus
It's you and me
We're friends as friends should be
I know it's me you see
It's you and me

I see it in your eyes
Looking deep inside
You know that I too
Reach for distant stars

We face the world outside
There's no more need to hide
We're more than we'll
Ever be on our own

As sure as all that's true
I've got a friend in you
Whatever comes my way
It'll be okay, cause...

Chorus

To share and understand
Come, hold my hand
Our circle carries room enough for all

We've all got what to say
Each in our own way
Step right inside so we can hear you too

Look around and see

We're friends as friends should be
Join hands with me
As friends should be

Here we stand, holding hands in the circle
Gather 'round, hear the sound in the circle
Open wide, step inside in the circle

Chorus

BRINGING HEAVEN DOWN TO EARTH

Rivka Leah Popack ©
Lead and backing vocals by Debra Jacobs
Album: Silent Prayer

There's a woman that I've met
No one knows she waits all week
To rise Friday morning
While all the world's asleep

She hurries to the synagogue
To sweep the dust and dirt
And as she gathers scattered prayer books
She brings heaven down to earth

There's a man that I've seen
At his fruit shop every day
He fills their empty baskets
He knows they cannot pay

His soft smile heals the sadness
And his kind words ease the hurt
As he fills another basket

He brings heaven down to earth

Chorus
Bringing heaven down to earth
Where mundane meets divine
Where every person finds the chance
To change a place in time
Bringing heaven down to earth
Where the unexpected lies
And the further out you reach
The more you touch the skies

There's a mother that I know
With her phonebook open wide
She reaches half across the world
Without stepping foot outside

She remembers the forgotten
She reminds them of their worth
And as tonight becomes tomorrow
She brings heaven down to earth

There's a bus driver in town·
His route's always the same
Yet nothing else is regular
He knows everybody's name

He asks, "How's life? The family?"
As if he's known each one since birth
And as he shares his morning's happiness
He brings heaven down to earth

Chorus

There's a truth I've been taught
That it doesn't take much
To find that piece of heaven
In everything we touch

When just one expectant moment
Becomes beauty wrapped in time
In a simple act of goodness
We make this world divine

Chorus

So let's bring heaven down to earth
Where mundane meets divine
Where each of us can find our chance
To change a place in time

Yes, let's bring heaven down to earth
Where the unexpected lies
And the further we reach out
Together we will touch the sky

🎧 DON'T WALK IN FRONT OF ME
Uncle Moishy

Don't walk in front of me; I may not follow
Don't walk behind me; I may not lead

Just walk beside me, and be my friend
And together, we will walk in the ways of *Hashem*

Ve'ahavta Lereyacho Kamocha
Zeh Klal Gadol Ba'Torah

וְאָהַבְתָּ לְרֵעַךָ כָּמוֹךָ]
[*זֶה כְּלָל גָּדוֹל בַּתּוֹרָה

You should love your fellow as yourself; [R' Akiva says] this is a basic principle in the Torah. -Talmud

🎧 AM YISROEL CHAI
Shaindel Antelis ©

I gotta tell you that there aren't many others
Like my Jewish sisters and my Jewish brothers
You gotta know that there's a spark deep inside you
And there will never ever be anyone like you

Chorus
Jump, jump higher, you can touch the sky
Sing a little louder and let your colors shine
You are perfect in G-d's eyes
Am, Am, Am, Am Yisroel Chai
[עַם, עַם, עַם יִשְׂרָאֵל חַי]
From New York to Spain
London to LA
Jo'burg Miami
Australia
Mexico to France
Let me see you dance
Canada and Israel
עַם יִשְׂרָאֵל
Jews all around the world
Jews all around the world
Jews all around the world
Jews all around the world

Know that you're never alone

We have our land to call our home
There's no limit to the joy that life can bring
There's always something to celebrate
Come on and sing
עם, עם, עם ישראל
עם, עם, עם ישראל

Chorus

Am Yisroel Chai, Od Avinu Chai
[*עם ישראל חי, עוד אבינו חי]
עם ישראל, עם ישראל, ישראל חי
עוד אבינו, עוד אבינו, אבינו חי, yeah
עם, עם, עם ישראל
עם, עם, עם ישראל

Chorus

From New York to Spain
London to LA
Jo'burg Miami
Australia
Mexico to France
Let me see you dance
Canada and Israel
עם ישראל

The nation of Israel lives; our Father lives on.

🎧 A FRIEND

Shaindel Antelis ©
Album: Live Today

Thank you for picking up the phone

I was feeling so alone
But you knew just what to say, what to say
A listening ear, a helping hand
Just someone who understands
Can take the dark clouds away
And I can't thank you enough
For lifting me up when I get stuck

Chorus
You're a friend always there for me
Like a lovely melody
You give not expecting anything in return
A friend always by my side
Even on the bumpy rides
How am I so lucky to have you
In my life, in my life

Today I was in a daze
Hoping that it was just a phase
But I felt like this last week too
But you always read my thoughts
And you free me when I'm caught up in nothing
And I can't thank you enough
For lifting me up when I get stuck

Chorus

Even when we're busy and don't speak in three months
You'll always have a place in my heart
I know that nothing can take this bond away
No matter how long we're apart

Chorus (x2)
So lucky to have you...

THE PALACE

Shaindel Antelis ©
Album: Live Today

The city is no place for princesses
Wandering to find their way
I really want to know what to make of this
So many are going astray
Know that you're not alone
G-d's waiting for you at His throne

Chorus
I'm ready to enter the palace
Won't You judge me favorably
Help me live peacefully
I'm ready to enter the palace
And all I want to be
Is what You ask of me

As I walk down the street, I see
So many people just trying to make ends meet
Life isn't simple
So many princesses and queens
Noblemen and kings
All living in false realities
Know that you're not alone
G-d's waiting for you at His throne

Chorus (x2)

Your will is my will
Do it, yes I will
'Cause no distance is too far

And Your love is so pure
Even though I'm unsure
But no decree is too harsh

Chorus (x2)

The city is no place for princesses
Wandering to find their way
I really want to know what to make of this
So many are going astray

BY YOUR SIDE

Shaindel Antelis ©

Put on a smile take off that frown
Something is happening something is going down
You've been suffering for way too long
Turn up the music and sing a new song
And don't keep your light hidden
Dance to your own rhythm

Chorus
Keep watching the birds fly
And soak in the sunlight
You'll be wonderful
Everything will be alright
Don't know how you'll get through
Get through this dark time
I'll be there with you
Standing by your side
Forever and ever never say never
Forever and ever we'll get through this together

Things could be better, but they could be worse

Count the blessings that you have
You gotta do that first
Even if every door is closed
Even if you can't make up your mind
You're trying to get ahead but keep falling behind
You'll find your place, I know
Just breathe and take it slow

Chorus

I've been through this so many times
Just trying to leave the past behind
And no, it isn't simple
We've all got things to figure out
And that's just what life is about
So love yourself a little

🎧 AM ECHAD

Song composed by Ari Goldwag and Yitzy Waldner ©
Song Concept by Ari Goldwag
Lyrics by Miriam Israeli

כְּשֶׁאֲנִי לְעַצְמִי
וְאַתָּה לֹא אִתִּי
מַה אֲנִי כְּשֶׁאֲנִי בְּנִפְרָד
כִּי אֲנִי יְהוּדִי
לֹא הוֹלֵךְ לְבַדִּי
רַק אִתְּךָ, יְדִידִי, יַד בְּיָד

Chorus
עַם אֶחָד, שִׁיר אֶחָד
בּוֹא אָחִי וְתֵן לִי יַד
וְנוּכַל לִשְׂמוֹחַ וְלִרְקוֹד יַחַד
כְּאִישׁ אֶחָד בְּלֵב אֶחָד

לֹא רוֹצֶה לִהְיוֹת לְבַד
רַק לָנֶצַח שֶׁבֶת אַחִים גַּם יַחַד(x2)

לִהְיוֹת מִשְׁפָּחָה
זֶהוּ סוֹד הַשִּׂמְחָה
כִּי בְּיַחַד הַכֹּל טוֹב יוֹתֵר
וַאֲנַחְנוּ שָׁרִים
כֹּל יִשְׂרָאֵל חַבֵרִים
עַל אַף אֶחָד לֹא נַסְכִּים לְוַותֵּר

Chorus

עַם אֶחָד, שִׁיר אֶחָד
בּוֹא אָחִי וְתֵן לִי יַד
וְנוּכַל לִשְׂמוֹחַ וְלִרְקוֹד יַחַד
אִם נַצְלִיחַ לֶאֱהוֹב
וְנַשִּׁיר הִנֵּה מַה טוֹב
הַמָּשִׁיחַ עוֹד יַגִּיעַ בְּקָרוֹב

...עַם אֶחָד, שִׁיר אֶחָד, עַם אֶחָד, שִׁיר אֶחָד

Translation:
When I am for myself
And you are not with me
What am I when I am separate?
For I am a Jew
I do not go alone
Just with you, my friend, hand in hand

Chorus
One nation, one song
Come my brother and give me your hand
And we will rejoice and dance together
As one person, with one heart

I don't want, want to be alone,
Just forever brothers sitting together (x2)

To be a family
Is the secret of joy
For everything is better together
And we sing
All Israel are friends
We won't give up on anyone

Chorus

One nation, one song
Come my brother and give me your hand
And we will rejoice and dance together
If we can successfully love
And sing "how pleasant..."
The *Moshiach* will come soon

One nation, one song, one nation, one song...

YOU MEAN THE WORLD TO ME

Rebbetzin Tap ©
Album: Shabbos & Holiday Collection

Life gets better every minute
The room gets brighter when you're in it
And when I'm feeling blue
I just stick with you
'Cause you'll always mean the world to me

You and I are birds of a feather
You help guide me in stormy weather

And when I'm filled with doubt
You make the sun come out
You'll always mean the world to me

Chorus
The memories that you and I share
The lifetime of love and care
In my heart, I will always find you there
Forever you and me
Oh, the memories that you and I own
The life of kindness that you've shown
In my heart, you will always have a home
Forever you and me

Every moment is a treasure
To be with you, is such a pleasure
And when I need a friend
On you I will depend
'Cause you'll always mean the world to me

Oh, life gets better every minute
The room gets brighter when you're in it
And when I'm feeling blue
I just stick with you
'Cause you'll always mean the world to me

Chorus

Forever you and me!

MY FELLOW JEW

Avraham Fried ©
Composed by Yossi Green
Arranged by Moshe Laufer
Album: My Fellow Jew

To Ariella Sapoznik for never turning your back
away and for being the definition of a true friend.
"So with all my heart and soul let me honor you."
- Mazaliya Mardakhayeva

G-d smiled in heaven, but His joy was not complete
The angels were singing, but their song had no wings
The world was freshly painted yet the sky was feeling blue
Something, something just wasn't right

Then with you came a G-dly light
That made the world complete
You gave the world its heart
You gave the world its soul
Now G-d can call this place His home
For now, there was you
For now, there was you
My brother/sister, my fellow Jew

Chorus
So with all my heart and soul let me honor you
A gentle people with a faith of steel
You teach the world how to live and how to give and
how to believe
If I could look into your heart, I would see the Face of
G-d
You have weathered all the storms they've all come and
gone
You are the unsung heroes of the world
And you were born of ancient days, and you will go on
and on
I've seen miracles before, but the greatest of them all is
you, my fellow Jew

Who can count the teardrops that have fallen from
your eyes
And who would dare to measure the pain that you have
known
Yet here you are undaunted with a mission and a
dream
You carry on when hope is gone
All that you live for will come true

And so when at times I'm feeling weak
It's you who makes me strong
And when at times I cannot speak
You become my song
I know I can do the impossible
When I think of you, my brother/sister, my fellow Jew

CHESSED TIME

Rebbetzin Tap ©
Album: Shabbos & Holiday Collection

That means it's time to do some *Chessed*
Time to get up and help our friends
Because when someone has a need
It's up to us to take the lead

We gotta go do
We gotta go do
We gotta go do some *Chessed*

Now off we go to do some *Chessed*
Off on our way to help our friends
Because when someone has a need
It's up to us to take the lead
For on each other we do depend
For on each other we do depend

SPECIAL CHILD

Chanale ©
Album: Believer

A meeting was held far from earth
With the angels and G-d above
They said it's time again for another birth
This child will need much love

And though her progress may seem slow
And accomplishments she may not know
Let's be careful where she's sent
We want her life to be content

Chorus
Please G-d find someone who
Will do this very special job for You
And let them realize right away
The leading role they're asked to play
And have them show her till the end
They'll always be there as her friend
And share a love so deep and strong
And that's the place where she'll belong

Make sure her parents hold her close
And never miss a smile
And when life gets hard, they'll always know
She's a gift to them this child
Give her a friend to hold her hand
Listen close and understand
Take the time to make her grin
Bring out her beauty from within

Chorus

SISTER, SISTER

Chanale ©
Album: Chanale and Friends

Sister, sister, remember
Not long ago when we were both young
Sure it seems like forever since we've
Skated holding hands in the sun
Now I'm watching the videos
Of the times when we were careless and free
And I notice that nothing's changed
'Cept I'm smarter, and it's clearer to see

Chorus
When I'm old, I'll still need you
You're my sister and my favorite friend
And I promise I'll be here
Like you've been there for me time and again

Sister, sister I wonder
What life would be without your sweet smile
Who would answer the phone so late
And listen while I talked for a while
You know I've kept every letter
That you wrote to me when we were apart
And when they tell me I look like you
Well I hope it's a resemblance of heart

Chorus

And when you need me, I'll be here at any time
I love you, sister of mine

🎧 A DIFFERENT KEY

Nechama Cohen ©
Album: Heartbeat

I'm trying to talk, but it seems nobody's here
Everyone's around, but they won't stop to care
I just wanna be heard, but no one's listening
The more I try, my voice is fading

Chorus
Everyone is singing, but they're singing their own song
Why can't we all join along?
Together in harmony, listening
to every note

If we blend our voices together in unison
We can make beautiful music
Don't sing too loud or you might miss out
On some other great melody
Even if it's on a different key

Everyone's busy; they don't want to hear
How my day was, and why I went where
Living their own lives, oblivious
Not realizing how much they're missing

Chorus

Everyone has a key that they live on
Some are high, some are low, and some are in between
Live and love, laugh and cry, just feel something real
Tune into what others are saying to you
There'll be so much more awaiting you
There's a lot you can learn it's not hard to find
if you open your mind

Chorus

A different key...

🎧 LET'S CHANGE THE WORLD

Composed and sung by Avraham Fried ©
Arranged by Yisroel Lamm
Shortened version adapted and sung by Racheli Jacks

You don't need a reason
Or season, my friend
You don't need fortune or fame

Go out of your way, make someone's day
Kindness, the friendly way
Cause, we are towers of light
We have the power to do what is right
Illuminating, making bright

Chorus
There is so much we CAN do
To make this world a kinder, better, happier place
There is so much we CAN do
To change the world
Let's change the world today

A SMALL PIECE OF HEAVEN

Composed and lyrics by Abie Rotenberg ©
Originally arranged by Yisroel Lamm
New arrangement by Eli Gerstner

Some people wonder
Others may say
Whenever adversity passes their way
Let me run let me hide
Oh I must close my eyes
By the time that they're open
It just might fade away

But not you dear friends
You know just what to do
When faced with a challenge
You always come through
And you've painted a smile

On the face of a child
Helping to make sure
That his dreams come true

Chorus
There's a small piece of Heaven
In everyone's heart
A glorious gift from above
It will sparkle and shine
If we each do our part
To reach out and touch it with love

So we thank you tonight
For doing your share
For the gift of bright sunshine
And fresh country air
But although that's a fact
You've done much more than that
You've shown these dear children
Just how much you care

Chorus

B'YACHAD

Composed by Mordechai Shapiro and
Yitzy Waldner ©
Lyrics by Miriam Israeli
Arranged by Ian Freitor

I like to draw and paint
I like to wake up late
But I don't like to clean my room
I like when Mommy bakes
The *Challah* and the cake

Sometimes I get to lick the spoon
I can get up and stand
If someone holds my hand
Then I can walk along my way
I like to talk to you
And when you listen to
Whatever I have got to say

Chorus
We can all sing
We can all sing
We can all sing *B'Yachad, Yachad*
We're creating *B'Yachad*
It's a special harmony (x2)

I like to ride my bike
And I enjoy a hike
I play piano, and I sing
I love my family
Sometimes I'd rather be
Alone away from everything

I like to be with friends
And to connect with them
I like to feel that I belong
We aren't quite the same
But really that's okay
I know that we can get along

Chorus

'Cause both you and I
See the same blue sky
We're under one star

Let's bridge the distances
Forget our differences
Wherever we are

Sometimes I'm really brave
Sometimes I feel afraid
And I don't always toe the line
Sometimes I fall and then
I get back up again
Nobody's perfect all the time

I like when people see
The good I have in me
We all can give in our own way
Let's spread the love around
Our differences don't count
Let's make the world a better place

Chorus

WHO AM I?

Abie Rotenberg ©
Album: Journeys Volume 3

I have trouble with my words
They don't seem to come out clear
But I want you all to know me, so I'll try
I'm asking one small question
It won't take up too much time
Can you tell me
Can you answer
Who am I?

Oh, I know I'm very different

By the things, I cannot do
Why I find it hard to tell you my own name
So you wonder just who am I
As you try to hide your eyes
But believe me
You and I are much the same

Don't you marvel at a sunset
As the rays shine through the clouds
And the night begins to take over the sky?
Don't you love the sound of laughter
And a lively happy tune?
Well then we are not so different, you and I

And when you see a mighty eagle
As it spreads its graceful wings
Don't you wish inside your heart
That you could fly?
And when you hear a crash of thunder
Don't you tremble out of fear?
Then we are not so different, you and I

Oh, I know my legs can't hold me
And I cannot shake your hand
And that looking at me makes you feel so strange
So you wonder just who am I
As you quickly pass on by
But believe me
You and I are just the same

Have you known the pain of sadness
And the feeling that it brings?
Yes, I'm sure there's been sometimes
You've had to cry

And that loneliness is worst of all
I'm sure that you'll agree
Then we are not so different, you and I

And do you know the joy of friendship
Of caring and of love?
Somehow I get the feeling that you do
For then we are not so different
We are very much the same
You do know who I am
Who I am, who I am, who I am, who I am
I'm just like you

WE'RE ALL THE SAME

Sheira Brayer ©
Album: Motiv8: 8 Songs to ROCK Your Own World

I often stop and wonder
Where we get all our thunder
When will the vicious cycle end
I cannot seem to understand
Why man is inhumane to man
When will we call each other "friend"?

Chorus
'Cause we're all the same
We laugh and cry
We're all the same
We all live and die
Let's make the journey matter now
Let's win the game
We're all the same
When cut we bleed

We're all the same
We all have a need
To love and to be loved
And to let peace reign
We're all the same

We've got so much to live for
Picture a world without war
Put all the hatred in the past
This would make quite a story
To leave our children glory
The kind of glory that will last

Chorus

Look at your neighbor
And think of what would happen
If danger came to our world
Wouldn't care about race or color
No, we'd be side by side with each other
Oh yeah, just like sister and brother
Oh, can't you see
How it could be

'Cause we're all the same
We laugh and cry
We're all the same
We all live and die
Let's make the journey matter now
Let's win the game

We're all the same
Under the skin
We're all the same

Deep down within
Want to be proud of who we are
Not be ashamed

We're all the same
Gonna make it real
We're all the same
Now let's start to heal
And take responsibility
Instead of blame

We're all the same
Oh, can't you feel it?
We're all the same
If we could only see it
Then we'd have everything
In the world to gain
'Cause we're all the same
We're all the same
After all, we're all the same

🎧 TO LOVE ANOTHER
Esther Freeman ©

When you look at me
Tell me what, do you see
Do you see a person staring back? When you insult tell
me what, do you feel
Do you think I feel any lesser than that?

Is it OK for me
To hurt like you do?
Would you want the same things done to you?

Am I allowed to breathe like a human does?
Please don't say these words to me just because

Chorus
Ve'ahavta Lereyacho [ואהבת לרעך]
Love your neighbor like you love yourself
Look inside your heart because that's where all the
Middos start
So think before you do and the same will be done unto
you
ואהבת לרעך
Love your neighbor like you love yourself
It's the basis of our Holy Torah
It's so important to love every Jew

Do you stare at me
Because I look differently?
Does everyone have to be like you?
When you judge me do you think you really know
All the things that I have been through?

So put yourself in my place before you disgrace me
You'll understand why I begin to cry
When you treat my feelings carelessly

Chorus

SAVE A LIFE

Debbie Friedman ob"m ©
Album: Songs of the Spirit: The Debbie Friedman
Anthology

Whoever destroys a soul, it is considered as if he
destroyed an entire world. And whoever saves a life, it is
considered as if he saved an entire world. — Babylonian
Talmud, Tractate Sanhedrin.

Broken hearts, shattered visions, pieced together one
by one
Hurt another and the world is destroyed
But save a life, and you will save the world

No more darkness, no more hiding, no more crying, no
more lies
Looking for the way back home again
Save a life, save a life and you will save the world

Darkness fades, the morning light appears
Shadows dance and come to greet the day
The voices of angels sing words of comfort, whispering
Save a life, and you will save the world

In the garden, voices singing, wipe your eyes now, no
more fears
Take my hand; we'll build the world together
Save a life, save a life and you will save the world

Morning comes, a new day has begun
See the light and come to greet the day
The voices of angels sing, words of comfort, whispering

Save a life, save a life and you will save the world

In the garden, voices singing, wipe your eyes now, no more fears
Take my hand; we'll build the world together
Save a life, and you will save the world

🎧 THE GIFT OF SONG

Sheira Brayer ©
Album: Motiv8: 8 Songs to ROCK Your Own World

Here is my present to you sweet child
It can make you sad
It can make you smile
It is not a doll or a game or a toy
But it will bring you eternal joy

Chorus
The gift of song
Will keep you young forever
Bring your friends and family together
You can't outgrow or lose
Music always seems to be
The one thing that breeds harmony
I hope someday my little girl
You will use your voice to heal the world

Chorus

You must always strive
To keep this precious gift alive
Remember to pass it on to the next generation

The gift of song
Will keep you young forever
Bring your friends and family together (2X)

You can't outgrow or lose
As long as you use
The gift of song

🎧 UNITY

Written and composed by Mordechai Ben David and Sheya Mendelowitz ©
Additional lyrics by Mordechai Ben David and Moshe Kravitsky
Album: MBD and Friends

Like angels in the sky
In a garden full of glory
The galaxies so brilliantly related
Ultimately high
On the first page of our story
Till the time our parents were created

Envious brother Cain
Threw a blow so mad and chilling
Tragically he never did recover
It's really so insane
All our selfishness that's killing
That stranger who's our sister and our brother

Chorus
Listen brother listen friend
Just a little smile, a helping hand
And our hearts will find a loving kind humanity
We must teach our children to

Treat their fellow friends like they were you
And then the world will find such peace of mind and
unity

Eagle soaring by
Could you lift him up with you now
And fly him home, with justice, pride, and freedom?
His eyes are gazing wide
From behind the bars, he prays now
With faith, with joy, oh how we wait to greet him

Ages rushing by
Writing chapters full of sorrow
Webs of self-destruction we are weaving
If we don't even try
There's no hope for our tomorrow
So what's it all worth if we are not achieving

Chorus (x2)

But one thing makes me smile
I can feel the happy ending
As justice will prevail, so delighted
In just a little while, we will join in freedom, singing
With peace and love across a world, united

FOREVER ONE

Avraham Fried ©
Arranged by Moshe Laufer
Album: Forever One

Look inside through the heart of a Jew
Open up its many doors
And the soul that you'll see there inside
Is a reflection of yours
For each soul is a part of one whole
That joins us to each other

We are all part of one another
And we have always been one
We are one since a way back in time
Unified at our start
We began as a nation to live
And believe with one heart

You and I we were all gathered there
As one we said we'll do and hear
We were born to belong together
And forever be one

Chorus
Forever one we will go far
It's not I am but who we are
We need just to reveal it
We need to try and feel it
And never are we alone
We have each other as our own
Nothing can divide us
For we are forever one

These are times when we might drift apart
And go our own separate ways
But the spark from above that we share
Is alive and ablaze
Soon *Moshiach* will gather each spark
And shine away the darkness
He will gather us all together
And we shall ever be one

Chorus

ONE DAY

Matisyahu ©
Album: Light

Sometimes I lay
Under the moon
And thank G-d I'm breathing
Then I pray
Don't take me soon
'Cause I am here for a reason

Chorus
Sometimes in my tears, I drown
But I never let it get me down
So when negativity surrounds
I know some day it'll all turn around because
All my life I've been waiting for
I've been praying for
For the people to say
That we don't wanna fight no more
There will be no more wars
And our children will play
One day, one day, one day

One day, one day, one day

It's not about win or lose
'Cause we all lose
When they feed on the souls of the innocent
Blood-drenched pavement
Keep on moving though the waters stay raging
In this maze, you can lose your way
It might drive you crazy but don't let it faze you, no way,
no way

Chorus

One day this all will change
Treat people the same
Stop with the violence
Down with the hate
One day we'll all be free
And proud to be
Under the same sun
Singing songs of freedom like
One day, one day, one day
One day, one day, one day

All my life I've been waiting for
I've been praying for
For the people to say
That we don't wanna fight no more
There will be no more wars
And our children will play
One day, one day, one day
One day, one day, one day

DEDICATED TO

Shoshana Yadel Ferber

BAT MITZVAH
TISHREI 22, 5778 -
SHEMINI ATZERES

יְבָרֶךְ הַשֵׁם וִיכָנֵסֵךְ לתורה
וְלֶחֻפָּה ולמעשים טובים

LOVE,
Ima and Abba

🎧 I AM AN ANCIENT WALL OF STONE

Abie Rotenberg ©
Album: Marvelous
Middos Machine
Volume 3

I am an ancient wall of
stone
Atop a hill so high
And if you listen with
your heart
You just may hear my
cry
Where has the *Beis
Hamikdash* gone?
I stand here all alone
How long am I to wait
for all my children to
come home?

A house of marble and
of gold once stood here
by my side
From far and wide all
came to see its beauty
and its pride
But *Sinas Chinam*
brought it down, and
with it so much pain
Now only *Ahavas
Yisroel* can build it once
again

Chorus
Together, together, you
stood by *Har Sinai*, my
daughters, and sons
Forever, forever, you
must stand together
forever as one

You come and stand
beside my stones to
raise your voice in
prayer
You ask, "When will the
Golus end, how much
more can we bear?"
But *Sinas Chinam* still
lives on; it lingers in
your heart
How can you come back
home to me, while you
remain apart?

Chorus

Together, together, you
stood by *Har Sinai, Bnei
Avraham*
Forever, forever, you
must stand together
forever as one

A NUMB WINTER COLDNESS

Recording by Chaviva Tarlow

A numb winter coldness
Pierced through the walls
Of a hut on the edge of the town

A woman lay dying,
She'd already stopped trying
To soothe the child, she had born

The *Alter Rebbe* feeling the pain
Alone, he went to her aid
Chopped wood for the fire
Warmed milk for the babe
While *Ne'ilah* was prayed

Going out of his way,
The *Rebbe* did portray
The importance of *Tzedakah B'Guf*

HARMONY

8th Day ©
Album: All You Got

Singing alone, I've been known to do
But it's not the same as singing with you
I've walked alone, yeah I know it's true
And it's not the same as dancing with you

Chorus
Life is so much better with harmony together
We could out storm any weather with harmony,
harmony together
Many colors blend as one - me, you and everyone
Our harmony is hard to fight; it could shine away the
darkest night
Soon they'll lay down their guns and knives
No more dark clouds in the skies
Enemies will walk away, singing softly as they say
Life is so much better with harmony together
Life is so much better with harmony together

I've seen the end, and there's nothing new
It's all about the unity of me and you
He may be different no matter what you do
But in his heart and soul, he knows these words are true

Chorus

Safta Nesia

In loving memory of my grandmothers
Nesia Geller & Bayla Elenberg

-NANETTE BRENNER

SHEYN VI DI LEVONE
Lyrics C. Tauber/Tauzberg

Sheyn vi di levone
Lichtik vi di shtern
Fun himel a matone
Bistu mir tzugeshikt!
Vayl/mayn glik hob ich gevunen
Ven ich hob dich gefunen
Sheyn vi toyznt zunen
Hostu/hot mayn hartz baglikt

Dayne tzeyndelech
Vays vi perelech
Mit dayne sheyne oygn
Dayne heyndelech, dayne herelech
Hot mich tzugetzoygn

Der moych is mir tzumisht
Ich gey arum tzuchisht

Chveys aleyn nit vos ich vil
Ich shem zich, ich bin royt
Di tzung is bay mir toyt
Ich ken nit zogn, vos ich vil
Du bist arayn tzu mir
In hartzn oyf kvartir
Khtrakh vi tzu zogn dir
Az du bist...

Chorus

Translation:
  AS BEAUTIFUL AS THE MOON

As beautiful as the moon
As radiant as the stars
You are sent from heaven
As a gift to me
I won good fortune
When I found you
As beautiful as a thousand suns
You have rejoiced my heart

Chorus
Your little teeth
Like little pearls
With your beautiful eyes,
Your flirting, your hair
Attracted me

My brain is mixed up
I go around confused
I myself don't know what I want
I'm embarrassed and red-faced
I've lost my tongue
I cannot explain what I want
You came to me
To remain in my heart forever
I'm thinking how to say to you
That you are...

Chorus

ALL IT TAKES IS ONE SMALL CANDLE

Abie Rotenberg ©
Album: Unforgettable Moments, Volume 2

All it takes is one small candle
One small flickering, shining candle
That is all it takes to penetrate the dark
And all it takes is one soft word
One soft, soothing, gentle word
That is all it takes to mend a broken heart

Chorus
When we put our hearts and minds together
A thousand glowing candles burning bright
Then we become a force that can't be measured
And together, we can drive away the night

All it takes is one small tear
One small, glistening, earnest tear
That is all it takes to melt a heart of stone
All it takes is one bright smile
One sweet, caring, loving smile
That is all it really takes to know you're not alone

Chorus

Together
Everyone together
Let's raise our voices in harmony
And someday soon we will all be free
If only we could all stand together

All we have is one small dream
One small, glorious, hopeful dream
And it's all we've ever had help to pull us through
All we ask for is one more miracle
One last long-awaited miracle
That is all we need to make our dreams come true

Chorus

So, let's all put our hearts and minds together
A thousand glowing candles burning bright
We'll become a force that can't be measured
And together, we can drive away the night
And together, we can drive away the night

אשר ישׁן עליו או בן יגח או בת יגח

שׁור או אמה כסף שלשים שקלים יתן לאד

יפתח איש בר או כי יכרה איש בר ולא י

בעל הבור ישלם כסף ישיב לבעליו והמ

את שׁור איש את שׁור רעהו ומת ומכרו

המת יחצון או נודע כי שׁור נגח הוא מ

לם ישלם שׁור תחת השׁור והמת יהיה כ

טבחו או מכרו חמשה בקר ישלם ת

יבמצא הגנב והכה ומת אין ל

ישלם אם אין לו ונמכר בגנב

Before Moshe *Rabbeinu*'s passing, he seriously yet lovingly spoke his final words to our nation in the song of *Parsha* of *Haazinu*. He instructed them, "*V'Atah Kisvu Lachem Es Hashira Hazos* — And now write this Song for yourselves." [Deuteronomy 31:19] The "Song" Moshe referred to is a euphemism for the entire Torah.

In those moments, Moshe understood that the people would uphold the Torah with greater devotion when it was transmitted through song. A song is not just borne upon the lips, but is seared into the memory and resounds in the heart of the listeners with joy. When we were small, our teachers taught us prayers, *Aleph Beis*, and other basics of Jewish life through a variety of songs. These are lessons we still remember and, G-d willing, will pass on to our children.

We can discover ways to make our learning joyful and infuse our observance with meaning; for through the study of Torah and the performance of its *Mitzvos*, we connect to *Hashem* and embrace the Infinite. Let's keep singing and burst into song, for we hold the precious gift of our inheritance.

"תּוֹרָה צִוָּה לָנוּ מֹשֶׁה מוֹרָשָׁה קְהִלַּת יַעֲקֹב"

"The Torah that Moshe commanded us is the heritage of the congregation of Yaakov." -Deuteronomy 33:4

QUESTION TO CONSIDER:
How can you make learning Torah and doing Mitzvos fun and joyful?

A TRIBUTE TO
Rabbi Moshe Snow
PRINCIPAL OF THE MORRISTOWN JEWISH CENTER HEBREW HIGH SCHOOL

[during my high school years and beyond!]

As a Conservative Jewish kid, I was first exposed to *love of Judaism* through a dynamic group of young teachers from Boro Park, Brooklyn. Weekly, they made their way out to the suburbs to run our Sunday Hebrew High School; they loved, taught and invited us to open our burgeoning minds to another way of seeing Gd and our Judaism. And, they literally invited us into their homes for *Shabbatons*, personal *Simchas* and shared their families and energy with us... through song! I didn't know then what I know now: Song is a window to the soul! Rabbi Snow brought his guitar and strummed his way into our hearts and minds, leaving behind touchstones to a past that—later—yielded a path to my future as well!

This song—did he just make it up? Is it a 'real' song? I was never able to tell, but I sang it as a lullaby to my two little Jewish daughters throughout their first years. And still, today—forty years later—I can bring it forth easily remembering every word, every note. Thank you Rabbi Snow—and team—for making us wise and teaching us straight.

With love,

Sue Lowenthal Axelrod
[Hebrew High School years: 1976-80]

Make the children happy
Help the children grow
Give them every
Opportunity to know
Make them wise
Teach them straight
For time – it passes us by
And it's too late

*Yismach Moshe, bmat-nat chelko
ki eved ne'eman karata lo* (x2)*

Make them wise
Teach them straight
For time – it passes us by
And it's too late

*Moses rejoiced at the gift of his destiny when You declared him a faithful servant adorning him as he stood in Your Presence atop Mount Sinai. -Shabbat Morning Liturgy

HOW BEAUTIFUL IS OUR HERITAGE

Morning Prayers Liturgy

אַשְׁרֵינוּ מַה טוֹב חֶלְקֵנוּ

וּמַה נָּעִים גּוֹרָלֵנוּ

וּמַה יָּפָה יְרֻשָּׁתֵנוּ

Translation:

Fortunate are we, how goodly is our portion

And how pleasant is our lot

And how beautiful is our heritage!

THE PLACE WHERE I BELONG

Abie Rotenberg ©

Album: Journeys, Volume 1

I was made way back in 1842

By a humble man, a real G-d fearing Jew

Who did his work with honesty, feeling and with pride

He was known in Kiev, as Yankele the Scribe

With loving care, his hand so sure and still

He formed me with some parchment, ink, and quill

Each day he'd slowly add to me, just a few more lines
With words to last until the end of time

And on the day that I was finally complete
The whole town came and filled the narrow street
And they sang and danced and held me high, and carried me away
To the little wooden *Shul* where I would stay

And as the Rabbi held me close against his chest
He spoke out loud and clear to all the rest
He said, "No matter if you're very young or even if you're old
Live by the words you'll find inside this scroll"

Three days a week they read from me out loud
It filled my soul with joy; it made me proud
They followed each and every verse with fire in their eyes
The words that told them how to live their lives

I watched the generations come and go
I saw the old men die, their children grow
But never in a century, did I miss my turn once
For the fathers, they had left me with their sons

But the hatred from the west came to Kiev
And they rounded up the Jews who had not fled
But Moishele the *Shammesh*
He was brave, and he was bold
He hid me in the cellar dark and cold

And for years and years, I waited all alone
For the people of my town to take me home

And they'd sing and dance and hold me high,
When they carried me away
To my little wooden *Shul* where I would stay

But it was someone else who found my hiding place
And to America, he sent me in a crate
And the men who took me off the boat,
They said I was a prize
But they were Jews I did not recognize

And in a case of glass, they put me on display
Where visitors would look at me and say,
"How very nice, how beautiful, a stunning work of art"
But they knew not what was inside my heart

And across the room, I saw upon the shelf
Some old friends of mine who lived back in Kiev
A silver pair of candlesticks, a *Menorah* made of brass
We'd all become mere echoes of the past

So if you hear my voice, why don't you come along,
And take me to the place where I belong,
And maybe even sing and dance when you carry me away
To some little wooden *Shul* where I could stay

And as the Rabbi holds me close against his chest
He'll speak out loud and clear to all the rest
He'll say, "No matter if you're very young or even if you're old
Live by the words you'll find inside this scroll"
Live by the words you'll find inside my soul

In loving memory of Eva Krenkel

Birthday: December 13, 1923 | Yartzeit: 8 Adar

🎧 AZ DER REBBE ZINGT

There are several variations provided for the lyrics of this Yiddish folk song. The version below and the English translation is adapted from Jane Enkin Music and Story.

Az der Rebbe zingt (when the rabbi sings)
Zingen ale Chassidim (all the Chassidim sing)
Tshiri biri bim tshiri biri bom
Zingen ale Chassidim

Az der rebe trinkt (when the rabbi drinks)
Trinken ale Chasidim (all the hasidim drink)
Yaba baba bay – LeChayim! Yaba baba bay – LeChayim! (to life!)
Trinken ale Chassidim

Az der Rebbe lacht (when the rabbi laughs)
Lachen ale Chassidim (all the Chasidim laugh)
Ha ha....
Lachen ale Chassidim

Az der Rebbe veynt (when the rabbi cries)
Veynen ale Chassidim (all the Chassidim cry)
Oy oy oy oy oy vey'z mir, oy oy... (oh, woe is me)
Veynen ale Chassidim

Az der Rebbe shloft (when the rabbi sleeps)
Shlofn ale Chassidim (All the Chassidim sleep)
(shh... yawn... hmmm...)

Az der Rebbe tantst! (when the Rabbi dances)
Tantsn ale Chassidim (all the Chassidim dance)
Ay didi day didi day, ay didi day didi day
Tantsn ale Chassidim

🎧 BAI MIR BISTU SHEIN

Bai mir bistu shein
Bai mir hostu chein
Bei mir bist eine oif der velt

Bei mir bistu git
Bai mir hostu it
Bai mir bistu teierer fin gelt
Fiel sheine meidlach hoben shoin
Gevolt nemen mich
Un fin zei alle ois gekliben
Hob ich nor dich
Bai mir bistu shein
Bai mir hostu chein
Bei mir bist eine oif der velt

Translation:
To me, you are lovely,
To me, you are charming.
To me, you are the
Only one in the world.
To me, you are lovely,
To me, you are charming,

To me, you are more precious than money.
Many pretty girls wanted me for a spouse
and among them all I chose only you.

THE SECRET

Shaindel Antelis ©
Album: Change

Questions echo in my mind
Is this true, or am I losing my head
I can't explain it, but I love it, I want more
I'm pretty sure I found what I've been looking for

Chorus
I may never know everything
But that's alright with me
I'll take it step by step
Until I see clearly

The Torah's filled with many pages
So many decisions, so many opinions, so many
changes
But it's all worth it, you can do it, of that I'm sure
Hashem is with you, and He's opening the door

Chorus

If you want the secret to happiness
It's written down right there
So open up, take a look
And don't be scared

Chorus

MY ZAIDY

Moshe Yess ob"m ©
Album: The Greatest Hits of Megama Plus!

My *Zaidy* lived with us in my parents' home
He used to laugh; he put me on his knee
And he spoke about his life in Poland
He spoke, but with a bitter memory

And he spoke about the soldiers who would beat him
And they laughed at him; they tore his long black coat
And he spoke about a synagogue that they burnt down
And the crying that was heard beneath the smoke

Chorus
But *Zaidy* made us laugh
Zaidy made us sing
And *Zaidy* made a *Kiddush* Friday night
And *Zaidy*, oh, my *Zaidy*
How I loved him so
And *Zaidy* used to teach me wrong from right

His eyes lit up when he would teach me Torah
He taught me every line so carefully
He spoke about our slavery in Egypt
And how G-d took us out to make us free

But winter went by
Summer came along
I went to camp to run and play
And when I came back home
They said, "*Zaidy* is gone"
And all his books were packed and stored away

I don't know how or why it came to be
It happened slowly over many years
We just stopped being Jewish like my *Zaidy* was
And no one cared enough to shed a tear

Chorus

And many winters went by
Many summers came along
And now my children sit in front of me
And who will be the *Zaidy* of my children?
Who will be their *Zaidy*, if not me?
Who will be the *Zaidy* of our children?
Who will be their *Zaidies*, if not we?

Chorus

WE'VE EXISTED SO LONG
Avremel Blesofsky

We've existed so long
'Cause the Torah kept us strong
And the Torah will never disappear
Through the ages, it was brought
By the children, who were taught
To follow it, and constantly declare

"I'm a Jew, and I'm proud
And I'll sing it out loud
'Cause forever, that's what I'll be
I'm a Jew, and I'm proud
And it's without a doubt
That *Hashem* is always watching over me" (x2)

KOL BAYAAR
Composed by the Shpoler Zeide, R' Aryeh Leib
Sung by H. M. Spalter and S. Levertov

English:
I hear in the forest a cry and a shout
A father seeks his children who have wandered about

"Children, children, where can you be
That you no longer remember me?
Children, children return to your home
For it's hard for me to be here all alone"

"Father, Father, how can we return once more?
The guards are all surrounding the door"

"Children, children, Torah you should learn
Then *Biyas Hamoshiach* you will surely earn
Very, very soon
In *Yerushalayim*, we will be
And we will see the miracles of old
In the *Bayis Hashlishi*"

Hebrew:
Kol Baya'ar Anochi Shomeya Av Levonim Korei
[קול ביער אנכי שומע אב לבנים קורא]

Yiddish:
A Geshrai A Gevald un A Gefilder,
A Foter In Vald Zucht Zaine Kinder

Russian:
Shum V'lesu Zvukayet, Batka V'lesu Sva-ich Detei
Shukayet

🎧 OIFEN PRIPITCHICK
M. M. Warshawsky ob"m

Dedicated to our beautiful, smart and talented
daughter Riva. We are so proud of you.
Love, Alex & Orit Taksir

Oyfn pripetshik brent a fayerl
Un in shtub iz heys
Un der rebe lernt kleyne kinderlekh
Dem Aleph Bais

Zogt zhe kinderlekh, gedenkt zhe, tayere
Vos ir lernt do
Zogt zhe noch a mol un takeh noch a mol:
Kometz-aleph: oh!

Lernt kinderlach, lernt mit freiyd
Lernt dem Aleph Bais
Gliklech iz der, vos hot gelernt Torah
Un dos Aleph Bais

Translation:
On the hearth, a small fire is burning
And in the room it's warm
And the Rabbi is teaching small children
The *Aleph Beis*

"See, children
Remember, dear ones, what you learn here
Repeat and repeat one more time:
Kamatz-aleph: oh!

"Learn, children, learn with enthusiasm
Learn the *Aleph Beis*
Happy is the Jew who knows the Torah
And the *Aleph Beis*"

IN LOVING MEMORY OF

Lillian Wasserman
Pesha Leah Bat Shaina Resha OB"M

YARTZEIT 5 SHEVAT

WE JOYFULLY REMEMBER HOW BUBBY WOULD SING "OIFEN PRIPITCHIK" TO HER CHILDREN AND GRANDCHILDREN.

SHE WAS OUR MOM

Written and sung by son Leonard Wasserman 1/17/05
To the tune of I Will Survive

Once there was a time, when I was just a child
Me and my brothers knew that something was so special in our lives
We saw her smile, we felt such joy and love
There was an angel looking down at us
An angel called our Mom
She was so kind
She kept us safe from harm
She protected us from evil
And taught us how to love
She was our mom
She kept us fed and clothed

And when we grew up to become young men
We moved out on our own
She was so sad
That we had left the nest
But that's just the way things happen
The way it's supposed to be
And then one day her youngest Rabbi son
Became so ill and left us
To be with *Hashem*
She stayed so strong and never failed us
She held us all together and taught us right from wrong
And when she reached the age of 90 — her treadmill sang it's song
And there she was — at age 96
Now we knew she really needed us
We rallied to her side
We did our best- to keep her safe from harm

Because she was our Mom
Her mind was clear — she still sang us songs
But we knew that time was running out
Our love for her still strong
She became weak
We shed so many tears
And when the day approached after so many years
We saw her strength just slip away
And then that fateful day
That really special day
Her Rabbi son's birthday
On 1/14 she is now in his hands
She was our mom and we will miss her so
But we will survive
She was our mom
We had to let her go
She was our mom

CHAPTER 6:
Soul & Faith

The *Tanya* teaches us that G-d created man with two souls, characterized by two vastly different inclinations. The first is the *Nefesh Elokis*, the G-dly soul; the second is known as the *Nefesh haBahamis*, the animal soul. In addition to that soul's physical desires and needs that make us human, negativity and undesirable traits also stem from the *Nefesh haBahamis*.

On the opposite end of the spectrum, the *Nefesh Elokis* epitomizes the positive and motivates the Divine attributes reflected within us of love, beauty, humility, and so much more. The *Nefesh Elokis* makes known to us that *Hashem* is always by our side and yearning for us to come closer. It's up to every individual human being to choose which of the two souls will hold the reins of their minds, emotions, and lives.

The G-dly spark within is an eternal flame. It cries out a message of possibility and hope and reminds us that *Hashem* believes in us — "*Rabah Emunasecha*, great is Your faith." It whispers to us, "You are vital in this place and time, so keep reaching higher and higher and singing your song." *L'Chayim!*

QUESTION TO CONSIDER:
Singing uplifts and reminds us to believe and live with joy.
Which song uplifts you and why?

AMEN

Rivka Leah Popack ©
Lead and backing vocals by Taliah Bloom
Album: Silent Prayer

There's a tune stirring deep in each soul
A tune we all know well
Of wonder, awe, and thanks
More than we can tell

There's a song lying deep in each heart
Deep where the soul knows no words
A song of creation
Waiting to be heard

Chorus
Shiru LaHashem Shiru Shiru
Shiru LaHashem Ki Tov
Shiru LaHashem Shiru Shiru
Ki Leolam Chasdoh
[שירו לה' שירו שירו
שירו לה' כי טוב
שירו לה' שירו שירו
כי לעולם חסדו*]

Every time you find strength in the words that you hear
Every time that you see the clouds start to clear
Every time that you manage to conquer your fear
See the blessing, say Amen

Every time you find wonder within the mundane
Every time that the sun shines right through the rain
Every time you discover the will, try again
See the blessing, say Amen

Chorus

Every time that you're warmed by the sun shining bright
Every time that you're able to stand for what's right
Every time that the moon lights your way through the night
See the blessing, say Amen

Every time you don't let a new day pass you by
Every time that you witness a bird soar the sky
Every time that you fall and find new chance to try
See the blessing, say Amen

Chorus

When you ask for blessing, and the rain keeps on falling
When the night ends and beckons the morning
Stop a moment, see the miracle
See the miracle

Every time a friend helps you when life's just too much
Every time you're inspired by love's gentle touch
Every time that you see that life is just such
A miracle, a miracle
Say Amen

Sing to G-d, for He is good, for His kindness is everlasting.

A TRIBUTE TO
Rivka Leah Popack
BRILLIANT SINGER/SONGWRITER, PRODUCER OF 'SILENT PRAYER'

Some songs find us at the exact right time. Almost never do you get to meet the person who wrote or sang that song. But I did.

At a time of personal transformation for me, I met Rivka Leah who freely and happily gave me her CD and asked me to pay special attention to her signature song, *Silent Prayer*. I did.

The words hit me with an impact clearly inspired by Hashem. Speaking to my own Divine message and coming at the exact right time, I listened to every word and sang it at the top of my lungs in my car [LOL]. Likewise with her *Ani Maamin*. Every song on her CD became etched in my memory, in my soul; filled and inspired me and lifted me up to be able to continue to joyfully lift up others.

Thank you Rivka Leah, for helping me find my Jewish soul.

With love,
Susan

www.rivkaleahmusic.com

🎧 SILENT PRAYER

Rivka Leah Popack ©
Lead vocals by Debra Jacobs
Backing vocals by Debra Jacobs and Taliah Bloom
Album: Silent Prayer

As you embark upon this journey
And I won't be there
I close my eyes and turn away
To pray this silent prayer

That you find the strength within you
To be more than you are
And the faith to believe
It's how you travel far

And whatever comes to pass
And where you might be
I pray you see the reason at the heart
To know it's meant to be

And when it seems that life's too much
I just hope you see it's true
That G-d wouldn't make you face a test
You couldn't follow through

May you discover the gift in giving
And find your peace of mind
Know that you're never alone
G-d is by your side

Find the will to make a difference
The will to live and learn

See the good in others
And do kindness in return

Make the most of what you're given
And what comes your way
Send off your own prayer
Live with purpose every day

And though the nest seems so much safer
Than the endless stretch of sky
I pray for you the courage
To spread your wings and fly so high

You can fly so high
You can reach the sky
There is nothing you can't do
When you know, G-d believes in you (x2)

Yehi Ratzon Milfanecha Hashem
Elokeinu V'Elokay Avoseinu
Shetishma Kol Tefillasi
Ki Atah Shomeya Tefillas Kol Peh

[יהי רצון מלפניך ה'
אלקינו ואלקי אבותינו
שתשמע קול תפלתי
כי אתה שומע תפלת כל פה*]

As you embark upon this journey
And I won't be there
I turn around and walk away
And send you with this prayer

**May it be Your will, Lord our G-d and the G-d of our fathers, that
You hear the voice of my prayer, for You hear the prayers of all.*

FOOTSTEPS

Rivka Leah Popack ©
Lead vocals by Chaya Sara Weiss
Backing vocals by Taliah Bloom
Album: Silent Prayer

I dreamed a dream, like none I've had before
So real, I can feel, the waves breaking on the shore
Of an empty beach, standing right there
With the ocean breeze, blowing through my hair

Stretching far behind me in the sands of time
Two sets of footprints, yours and mine
There through the gentle tides, you held my hand
But there's one thing I just can't understand

In the times that were rough
Through the dark and stormy seas
My heart called to you, but a whisper on the breeze
As the cold set in deep, headed towards dry land
I saw only one set of footprints in the sand

Dear child of mine, I'm right here by your side
I've watched your world unfold with such delight
Beneath the sheltered clouds, and the guiding light ahead
You walked the hidden path, not knowing where it led

With the dawn of each new day, the wonder in your eyes
Horizons opened up; you discovered freedom skies
Blessing each new breath, I watched you learn and grow

Yes, there's something that I need you to know

In the times that were rough
Through the wind and through the rain
I heard your voice; I heard you calling my name
I was there, in your prayer, as your heart whispered its psalms
I lifted you and carried you in my arms

Walking through sands as they shift beneath your feet
Never quite knowing what you're gonna meet
On these forty-two journeys of life
Hear me now, hear me now

On the road that lies beyond
Through the bitter and the sweet
You'll find my light, emerge from night
Where earth and heaven meet
Footsteps behind, I trust you'll find, that deep inside you know
I'm here with you, as you leave your home, to the land that I'll show

INSPIRATION

Rivkah Krinsky ©

Dedicated to Susan Axelrod for your dedication to our Jewish daughters and for your smile and words that uplift our hearts and souls.
Love, Nechama and JGU Online Students

I'm looking for a smile
That warms my soul
That makes me feel whole

Like home

I'm looking for those words
To fill my heart
Inspiring a new dawn
A new start

Where's the song
That fans the flame
I know...

Chorus:
All I have to do
Is take a look at you
And I can find who I really am
You make me want to try
Whilst on your wings I fly
You're my inspiration

I'm searching for the one
Who dares to dream
In spite of how lofty
It may seem

I'm searching for that someone
Whose faith is strong
Unwavering no matter
How long

And in this madness
With all the sadness
I know...

I can see it clearly now

I can breathe
You are the wind behind my back
I can breathe

🎧 SHALL WE WALK?

Shall we walk in light or darkness?
Night must fall, still, the choice is ours
To look and just see shadows
Or raise our eyes and search the sky for stars

Let there be music, oh yes, let there be joy and light
Laughter and song to brighten the darkest night
Trust and faith that everything's going right
Ivdu Es Hashem Besimcha
[*עבדו את ה' בשמחה]

Serve G-d with joy. -Psalms 100:2

🎧 I BELIEVE
Chaim Fogelman and Chony Milecki ©

I've seen the Eiffel Tower
And I've seen Trafalgar Square
I've seen the sunrise on the ocean
And I know that You are there
From our Holy Land Israel
To the Jewish plight, we all know too well
I know You are there
And I know, I know You care

Horrified, we watched the Towers fall
As my soul froze somehow
I wondered G-d, where are You now?

But as the people ran in fear
I know You were standing there
And as our heroes went to die
I think I heard You start to cry

Chorus (x2)
And I believe You are listening to me
And I believe You are standing here with me
And the footprints in the sand, oh no they're not from me
I believe they're all from You, my G-d when You carried me

The storms in our life
They come riding in like the wind
And turn us inside out
Just to fill our hearts with doubt

But You're my strength; You're my power
You're my hero, You're my tower
You're my life-line in the sea
And it's You who carries me

Chorus

I believe, ooohhh
I believe, ooohhh
I believe, ooohhh
I believe, I believe
Yes, I still believe (x2)

🎧 YOU'RE NEVER ALONE

Melody composed by Mirele Rosenberger
Lyrics by Avraham Fried ©
Album: You're Never Alone

Sometimes when you're feeling all alone
You need some happiness to call your own
Nothing is going the way it should
You're trying to do the best you could

Lift up your eyes to the skies
Your life's in His hands, trust in Him, He will reply
Guiding all your steps always at your side
You are His joy and pride

And don't you know, you're never alone
It doesn't matter where you are
There's nothing in His eyes more special than you
Wherever you go, *Hashem* goes with you (x2)

🎧 IVDU

Benny Friedman
Composed by Yoni Eliav and Benny Friedman ©
Arranged by Yaron Gershovsky
Album: Yesh Tikvah

טוֹב־ה' לַכֹּל וְרַחֲמָיו עַל־כָּל־מַעֲשָׂיו
עִבְדוּ אֶת־ה' בְּשִׂמְחָה בֹּאוּ לְפָנָיו בִּרְנָנָה

Translation:
The Lord is good to all, and His mercies are on all His works. -Psalms 145:9
Serve the Lord with joy, come before Him with praise. -Psalms 100:2

DEDICATED TO

Yaffah Nessyah Ferber

BAT MITZVAH
ADAR II 26 5776

יְבָרֶךְ הַשֵׁם וִיכַנֶּסֵךְ לַתּוֹרָה
וְלַחֶפָּה וּלְמַעֲשִׂים טוֹבִים

LOVE,

Ima and Abba

SHOOTIN' FOR THE MOON

Michoel Pruzansky
Composed by Elie Schwab ©
Additional composition by Yochanan Shapiro and
Michoel Pruzansky
Lyrics by Elie Schwab and Miriam Israeli
Arranged by Eli Klein and Yitzy Berry
Additional music and mixing by Eli Gertsner
Album: Shootin' for the Moon

Chorus
I'm shootin' for the moon tonight
I ride the winds at the speed of light
I've set my goals; I made my mind
And if I miss I'll make it to the stars
We're gonna make it to the top
I'm shootin' for the moon tonight
And if I miss I'll make it to the stars

Looking up, standing on the ground
Me and my dreams galaxies apart
But I know, somewhere deep inside
I've got the strength to get that far
Climbing on a ladder in the sky
Though I'm not an angel, maybe I can fly
Pushing through still another mile
All I gotta do is try

Chorus

Sending up yet another prayer
Father, I know you believe in me

When its rough, and I'm feeling doubt
You can raise me up above the clouds
I can feel the power of a dream
Giving me wings, taking me beyond
All the pain, all the broken hopes
Gonna leave it all behind

Chorus

Never gonna break apart, till I reach my destination
Never gonna lose the spark in my soul
Gonna be a shining light, gonna be an inspiration
Never giving up the fight towards my goal

Chorus

🎧 IVRI ANOCHI

Benny Friedman
Composed by Ari Goldwag ©
Lyrics by Ari Goldwag, Shmuel Marcus, Miriam Israeli
Arranged by Ian Freitor and Daniel Kapler

Rabos Aveir Ha'am Hazeh Baderech
V'ani Holech Im Rosh Lema'alah
Kol Echad Hu Ben Oh Bas Shel Melech
Kach Hayah Vekachah Zeh Gam Halah
Yehudi Im Neshama Bo'eres
Bechol Makom, Uvechol Eretz
Lo Rotzeh Sheyihiyeh Acheres
Yehudi Ani
Zeh Mashehu Nitzchi
[רבות עבר העם הזה בדרך
ואני הולך עם ראש למעלה
כל אחד הוא בן או בת של מלך

כך היה וככה זה גם הלאה
יהודי עם נשמה בוערת
בכל מקום, ובכל ארץ
לא רוצה שיהיה אחרת
יהודי אני
[זה משהוא נצחי*]

Bnei Avraham, Yitzchak v'Yaakov
Bnei Sarah, Rivkah, Rachel v'Leah
[בני אברהם יצחק ויעקוב
[**בני שרה רבקה רחל ולאה] (x2)

Chorus
Ivri Anochi, V'Es Hashem Elokay Hashamayim Ani Yareh
[***עברי אנכי ואת ה' אלקי השמים אני ירא] (x4)

A little bit of history I've been through
Ask me where I'm from, and I will tell you
I'm a Jew, and every Jew's a proud Jew
Not just me, my sisters and my brothers
Never be ashamed to be a proud Jew
It's not what you've done; it's how He made you
So sing this song and spread the pride around you
יהודי אני, eternally!

בני אברהם יצחק ויעקוב
בני שרה רבקה רחל ולאה (x2)

Chorus

I'm a Jew, and I'm proud
And I'll sing it out loud
'Cause forever and ever

That's what I'll be
I'm a Jew, and I'm proud
And without a doubt
Hashem is always watching over me

(x2) עברי אנכי ואת ה' אלקי השמים אני ירא

Chorus

יהודי אני...

*Many people passed this way, and I go with my head up. Each one is the son or daughter of a king; so it was and so on, a Jew with a burning soul, everywhere, and in every country. I do not want it to be any different. I am a Jew — it's something eternal!
**The children of Abraham, Isaac, and Jacob, the children of Sarah, Rebecca, Rachel and Leah
***I am a Hebrew [a Jew] and the Lord, G-d of the heavens [is the One] I fear. -Jonah, 1:9*

YESH TIKVAH

Benny Friedman
Composed by Ari Goldwag ©
Original lyrics by Miriam Israeli and Ari Goldwag
English lyrics by Rabbi Eli Friedman
Arranged by Ian Freitor
Album: Yesh Tikvah

תִּסְתַּכֵּל פֹּה וְשָׁם
מִסָּבִיב לְעוֹלָם
יֵשׁ צָרוֹת, דְּאָגוֹת
הַחִיּוּךְ נֶעֱלָם
אַךְ אַל תִּרְאֶה רַק שָׁחוֹר
כִּי גַּם זֶה יַעֲבוֹר
וְהַכֹּל יִסְתַּדֵּר

כִּי ה' יַעֲזֹור

Chorus

יֵשׁ תִּקְוָה
אִם נָשִׁיר כּוּלָּנוּ יַחַד
יֵשׁ אֱמוּנָה חֲזָקָה מִכֹּל הַפַּחַד
לֹא נִפּוֹל, לֹא נִרְעַד
כִּי אֲנַחְנוּ לֹא לְבַד
יֵשׁ לָנוּ ה' אֶחָד

בּוֹא אִיתִי
שִׂים יָדְךָ בְּיָדִי
אַל תִּדְאַג, אַל תִּפְחַד
כִּי נִצְעַד יַד בְּיָד
הַקָּדוֹשׁ בָּרוּךְ הוּא
אֶת כּוּלָּנוּ אוֹהֵב
עוֹד תִּרְאֶה שִׂמְחָה
יִיגָמֵר הַכְּאֵב

Chorus

Translation:
Look around, far and near
Where's the joy, where's the cheer
Why the fear, why the frown
Why the smile upside down
Shake yourself from the dust
Scrape your soul from the rust
Know that this too shall pass
For in G-d we trust

Chorus
There is hope
If we sing our hope together

We have faith that is stronger than the terror
No despair, no dismay
Everything will be okay
He is with us night and day

Brother dear
Dry your tears
Take my hand, never fear
Let's advance, side by side
And let's cast our fright aside
Don't forget all the love
That we have from Above
And you'll see with the dawn
All the pain will be gone

Chorus

HASHEM LOVES YOU

Ari Goldwag ©
Sung by Ari Goldwag and Sheves Chaverim
Album: A Capella Soul

Sometimes you're feeling down
Things haven't gone your way
So you're looking all around
To find someone who'll save the day
There's one Place you can turn
He'll never turn you back
When you look to *Hashem*
You're always back on track

Chorus

'Cause *Hashem* loves you
You're His greatest pride
Yes, *Hashem* loves you
He's always by your side
You can see it too
All the good you have inside
It's up to you
All you need is to decide

One thing you've got to know
Is no matter what you do
No strings are attached
To the love *Hashem* will show to you
Just got to hold on tight
Put your trust in Him
Keep your head held high
Let your soul just start to sing

Chorus

You'll walk a different walk
With confidence in your stride
When you think of *Hashem's* love
And you know you're always on His mind
There's a light you've got to shine
A job no one else can do
Hashem's given you the tools
Now the rest comes down to you

Chorus

He loves you...

🎧 LO NAFSIK LIRKOD

Song composed by Ari Goldwag & Yitzy Waldner ©
Song concept by Ari Goldwag
Lyrics by Miriam Israeli
Album: Lo Nafsik Lirkod

זֶה שִׁיר שֶׁכָּל אֶחָד יוֹדֵעַ
כָּל אֶחָד שׁוֹמֵעַ
הוּא הוֹפֵךְ אֶת כָּל הָרַע לְטוֹב
הוּא נוֹתֵן לָנוּ הַכֹּחַ
לְהַמְשִׁיךְ לִשְׂמוֹחַ וְלִרְקוֹד (x2)

לֹא נַפְסִיק לִרְקוֹד
תָּרִימוּ אֶת הָרַגְלַיִם
הַשָּׁמַיִם הֵם הַגְּבוּל עֲדַיִין
לֹא נַפְסִיק לִרְקוֹד
יָבוֹא מַה שֶׁיָּבוֹא
לֹא נַפְסִיק לִרְקוֹד

זֶה שִׁיר שֶׁיֵּשׁ לוֹ אֶת הַקֶּצֶב
אֵין בּוֹ אֶת הָעֶצֶב
זֶה נִיגּוּן שֶׁשָּׁר טוֹב לְהוֹדוֹת
נַעֲשֶׂה יַחַד לְחַיִּים
נְשַׁלֵּב יָדַיִם וְנִרְקוֹד (x2)

Chorus

Translation:
This is a song that everyone knows
That everyone is listening to
It turns all the bad into good
It gives us the strength
To continue to rejoice and dance (x2)
We will never stop dancing

Pick up your feet
The sky's still the limit
We will never stop dancing
Come whatever comes
We will never stop dancing

This is a song that has the beat
It doesn't have any sadness
This is a tune that sings, 'It is good to give thanks'
Let's make a *L'chaim* together
And dance together arm in arm (x2)

🎧 ET REKOD

Yaakov Shwekey ©
Album: Kolot

לְכָל זְמַן, לַכֹּל זְמַן וָעֵת
לְכָל זְמַן, לַכֹּל זְמַן וָעֵת
עֵת לֶאֱהוֹב, עֵת לִשְׂנוֹא, עֵת מִלְחָמָה,
וְעֵת, וְעֵת שָׁלוֹם (x2)

אֲבָל הַלַּיְלָה הַלַּיְלָה הַזֶּה
אֲבָל הַלַּיְלָה הַזֶּה
כֻּלָּנוּ בְּשִׂמְחָה לָנוּ הַלַּיְלָה
עֵת רְקוֹד, עֵת רְקוֹד, עֵת רְקוֹד
כֻּלָּנוּ בְּשִׂמְחָה לָנוּ הַלַּיְלָה
עֵת רְקוֹד, עֵת רְקוֹד, עוֹד וְעוֹד

Translation:
There is a time for everything
A time for love, a time for hate
A time for war and a time for peace (x2)

But tonight we are all happy
It's time to dance!

🎧 L'CHI LACH

Debbie Friedman ob"m ©

This song, based on Genesis 12:1-2, shares a piece of the story of Abraham and Sarah as they began a journey of faith, while also calling to a contemporary Jew as a reminder of a promise to be blessed on a journey.

L'chi Lach, to a land that I will show you
Lech Lecha, to a place you do not know
L'chi Lach, on your journey I will bless you

And you shall be a blessing
You shall be a blessing
You shall be a blessing, *L'chi Lach*

L'chi Lach and I shall make your name great
Lech Lecha and all shall praise your name
L'chi Lach to the place that I will show you

L'Simchat Chayim
L'Simchat Chayim
L'Simchat Chayim, L'chi Lach

L'chi Lach, to a land that I will show you
Lech Lecha, to a place you do not know
L'chi Lach, on your journey I will bless you

And you shall be a blessing
You shall be a blessing
You shall be a blessing, *L'chi Lach*

And you shall be a blessing, *L'chi Lach...*

🎧 COMPASS

Chanale ©
Album: I Am the Land

Yeah, it's been a bumpy road
Roller coasters high and low
There's a map that tells the way
Let it help you navigate
You don't have to go that far

Chorus
You want to give up 'cause it's hard
But someone knows just where you are
So let *Hashem* above be your compass when you're lost
And you should follow Him wherever you may go
On a path that is true
There's direction for a Jew
And no matter what you'll never be alone
Never be alone, oh oh oh
Never be alone, oh oh oh

You've lost your courage on the way
Don't close your eyes, don't be afraid
Put all your faith into His hands
Though he knows just where you stand
Follow Him, you'll be okay

Chorus

On a path that is true
There's direction for a Jew
And no matter what you'll never be alone

🎧 PLAYING WITH FIRE

Avraham Fried ©
Album: Bring the House Down

There's a place in your heart deep within
Known as the *Kodesh Hakodashim*
There's an altar there
With a heavenly fire burning
That's why you're always yearning
That's why you're always yearning

Chorus
This fire takes you higher
If you let it burn
Inspire your desire
To live and learn
If you ignore it
And don't absorb it
Brother, you're playin' with fire
Your heavenly fire
It's there to take you higher
And higher, and higher, and higher

🎧 HOLD ON TO YOUR FAITH

Rebbetzin Tap ©
Album: Shabbos & Holiday Collection

Sometimes, you don't know what to do
You've thought it all through
A rescue's overdue
Sometimes, you don't know where to turn
Your head's filled with concern
That's the time to learn

Chorus
To hold on to your faith
Open your heart
When times are hard, you will get through
Hold on to your faith
Open your heart
When times are hard, you're not alone

Sometimes, it's hard to understand
When everything you've planned
Is slipping through your hands
Sometimes, it seems so hard to cope
At the end of your rope
Just never lose hope

Chorus

Can we do it?
Yes, we can... (x4)

DOING FINE
Chany Levy ©

Sorting through the voices in my mind
I try to move, but I can hardly find
Strength to pick me up from where I am
I'm here again, and everything's the same
Same old struggles showing up
I tried so hard, but it's not enough
I'm racing toward the finish line
But it takes time

Chorus
Each day I get a little stronger
Each year I live a little longer
And each challenge shows me how much farther
I've moved ahead
So when I stare at my reflection
I dare not pressure for perfection
It's one step at a time
Breathing in
I am doing fine

Silently I sink into myself
Get me out
But no one's there to help
I'm running out of patience, out of hope
I'm holding on
I need to know
Hashem, He counts the tears and sweat
And though I may not be there yet
There's a welcome sign at every step
And I'm okay

Chorus

Thank You for this melody divine
Clarity is often hard to find
Life's a journey; life is not a race
And I need time to figure out my place
Round and round
It sure is tough
But it's a spiral, and it's going up
Feel the raise in every rise
Stop, take pride

Each day I get a little stronger
Each year I live a little longer
And each challenge shows me how much farther
I've moved ahead
So when I stare at my reflection
I dare not pressure for perfection
It's one step at a time
I'm letting go, and I will be just fine
Believing that I am doing fine

TO BUILD AND REBUILD
Chaya Aydel Lebovics ob"m
To the Tune of A Sukka'leh A Kleine

Many years ago, in the *Midbar* we know
That our parents had to build and rebuild
The *Mishkan* by following the plans of *Hashem*
And the Clouds of Glory rested on them, da da da da
The *Mishkan* by following the plans of *Hashem*
And the Clouds of Glory rested on them

Throughout many years, through suffering and tears
Our fathers learned to build and rebuild
A fine Jewish home; they were never alone
Hashem strengthened them and wiped off their tears,
da da da da
A fine Jewish home; they were never alone
Hashem strengthened them and wiped off their tears

With joy and with pride, our children at our side
We build our dear *Sukkah'le* today
We pray and we long, "Please keep our faith strong
And please send *Moshiach* our way," da da da da
We pray and we long, "Please keep our faith strong
And please send *Moshiach* our way"

🎧 SUPERHERO
Esther Freeman ©

Since I was young, I dreamed of changing the world
"It's absurd," they would say, "You're just a little girl
Forget your childish dreams
You cannot be a superhero
Grow up and live your life, walk away"

Chorus
They keep telling me I cannot change the world
But in my heart I know I'm not just a little girl
I feel this power invested in my soul
And I know I can be a superhero

I tried to grow up and fast
And forget all my silly little dreams
And listen to what they said is reality
But the void in my heart
Still remained quite a part of who I am today and

meant to be
Chorus

Olam Katan Zeh Adam
[*עוֹלָם קָטָן זֶה אָדָם]
If I change the world that's me, the rest will follow
naturally
I'm a powerful little girl, and I can change the world
So here I am I'm going to be strong
If I can save myself, I've saved it all
No matter what they see, this is the reality
I'm a superhero, and I can change the world
By changing myself

Chorus

*Man is a small world. -Talmud

🎧 MAN PLANS AND G-D LAUGHS
Esther Freeman ©

We keep fighting, denying
The One True Source
We're choosing, refusing
The Ultimate Force
And though we've known it all along
Maybe we've been seeing it wrong

Oh, we walk about our daily lives
Thinking we're in control
The lines we say, the parts we play
It's just not our role
So just sit back and let it go

And let G-d run the show

Chorus
Mentch Tracht Un G-tt Lacht
[מענטש טראַכט און ג-אָט לאַכט*]
But we're still making our own plans
When it seems like everything's going wrong
It's all within His hands
Don't let anything get you down
Remember this one thought
When *Hashgocha Protis* plays its part
Don't forget what we've been taught

We need to stop trying to run
A world that does not belong to us
Lift your hands unto to the sky
And stop questioning why

Chorus

*Man plans and G-d laughs.

🎧 VANITY
Esther Freeman ©

In this time we call life
There's a mission on which to hold
Some get sidetracked on the way
Lose their sight, so I'm told
But I know there's more to see
Yes, I know there's more for me
Some look for fame and fortune
Get all caught up in hot air
It's about style, name, reputation

Who you know not, do you care?
But I know it doesn't last
Yes, I know it passes fast

Chorus
Yes, this is the only way for me
Siz Doch Altz Hevel Havalim
*Ein Od Milvado**

What the eyes see is very different
From the true reality
Take a second, see the bigger picture It's nothing but vanity
'Cause I know there's more to life
Yes, I know what is right

Chorus

Superficial, latest trending, am I cool enough for you?
The deception's so compelling
But it ain't so true
As you look now in the mirror
The reflection through your eyes
Don't be fooled by all the glory
Of vanity's disguise

Chorus

*It is all vanity of vanities; there is naught but Him. –Ecclesiastes

🎧 SEASON OF CHANGE
Dalia Oziel ©

You're cold inside

The sky is bleak
There's been no sun
You're feeling weak
You try to source
Your inner strength

Winter's cold
But we build with snow
Fall shows the beauty in letting go
And summer's warmth
Is captivating
Seasons keep changing
And so do me and you
We all have the winters
We have to go through
A change of season, or a season of change
Find your perspective, have the words rearranged

Chorus
We're strong when we hold each other's hands
Facing struggles in the Master plan
He smiles when He sees us all unite
When we help each other fight
It's the season of change
We're stronger together
No matter the weather
It always gets better
It's the season of change
Let's strengthen each other
We're sisters and brothers
Through sunshine and thunder
It's the season of change

No winter lasts

No spring skips its turn
Autumn comes, to sooth the summer's burn
The force of nature proves that things will change
You'll never live a life full of pain

The ups and downs
is what it's all about
And when you're feeling good
It's time for branching out
We'd grow faster in our time of need
If we'd nurture each other's seeds

Aleh Katan...
Na na na na na na na na na na... (x4)

Take the leap
Have the courage to fall
Unleash your colors - it is you after all
Feel the breeze - it is just time to be
Don't forget you're "*Aleh Katan Sheli* [עלה קטן שלי*]"

Chorus (x2)

*My little leaf

🎧 INSIDE OUT
Nechama Cohen ©
Album: Heartbeat

I heard from a smart guy the outside is just a lie
When joy is not flying in your heart, you can't start to soar
You gotta live life to the beat of your soul
It feels right when it's not just a show anymore

I, I wanna try
I, I wanna fly

Chorus
Happiness only comes from the inside, inside, inside
out
It's only real when it comes from the inside, inside,
inside out
When you find that spark in you that shines like a
glowing light in the darkest night
Happiness only comes from the inside, inside, inside
out

I heard from a smart man it's not about running
around
You're just running away from the pain you've found
You gotta live creating the joy you'll have
Music's playing inside though you hear no sound

I, I'm gonna try
I, I'll find a way to fly

Chorus

Though it's not easy to find that feeling of elation
I'm gonna search from deep inside and follow my
intuition
I know though the instant is fast, it won't last very
long
Day by day, I'll take it slowly from the inside out
Until I'm strong

Happiness only comes from the inside, inside, inside
out

It's only real when it comes from the inside, inside,
inside out
So bright like a shooting star across the black sky
Shining rays of light
Happiness only comes from the inside, inside, inside
out

Inside, inside out...

🎧 HEARTBEAT

Nechama Cohen ©
Album: Heartbeat

Sometimes your faith
Seems to escape through
The cracks that you never knew you made
Sometimes the pain
Tries to consume you
But time keeps on turning and things change

Chorus
Just like a heartbeat
That's rising and falling
Sinking and soaring
It keeps you alive
There will always be ups and downs
There's no time to waste for staying on the ground
A struggle makes you stronger in the end
Believe that it's true
You know you'll survive
When you hear
Your heartbeat, your heartbeat

Sometimes you smile,
The world smiles back at you and understands your
spirited mind
Sometimes you fly,
The view is so beautiful
But even birds land once in a while

Chorus

And life goes on when you don't think it can
And when you fall, you'll learn how to stand
'Cause the road will never be smooth
The ins and the outs are what life's all about
And learning how to smile through it all

Just like a heartbeat
That's rising and falling
Sinking and soaring
It keeps you alive
There will always be ups and downs
There's no time to waste for playing around
Believe that you're stronger than you think
You'll see that it's true
You know you'll survive
When you hear
You know you'll be fine
'Cause you feel
Your heartbeat, your heartbeat

SHINE

Nechama Cohen ©
Album: Heartbeat

I wake up to the rain outside my window
Every drop a reflection of my inner pain
I gather my strength to get up again somehow
Hide the tears that are lingering on my face

My act can fool for a while
Though inside I'm crying
I know all the reasons to smile
Still, my spirit is dying
I keep telling myself

Chorus
The sun does shine, underneath
Ever so brightly, but I just don't see past the cloudy
line
The sun does shine, underneath
Forever faithfully, it will always be
There for me to see

I'm walking along the lines of monotony
Never straying, I'm praying to just get somewhere
I'm hearing my footsteps as if it's not me
In my mind, my real life is so far away from here

My act can fool for a while
Though inside I'm crying
I know all the reasons to smile
Still, my spirit is dying
I keep reminding myself

Chorus

It's shining on me
Melting away my fear
I have to believe
I may not see it, but it's always there

Chorus

NESHOMO'LE

Abie Rotenberg ©
Album: Journeys, Volume 2

"Come with me, little *Neshomo'le*
Let me hold you in my hand
And we'll fly away, you and I together
To a place down on the land"

"Come with me, little *Neshomo'le*
Don't shy away, do as your told
There's a little child waiting to be born today
You're to be his spark, his soul"

"But dear *Malach'l*, no, I don't want to go
There is so much pain and evil on the earth below
Let me stay here up in heaven where it's safe, and I'll be pure
Please don't make me go away, can't you see I'm so afraid?"

"Come with me, little *Neshomo'le*
It's time you faced your destiny
And as we fly beneath the clouds now
I will show you; there is so much you can be"

"Yes, dear *Malach'l*, I can see *Kedushah* over there
Look, someone's learning Torah, and there's another deep in prayer
I will stay here if you answer me, it's all I need to know
You must promise me, dear friend, that I too will be like them"

"Come with me, little *Neshomo'le*
Oh it's a task that I must do
As I tap you on the lip, you will forget me
You're on your own; it's up to you"

"Come with me, little *Neshomo'le*
Let me hold you in my hand.
And we'll fly away, you and I together
To a place above the land."

"But dear *Malach'l*, no, I don't want to go I'm not ready to go with you, where you take me, I don't know
Let me stay right where I am there's so much more I need to do
Please don't make me go away can't you see I'm so afraid"

"Come with me, little *Neshomo'le*
I've only come to take you home.
And there is no need to fear your destination
You've earned a place right by the throne..."

"A place right by the throne..."

MELECH MALCHEI HAMLACHIM

Rivky Saxon ©
Music by Eyal Golan
English lyrics by Shayna Mushka Saxon

The thoughts they come in
Power we have within
To change them
To redirection
Put a finger on it
Don't get scared
Use courage
But we are not
Submissive to it

Handed to me
Responsibility
On what I choose to focus on
Yet only identifying
What is there
Can I activate
With mental steer

Melech Malchei Hamelachim
Is staring at me
He trusted the key within me
Even when hard it does get
To go on, just forget
He believes I can responsibly

Testing me initially
The thoughts constantly

The subconscious I can't control
But, Hashem does expect then
To give it direction
To change the channel in my head

Fear I then feel,
Oh, how can I heal
The imagined danger I see?
Take the thoughts that come up
Look time down the line
In a year will it matter to me?

Wouldn't it be easier
To just fly above it
And never have these on my head?
Yes, sometimes I can
But when they still happen
I want to know how to respond and say

Melech Malchei Hamelachim
Thank You for everything
There's so much You've given to me
Brothers, and sisters, so dear
And parents who care
And friendships
With people I share

My ultimate Father, my King
So much *Chessed* You bring
When I think about it consciously
I can relax, logically
It will all be okay
I can lower the intensity

Hashem, You're really my Best Friend
You're in me; You're in them
You're gonna make sure it's okay
As long as I just do my best
I can really go rest
And let You, *Hashem* run the scene

Melech Malchei Hamelachim
Thank You for everything
So many good things to realize
As I open my eyes
Hashem is "*Pokeyach Ivrim* [*פוקח עורים]"

*Opener of the eyes. –Morning Blessings Liturgy

🎧 HONEY, YOU'LL SURVIVE

Rivky Saxon ©

All these teenagers walkin' down the street together
"Man, it looks so fun," says one friend to another
But they don't have a clue what's really going on
'Cause when you're so concerned, how can you have fun?

'Cause half the girls are worried what the other half thinks
And half the boys are showin' off their brand new bling
And it's all superficial when you stand back and watch
You'll find out you ain't missing out on much
"But it's so dang fun!"

Chorus
Honey, you'll survive without it, believe it

It's a major drag when you see it from the outside
Honey, you'll survive without it, you'll see it
When you're outta the scene
You'll feel a whole lot more pride

Come on!

"I can't talk to girls," says a bunch of them
"I simply get along much better with boys"
But if you're honest with yourself then a lot of the time
It's just another ploy

Chorus

You don't need no validation from the guys
Who for the most part only want one thing
And you're way better than their opinions and their judgments
And the lies and the compliments
Ooohhh…

Not everything is the way it seems
Sometimes it's hard to see through the internal schemes
And the fronts that people put up
When you look closely, you'll see it's all made up
All the drama and rumors around
Like, who in their right mind would ever want that?
But there's fear of missing out
There's peer pressure and doubt
And you want to feel included
You wanna be with that crowd
But it's not all it's cracked up to be
You'll see if you ever get out

'Cause once you start, everything can go south from there
Like a drug that you can't get enough of
When push comes to shove, no, it's never enough
So why not quit while you're ahead?
Don't join in the first place
'Cause once you're in it
You'll find out it ain't worth it
So stand up to the crowd and look alive
Hold your head high
'Cause honey; you'll survive

Honey, you'll survive without it (x4)

Chorus

DEAR COMPUTER
Rivky Saxon ©

Whoaa, yeah, yeah, yeah, yeah
I'm getting up
Out of this place
No, I'm not doing this
You think you can
Entrap me again
Well, I'm not gonna let you
Pull me down
Oh, pull me down
No
This chair has been
Sat in for too long
It's time I stretched my legs
I'm coming clean
You know you're addicting

I'm gonna get cured
From this disease
This virtual reality

Chorus
And you can't stop me now; I'm shutting you down
Though you seduce me with your lights and sounds
But you're not worth it
And I can't waste more time
Dear computer

So many sites
So many ads
So much stimulation
I really don't need this in my life
I'd rather spend time with actual people
Who don't need to be plugged in every four hours

Chorus

Whoa... Whoa...
I can't waste more time, can't waste more time
Can't waste more time, can't waste more time

My eyes are bloodshot
Can't stop lookin' at the screen
I'm at your mercy
Why do you do this to me?
It's almost like you love seeing me like this
Hopelessly devoted
And wasting my time on you
Oh, on you
You love it, don't you?
Hopelessly devoted

And wasting my time

Chorus

Dear computer (x4)

Time to say goodbye
I'm leaving you
I guess I'll see you around
But you follow me
And don't let me sleep
You're everywhere I go
In every spot all around town

But you can't stop me now; I'm shutting you down
Though you seduce me with your lights and sounds
But you're not worth it
And I can't waste more time
No
You're not worth it
I've got to live my life
Dear computer

🎧 GAM ZU

8th Day ©

Cold winter nights, came and stole my flame
Took my lights, whispering my name
Midnight storm shattered all my dreams to the ground
Scattered memories
When the clouds go dark
And it's raining gray
I'll need that spark

Like Nochum would say
If I knew then what I know now
Would I feel so down?

Chorus
Gam Zu [גם זו]
Heaven's looking down for you - גם זו
Every single thing you do - גם זו
In your reflection - גם זו
He really knows the best for you – גם זו
One day He'll make it all come true – גם זו
In your reflection (x2)

Gam Zu Letovah [*גם זו לטובה]...

It's hard to know
What's in those Heavens' rhymes
Is this life
A riddle all the time
When your clouds go dark
And it's raining gray
You'll need that spark
Like Nochum would say
If I knew then what I know now
Would I feel so down?

Chorus

גם זו לטובה...

They say, "I think it's gonna snow"
They say, "Canceling the show"
They say, "See, I told you so"
I say, "You never, never know"

They say, "I think it's gonna snow"
They say, "Canceling the show"
They say, "See, I told you so"
But I say

Chorus

‎גם זו...

*"This too is for the good." -R' Nochum Ish Gamzu

🎧 DON'T SHY AWAY

8th Day ©
Album: Slow Down

You can't say goodbye if you want one more try
You can't tell the truth with a lie
A man can't be honest without being strong
And you can't be a singer without a song

Are you really so bold if you're ready to fold
Fashion, it changes, I'm told
I can't always be right, yet, maybe I'm wrong
But you can't be a singer without a song

Chorus
So don't shy away from your light
Stand up for what's right

Get up, get up, get up
Don't shy away, shy away

You can't reach for heaven if you're stuck on seven
And you can't share a slice all alone

Boats don't cross rivers with shoulders of shivers
And you can't be a singer without a song

Chorus

Don't shy away from your light...

🎧 ALL YOU GOT

8th Day ©
Album: All You Got

After one hundred and twenty-five years
You go up to heaven; you climb all those stairs
They won't ask you were you wise like Solomon
They won't ask you were you strong like Samson

They'll ask just one question
And you give just one answer
It's the end of the game
And only one thing matters
They'll say, "Did you give it all you got?"

Chorus
'Cause in this life you only have what you got
So give it all you got
In this world, we only have what we got
So give it all you got
If you say it's easy, I'll say it's not
You gotta give it all you got
If you say it's not for you, I'll say it's your lot
You gotta give it all you got
If you say you're tired I'll say tick-tock
You gotta give it all you got
You could put my album on the shelf to rot

Just give it all you got

After working so hard and wiping those tears
You look in the mirror; you face all your fears
Don't be a fool trying to be wise like Solomon
Only the weak try to be strong like Samson
I did what I said
I got no one to blame
'Cause only one thing matters
At the end of the game
They'll say, "Did you give it all you got?"

Chorus

🎧 MOSES IN ME

8th Day ©

Knock, knock, Pharaoh's at my door
Oh, he still comes around
He changed his name, but I can hear his sound
Knock, knock, Pharaoh's at my door
He's bringing slavery
To tie my hands and blind my eyes to see

Chorus
But I've got a little bit of Moses in me
I've got the power, power to break free
This bloody river is gonna split before me
I've got a little bit of Moses in me

Knock, knock, Pharaoh's at my door
Oh, he still comes around
He changed his name, but I can hear his sound
Knock, knock, sorrow's at my door

He wants to drown my faith
To push me down and hold me to the floor

Chorus (x2)

No gate is high enough to keep me from my land
This desert's burning up, I think you understand
No Pharaoh's big enough to tell me what to do
I've seen you working hard, and I believe in you
Yes I believe in you

'Cause I've got a little bit of Moses in me
I've got the power, power to break free
This bloody river is gonna split before me
I've got a little bit of Moses in me

Chorus

I've got a little bit of Moses in me...

🎧 MA'AMIN BENISIM

Yaakov Shwekey ©
Lyrics by Miriam Israeli
Composed by Yitzy Waldner
Arranged by Ravid Kashti
Album: We Are a Miracle

לִפְעָמִים מַרְגִּישִׁים
שֶׁהַחַיִּים כֹּל כָּךְ קָשִׁים
מַה יִהְיֶה עוֹד יוֹם עוֹד שָׁנָה
אֲבָל אֲנִי מְחַיֵּךְ
לֹא דוֹאֵג לְהַמְשֵׁךְ
כִּי יֵשׁ לִי, יֵשׁ לִי אֱמוּנָה

Chorus

אֲנִי מַאֲמִין בְּנִסִים
אֲנִי יוֹדֵעַ שֶׁיֵּשׁ אֱלוֹקִים
וְהוּא בּוֹרֵא עוֹלָם
הַכּוֹחַ שֶׁל כֻּלָם
שׁוֹמֵעַ אֶת קוֹלִי

אֲנִי מַאֲמִין בְּנִסִים
אֲנִי יוֹדֵעַ שֶׁיֵּשׁ אֱלוֹקִים
וְהוּא בּוֹרֵא עוֹלָם
הכוח של כולם
יִשְׁלַח לִי אֶת הַנֵּס
יִשְׁלַח לִי אֶת הַנֵּס שֶׁלִי

תֶן חִיּוּך בנאדם
יֵשׁ נִיסִים כל הַזְמַן
לֹא לִבְכּוֹת הַכֹּל לְטוֹבָה
אָסוּר לְךָ לְהִתְיַאֵשׁ
רַק תַמְשִׁיךְ לְבַקֵשׁ
תִּשְׁמוֹר תִּשְׁמוֹר אֶת הַתִּקְוָה a(x2)

Chorus (x2)

Translation:
Sometimes we feel
That life's so difficult
What will another day, or year bring
But I smile
I don't worry to keep going
Because I have faith

Chorus
I believe in miracles!
I know there is a G-d

And He's the creator of the world
The force behind everyone
Who hears my voice
I believe in miracles!
I know there is a G-d
And He's the creator of the world
The force behind everyone
Send me a miracle
Send me my miracle

Smile, son of man
There are miracles all the time
Don't cry - it's all for the good
You just can't despair
Just keep on seeking
And hold on to hope (x2)

Chorus (x2)

WE ARE A MIRACLE
Yaakov Shwekey ©
Composed by Yitzy Waldner
Lyrics by Sophia Franco
Mixed by Ian Freitor
Album: We Are a Miracle

A nation in the desert
We started out as slaves
Made it to the motherland
And then came the Crusades
It's been so many years
Crying so many tears
Don't you know
Don't you really know?

We are pushed to the ground
Through our faith, we are found
Standing strong

The Spanish Inquisition
Wanted us to bow
But our backs ain't gonna bend
Never then, and never now
It's been so many years
Crying so many tears
Don't you know
Don't you really know?
We are pushed to the ground
Through our faith, we are found
Standing strong

Chorus
We are a miracle
We are a miracle
We were chosen with love
And embraced from above
We are a miracle

Extermination was the plan
When the devil was a man
But the few who carried on
Live for millions who are gone
It's been so many years
Crying so many tears
Don't you know
Don't you really know?
We are pushed to the ground
Through our faith, we are found
Standing strong

Chorus

Every day we fight a battle
On the news, we are the stars
As history repeats itself
And makes us who we are
Hate is all around us
But we'll be here
To sing this song
Sing this song
Sing our song

Chorus

We are a miracle
We are a miracle
Through it all, we remain
Who can explain?
We are a miracle

🎧 I CAN BE

Yaakov Shwekey ©
Composed by Yitzy Waldner
Lyrics by Sophia Franco
Arranged by Udi Damari
Mixed by Ian Freitor
Album: I Can Be...

Dedicated to our daughter Rivka Feldman. May
you continue to shine and be all you can be!
Love, Mommy & Tatty

I am a child
And the road ahead is paved with possibility
Laughter and smiles
When I'm with you, I'm soaring high and free
When you're in my world
I believe in me
I look into your eyes and see that

Chorus
I can be stronger
I can be braver
I can be, I can be anything
Anything I wanna be
Ooohh anything I wanna be
I have the power
I have the courage
I am a hero
Everything I need is inside of me
Is inside of me

Life throws me fire
And fate will test me ten million ways

Sometimes I'm tired
It's hard to see the light of better days
But then I dare to dream
I find the hope for more
I reach for all you gave and see that

Chorus

Life is the people we love
And what we give to one another
Loving is giving, giving is life (x2)
Na, na, na, na, na, na, na ooohh

Chorus

I am a fighter
I am a dreamer
I am a hero
Everything I am
'Cause you believed
'Cause you believed in me

Chorus

🎧 CHANGE

Shaindel Antelis ©
Album: Change

Been going through a rough time now
Wanna fix it, but I don't know how
These tears don't seem to mend my fears
My frustrations come and go
But they're helping me I know
The pain just makes me strong

Now I gotta move
Gotta prove
Gotta do all I can

Chorus
'Cause I will make a change
I want to pull down all the barriers that hold me back
And I will make a change
Change, change, change, change

I turn to G-d and ask Him why
How many times a day do I need to cry
I'm ready to fly
So help me find my wings so I can soar
Find out what I'm living for
Now I gotta move
Gotta prove
Gotta do all I can

Chorus

Now I want to fly, though I fall
I know You'll catch me
When You're by my side, I can do anything

FATE
Shaindel Antelis ©
Album: Heart and Soul

I was ready to give up
My emotions all bottled up
Suddenly it became clear
The light at the end was coming near
Chorus

Fate is not in my possession, oh no
After all, I've learned
After all, I've seen
I have one confession
I used to think my
Life was according to my plan
But now I see that
It's really in the palm of G-d's hand

Stop thinking so hard
Give your aching head a break
Be careful of what you feed your soul
G-d's watching you, and He's in control

Chorus

I didn't know
The direction of my path
Now I found some clarity at last
And I know that

Chorus

HASHEM IS HERE
Surie Levilev ©
Album: Mommy and Me with Morah Music

Hashem is here, *Hashem* is there
Hashem is truly everywhere (x2)

Up, up, down, down
Right, left, and all around
Here, there, and everywhere
That's where He can be found (x2)

DADDY COME HOME

The Yeshiva Boys Choir
Composed and arranged by Eli Gerstner ©
Choir conducted by Yossi Newman

Daddy's been gone
Gone for so long
For him, I pray
He joined the Corps
Fighting a war
Somewhere far away

He promised me he'd return
When the *Chanukah* candles burn
So here I wait
The blessings I recite
By the candle-light
But it's getting late

Chorus
Daddy come home
Stay with me
Let me hold your hand
Let me sit upon your knee
I see fear
In Mommy's eyes
Every time she cries
And tries to comfort me

It's scary here at home
My mind begins to roam
Have I lost you?
I hear the phone
Mommy's mournful moan
It can't be true

Chorus

Where has he gone?
How will I carry on?
Tell me what can I say?
I need to pray
Please hear my plea
Send my Daddy home to...

...Who's that I hear
Calling my name?
I run into his arms
Yes, my Daddy came
Home to me
He's on his knees
Now he's holding me
For all eternity

Now, as night falls
We stand tall
Eight candles burning bright
And they're lighting up the night
Home at last
Eyes aglow
I hug my Daddy tight
And I'm not letting go

🎧 RIDE THE TRAIN

Abie Rotenberg ©
Album: Journeys, Volume 2

Come on and ride the train
Step on board, take your ticket, no two are the same
You'll soon be going for a ride
There's nowhere to run, no place to hide
You're ridin', ridin', ridin', on the train

But you try to check your ticket,
And you don't know what it means.
Will you get to sit on velvet and dine on fine cuisine?
Or is it your place to be upon a worn-out wooden seat
With a slice of old and crusty bread,
Your only food to eat

Come on and ride the train
The doors are closed, the whistle's blowing,
Now you must remain
The locomotive's on a roll
There's just some things you can't control
You're ridin', ridin', ridin' on the train

So you ask an older passenger, "How long will this ride be?"
He says, "Sorry son, I can't say there is no guarantee
It might be the next station; we'll be there in no time
Or maybe if you're lucky, you can stay till the end of the line"

Then you take a walk all through the train, each boxcar one by one
Most are filled with people saying, "This ride's just for fun
Why think about tomorrow when you've got today instead?
Sit back, enjoy the view
There's miles and miles of rail ahead"

Ride the train, oh ride the train
Come on everybody, ride the train (x2)

But one car seems so different
Inhabited by few, who say there is no time to waste
We're only passing through
The choices that you make today are all that's gonna last
This train is moving down the track, and it's moving awful fast

Come on and ride the train
Step on board, take your ticket, no two are the same
You'll soon be going for a ride
There's nowhere to run, no place to hide
You're ridin', ridin', ridin', on the train

YISROEL

Dov Levine ©
Album: Kumzits Classics

Yisroel, Yisroel
Where have you been all these years?
I've been awaiting your return
Come on home, let me dry off your tears

I recall as a young bride
How you were faithful and true
But since then you've wandered to strangers
Who tried to make a traitor of you

Don't you be fooled by their lies
Their only aim is to lure you away from me
Won't you believe that it's true?
I'm the only one for you (x2)

How long, till when
Will you endure all their scorns?
Though you've been beaten by wind and rain
You still are a rose among thorns

Battered crown, tattered gown
Your garments are covered with mud
Still, you continue to wander
Though the earth has been soaked with your blood

What are you hoping to find?
Haven't I given you all you could wish for?
Come back, and we'll start anew
I'll be here waiting for you (x2)

Oh, to behold your countenance
Let the sound of your voice fill My palace
Only then, My dear one
Will you experience true happiness

Tell me it's only a dream
Tell me that your heart and your soul are still here
with me
Wake up, and we'll be together
Yisrael Vikudsha Berich Hu
[*ישראל וקודשה בריך הוא] (x2)

Chad Hu [**חד הוא]

*Israel and G-d -Zohar
**He is One -Zohar

MAAMINIM

Mordechai Ben David ©
Mixed by Eli Lishinsky
Album: Maaminim Bnei Maaminim

אֲנַחְנוּ מַאֲמִינִים בְּנֵי מַאֲמִינִים, וְאֵין לָנוּ עַל מִי לְהִשָּׁעֵן,
אֶלָּא עַל אָבִינוּ שֶׁבַּשָּׁמַיִם

יִשְׂרָאֵל בְּטַח בַּה', עֶזְרָם וּמָגִנָּם הוּא

Translation:
"We are believers, children of believers, and we have
none [else] to rely on but on our Father in heaven."
-Midrash
"Israel, trust in *Hashem*; their help and their shield is
He!" -Psalms 115:9

EVERYTHING IS GOOD

Composed by Yoni Shlomo and Moshe Laufer ©
Sung with the Yedidim Choir

This song is based on the teaching of the Alter Rebbe in the Tanya (Igeres Hakodesh, Chapter 11), that, "No evil descends from above," and everything is good.

והכל טוב, אין רע יורד מלמעלה
אבל באמת, אין רע יורד מלמעלה
והכל טוב, אין רע יורד מלמעלה
ועל כן, ראשית הכל, שישמח האדם ויגל בכל עת ושעה
והכל טוב, אין רע יורד מלמעלה
ובאמונה זו באמת, נעשה הכל טוב גם בגלוי
והכל טוב, אין רע יורד מלמעלה

Translation:
In truth, however, "No evil descends from above," and everything is good. Accordingly, everything is absolutely good, except that it is not apprehended as such by man. Therefore, first of all, man ought to be happy and joyous at every time and hour. When one believes this truly, everything becomes good even on a revealed level.

KOL HA'OLAM KULO

Lyrics by R' Nachman of Breslov
Composed by Franciska ©

כָּל הָעוֹלָם כֻּלּוֹ גֶּשֶׁר צַר מְאֹד
וְהָעִיקָר לֹא לְפַחֵד כְּלָל

Translation:
The whole world is a very narrow bridge
But the important thing is not to fear at all

Y'HI SHALOM

Psalms 122:7-9
Shalsheles
Composed by Yitzchok Rosenthal ©
Arranged and conducted by Yisroel Lamm
Album: Shalsheles, Volume 2

יְהִי־שָׁלוֹם בְּחֵילֵךְ שַׁלְוָה בְּאַרְמְנוֹתָיִךְ
לְמַעַן־אַחַי וְרֵעָי אֲדַבְּרָה־נָּא שָׁלוֹם בָּךְ
לְמַעַן בֵּית־ה׳ אֱלֹהֵינוּ אֲבַקְשָׁה טוֹב לָךְ

Translation:
May there be peace in your wall, tranquility in your palaces.
For the sake of my brethren and my companions, I shall now speak of peace in you.
For the sake of the house of the Lord our G-d, I shall beg for goodness for you.

ASHIRA

Psalms 104:33-35

אָשִׁירָה לַה׳ בְּחַיָּי אֲזַמְּרָה לֵאלֹקַי בְּעוֹדִי:
יֶעֱרַב עָלָיו שִׂיחִי אָנֹכִי אֶשְׂמַח בַּה׳
יִתַּמּוּ חַטָּאִים מִן־הָאָרֶץ וּרְשָׁעִים עוֹד אֵינָם
בָּרְכִי נַפְשִׁי אֶת־ה׳ הַלְלוּ־הּ

Translation:
I will sing unto the Lord as long as I live; I will sing praise to my G-d while I have any being. Let my musing be sweet unto Him; as for me, I will rejoice in the Lord. Let sinners cease from the earth, and let the wicked be no more. Bless *Hashem*, O my soul, *Halleluy-ah*!

CHAPTER 7:

Niggunim

Each soul descended from a very lofty and heavenly abode and is truly a spark of G-d above. The soul is like a princess who traveled from her palace to a chaotic and foreign location, where the customs are vastly different from her own royal home, and the language she cannot understand. She yearns to return to her home where she feels warm and safe. Our soul, clothed in our bodies and made to live in a mundane world, cries as she searches for the only truth — *Hashem* is One and His Name is One and "there is nothing but Him!" Unfortunately, as we are too often enmeshed in the hustle and blur of our daily lives and business, the soul's cry is ignored, and she waits to be heard and unlocked.

A *Niggun* is a — usually wordless — Chassidic melody. As we croon and thrum with a timeless rhythm, we silence our chatter, worries, and even our mind's apathy, and tune into the soul's whispers, allowing her plight and love for *Hashem* to wash over our hearts. She inspires our whole being with a greater awareness of *Hashem* and a yearning to cleave to Him. It gives us an experience of fusion so powerful that mere words are inadequate to express it. All it can give birth to is an unrestrained cry of joy, a scream from the depths of the heart, a song of sheer delight that breaks all barriers.

Our most profound desire transcends all words and is like a river obstructed by a levee. But your voice of song is the mechanism to break that levee down. Unleash your *Neshama* through the redemptive power of a *Niggun* melody, and let her burst forth.

QUESTIONS TO CONSIDER:
A soulful Niggun quiets the chaos so we can hear the whispers of our soul!
What is your soul's yearning?
How can you remove the distractions to express your soul's desires?

🎧 KELI ATOH

Psalms 118:28
Alter Rebbe, R' Schneur Zalman of Liadi
Recording by Chaviva Tarlow

כֵּלִי אַתָּה וְאוֹדֶךָ אֱ-לֹקַי אֲרוֹמְמֶךָ

Translation:
You are my G-d, and I shall thank You; the G-d of my father, and I shall exalt You.

🎧 KAPELYA

Composed by the 2nd Chabad Rebbe, Mitteler Rebbe's Kapelya (choir)

This melody's four divided sections hint to the deep symbolism of the four-rung ladder of humankind's devotion to G-d and approach to His Divine service. The Mitteler Rebbe's was of such unparalleled lofty caliber, that he was risk of ceasing from earthly existence and reabsorbing into G-dliness. Thus, his Kapelya, or orchestra, played for him occasionally to keep him 'grounded' so to speak, as his son-in-law and successor once disclosed.

🎧 YEMIN HASHEM

Psalms 118:16
Tzemach Tzedek, R' Menachem Mendel Schneerson

יְמִין ה' רוֹמֵמָה יְמִין ה' עֹשָׂה חָיִל

Translation:
The right hand of the Lord is exalted; the right hand of the Lord deals valiantly.

🎧 LECHATCHILA ARIBER

Attributed to the Rebbe Maharash, this Niggun's melody and name represent his famed dictum on dealing with challenges: "The world says, 'If you can't crawl under an obstacle, try to climb over,' but I say, 'At the outset, climb over!'"

🎧 NIGGUN HACHANA

Cherished by the Rebbe Rashab, Niggun Hachana, the "Melody of Preparation" (also known as the Rostover Niggun for its birthplace in Russia), aids the soul in its liberation from the chains of physicality and primes it to absorb the G-dly essence of Torah. If was often sung to ready oneself to chant the Alter Rebbe's heavenly tune, "Daled Bavos."

🎧 NIGGUN BEINONI

Composed by R' Aharon Charitonov of Nikolayev, Ukraine
Lyrics by Shlomo Sternberg
Music by Yossi Cohen
Mixed and edits by Berry Cohen
Sung by the Kapelle

"Beinoni" typically translates as "average" or "in-between," but it is understood on a deeper note by R' Schneur Zalman of Liadi in his pivotal work, the Tanya. This steady, pulsating melody, composed by R' Aharon Charitonov of Nikolayev, reflects the constant struggle characteristic of the Beinoni. Though he inevitably experiences fluctuating moments of frustration and joy, his consistency — his clear goal and tenacity to sanctify G-d with joy and order in everything he does — are

what define him. Therefore he is not described as "Eved Hashem — a servant of G-d," but as "Oveid Hashem — one who continually serves G-d," indicating a living, developing effort and devotion.

The Beinoni is neither righteous nor wicked but has full control over his evil inclination. Spiritual perfection is not organic to the Beinoni the way it is innate to the Tzaddik; and as the majority of us today are aspiring Beinonim, we realize sincere work is required to refine ourselves as a "chariot for G-d." The strength is within us to choose the right path. Each small step towards the light of Torah is our service of G-d. And with each rung we ascend, we rise higher than the angels.

A typical *Chossid*, sitting and reflecting
The bitter taste of failure fills him
Where am I heading?
I fought with all my might
I've done all I can do
Yet it doesn't seem the change in me is real and true
Though I know the truth
I feel I cannot reach it
I do the act, yet my heart doesn't feel it
My inspiration short, the battle long
My efforts are all worthless
Oh, it feels so wrong

For an answer, to the *Rebbe* he turns
As he is told, a *Perek Tanya* he learns
A deep and new perspective *Chassidus* does show
My dear *Chossid*, this is what you must know

All the millions of *Malachim* in the sky
And *Tzaddikim* rising high in love and fear
All so dear, but don't come near
To *Kol Dichiya Udichiya* [*כל דחיה ודחיה], even one

Each struggle you overcome, each battle won
Every *Tefillah*, every *Mitzvah* that is done
Your *Avodah* gives Him *Nachas* and pleasure
To *Hashem*, you're the most precious treasure
You build His *Dirah* in your world and heart
Through every soldier conquering his little part

Through כל דחיה ודחיה, even one
Each struggle overcome, each battle won
Every *Tefillah*, every *Bracha*
Every single word of Torah, day or night
Each *Shema Yisroel* you recite
Each bit of light
Is infinite and reaches to the greatest height
This is your truth
So start with one step towards it
It's not an act, for deep inside you mean it
Although perfection you may never see
Yet to *Hashem* the battle is the victory
Yet to *Hashem* the battle is the victory

*With each and every rejection [of evil]. -Tanya

🎧 ATAH BECHARTONU

Holiday Liturgy
Taught by the Lubavitcher Rebbe, R' Menachem Mendel Schneerson

אתה בחרתנו מכל העמים, אהבת אותנו ורצית בנו
ורוממתנו מכל הלשונות וקדשתנו במצותיך
ושמך הגדול והקדוש עלינו קראת

Translation:
You chose us from all the nations, You loved us and desired us.
You elevated us over all tongues (nations) and sanctified us with your commandments;
And Your great and holy name You proclaimed on us.

🎧 HU ELOKEINU

Shabbat and Holiday Liturgy
Taught by the Lubavitcher Rebbe, R' Menachem Mendel Schneerson

הוא א-לוקינו, הוא אבינו, הוא מלכנו, הוא מושיענו
הוא יושיענו ויגאלנו שנית בקרוב, וישמיענו ברחמיו לעיני כל חי לאמור
הן גאלתי אתכם אחרית כבראשית להיות לכם לא-לוקים

Translation:
He is our G-d, He is our Father, He is our King, He is our Redeemer, He is our Deliverer.
He will deliver us, and redeem us once more, shortly; and in His mercy He will let us hear, in the presence of all living, proclaiming: "Behold, I have redeemed you at the end of time as in the days of yore, to be to you for a G-d."

🎧 ANIM ZEMIROT

Shabbat Morning Liturgy
Taught by the Lubavitcher Rebbe, R' Menachem Mendel Schneerson
Recording by Chaviva Tarlow

אַנְעִים זְמִירוֹת וְשִׁירִים אֶאֱרֹג כִּי אֵלֶיךָ נַפְשִׁי תַעֲרֹג
נַפְשִׁי חָמְדָה בְּצֵל יָדֶךָ לָדַעַת כָּל רָז סוֹדֶךָ

Translation:
I sing hymns and compose songs because my soul longs for You.
My soul desires Your shelter to know all Your ways.

🎧 KI ANU AMECHA

High Holidays Prayers Liturgy
Taught by the Lubavitcher Rebbe, R' Menachem Mendel Schneerson

כי אנו עמך ואתה א-לוקינו
אנו בניך ואתה אבינו

Translation:
For we are Your people, and You are our G-d.
We are Your people, and You are our Father.

🎧 TZAMAH LECHAH

Psalms 63:2-3
Alter Rebbe, R' Schneur Zalman of Liadi

צָמְאָה לְךָ | נַפְשִׁי כָּמַה לְךָ בְשָׂרִי בְּאֶרֶץ־צִיָּה וְעָיֵף בְּלִי־מָיִם
כֵּן בַּקֹּדֶשׁ חֲזִיתִךָ לִרְאוֹת עֻזְּךָ וּכְבוֹדֶךָ

MAZEL TOV *Tzipporah Raizel*
ON YOUR MANY ACCOMPLISHMENTS, THUS FAR.
WE ARE SO PROUD OF YOU. MAY YOU CONTINUE
TO BLOSSOM TO YOUR FULL POTENTIAL.
WITH ALL OUR LOVE AND SUPPORT,
Ima, Abba and the boys

MAZAL TOV TZIPPORAH ON THIS TRULY WELL DESERVED
HONOR. WE LOVE YOU AND WE ARE SO PROUD OF YOU!

Bubbie Naomi, Uncle Josh & The Rosenzweigs

MAZAL TOV TZIPPORAH! WE LOVE YOU!
Your New York Cousins

"I love the niggun Anim Zemiros. The melody uplifts, inspires and invigorates me; and what's more, it reflects my inner song, the energy motivating me to keep reaching higher, closer to my soul and Hashem: "Nafshi chamda b'tzeil Yadecha lada'as kol raz sodecha - My soul desired the shelter of Your hand, to know every mystery of your secret." This is truly the deepest desire of every single one of our neshamos." -Tzipporah Prottas

Translation:
My soul thirsts for You; my flesh longs for You, in an arid and thirsty land, without water.
As I saw You in the Sanctuary, [so do I long] to see Your strength and Your glory.

🎧 UFARATZTA

Genesis 28:14
Taught by the Lubavitcher Rebbe, R' Menachem Mendel Schneerson

וּפָרַצְתָּ יָמָּה וָקֵדְמָה וְצָפֹנָה וָנֶגְבָּה וְנִבְרְכוּ בְךָ כָּל-מִשְׁפְּחֹת הָאֲדָמָה וּבְזַרְעֶךָ

Translation:
And you shall gain strength westward and eastward and northward and southward, and through you shall be blessed all the families of the earth and through your seed.

🎧 NIGGUN SHAMIL

Taught by the Lubavitcher Rebbe, R' Menachem Mendel Schneerson
Lyrics by Shlomo Sternberg
Music by Yossi Cohen, Yehuda Piamenta, and Yitzchok Hurwitz
Arranged by Yossi Cohen
Sung by The Kapelle

A story is told of multi-tribal leader named Shamil, in Russia's Caucasian Mountains over a century ago. The Russian army intended to subjugate the people but was continually repelled by its staunch warriors.

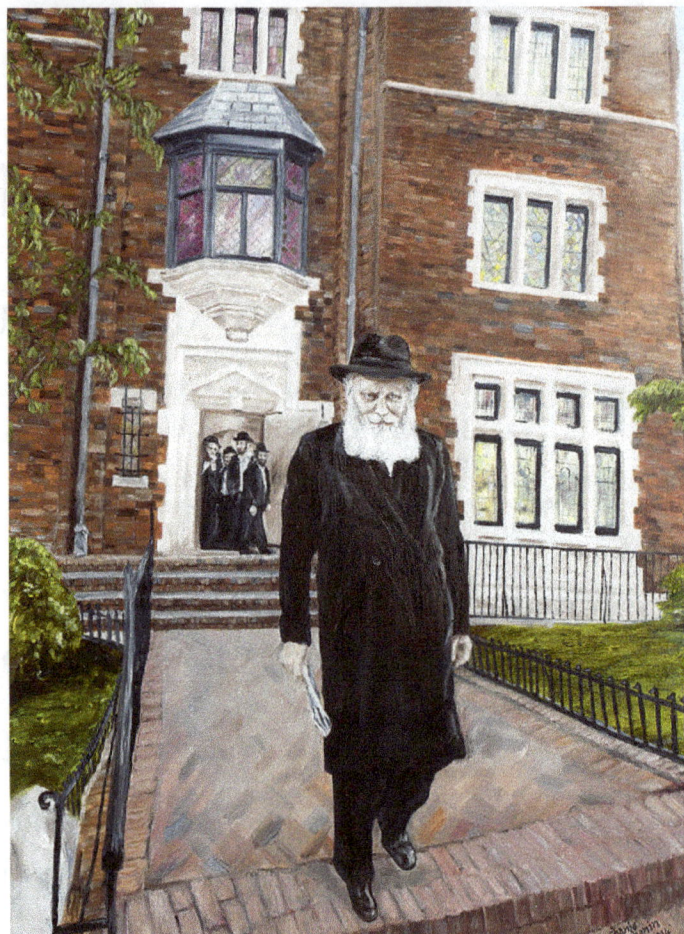

The Russians thereupon proposed a false peace treaty, leading the tribes to lay down their arms, and ultimately they captured the tribal leader. Imprisoned and forlorn, Shamil yearned for his liberty and fortune but found comfort in the knowledge and vision that one day he would surely ascend to greatness with even more grandeur than before. His intense yearning, expressed in song, is a profound allegory for the soul's rise and fall. During its exile from the pure heavens that are its origins, the soul, eternally beset with longing for spiritual freedom and fulfillment, mourns its captivity in a physical body

ruled by physical desires. Nevertheless, in the face of its plight, it commits itself to rouse the body to engage in Torah and Mitzvos, thereby embracing the infinite and soaring higher than possible before.

In a beautiful palace on a mountain so high
Shamil rules his kingdom with pride
His enemies defeated in fight after fight
His advantage is clearly his height
To a false call for peace, he agrees to come down
Enslaved and imprisoned, his pain knows no bounds
Yet his spirit is high, for he knows he'll ascend
And be with his nation again
Thought it seems so unreal, he is confident and sure
He'll rise more than ever before

Standing as one with her Father above
Serving with fear and with love
Her emotions and knowledge were G-dly and pure
The *Neshama* was safe and secure
To the lowest of low, she is sent with a goal
But countless distractions are drowning the soul
From the depths of the *Mayim Rabim*, she cries
She longs for her source up on high
She knows from down here she could rise even more
Much closer to *Hashem* than before

At *Farbrengens* and rallies, they merited to be
The *Rebbe* they'd hear, and they'd see
His devotion to them was so easy to feel
Their *Hiskashrus* so deep and so real

Our connection was challenged by a darkness so strong
"*Ad Mosai, Hashem?*" this is taking so long

Yet he leads us and guides us as *Chassidim*, we're sure
He is with us now more than before
So devoted we stand to fulfill his command
Oy, *Rebbe*, we'll do all we can
Yes, we know beyond doubt that the best days at last
Are in the future and not in the past
With a swing of your hand, all the darkness will end
*Oy Rebbe Mir Velin Zich Zen**

**Oy Rebbe, we will see you!*

🎧 TERANEINA SIFASAI
Psalms 71:23-24

Dedicated to every single Jew who has the spark of *Moshiach* inside them that is waiting to burst into flame through the *koach* of the *Rebbe* and *Rebbetzin*.
–Nechama Dena Zwiebel

This Niggun empowers us to sing our personal song, the song that emerges through our personal redemption. Our personal song joins with all others to form the final tenth song of Redemption.

תְּרַנֵּנָּה שְׂפָתַי כִּי אֲזַמְּרָה־לָּךְ וְנַפְשִׁי אֲשֶׁר פָּדִיתָ

גַּם־לְשׁוֹנִי כָּל־הַיּוֹם תֶּהְגֶּה צִדְקָתֶךָ כִּי־בֹשׁוּ כִי־חָפְרוּ מְבַקְשֵׁי רָעָתִי:

Translation:
My lips will sing praises when I play music to You, and my soul, which You redeemed.
Also my tongue will utter Your righteousness all the days, for those who seek my harm are shamed, yea, for they are disgraced.

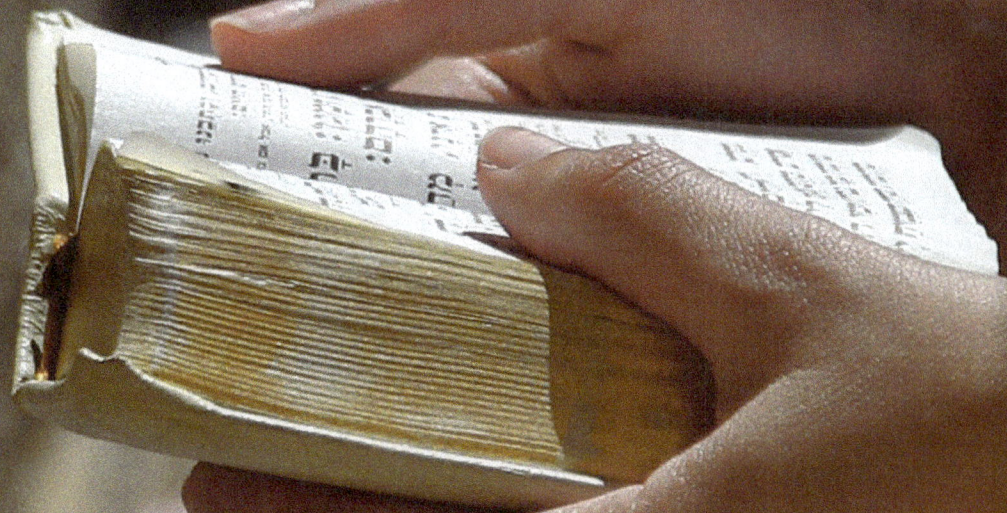

CHAPTER 8:
Prayer

The Talmud declares, *"Bamakom Rinah Sham T'hay Tefillah — Where there is song, there is prayer."* A wise teacher once illuminated this statement in the following way: Song and prayer are in essence the same. When you sing, your song comes from such a deep place. It is a gift and offering of your very soul, a prayer to *Hakadosh Baruch Hu*, our G-d. Similarly, as *Chassidus* teaches, when we pray, our *Tefillah* should be beautifully and pleasantly sung!

Almost every service in the *Beis Hamikdash* was accompanied by the music and song of the *Levi'im*. Is it possible for us to maintain that elation in serving *Hashem* even when we lack the Holy Temple? The Talmud teaches us the solution, as it also points out, *"Tefillos K'neged T'midim Tiknum —* prayer was established in place of the sacrifices."

As you talk to *Hashem*, like one does with her close friend, don't be afraid to sing your heart out. Your sweet voice, heartfelt words, focused thoughts, and precious *Neshama* are all instruments with which you can play to *Hashem*. He cannot wait to hear your soul's symphony!

QUESTION TO CONSIDER:
What is your favorite song from our prayers, and what is its meaning?

🎧 TELL THE SUN TO RISE

Rivka Leah Popack ©
Lead and backing vocals by Sarah Kisilevich
Album: Silent Prayer

I woke up to the day, sun on my face
I started walking; I set my pace
The road split in two
I asked which path's for me
He said it all depends
Where you wanna be
I said, well I don't care
I just wanna keep my pace
The day woke me, sun on my face

Eyes wide open, soul asleep
You slumber deep inside
And your soul don't see
Running ahead but your soul's far behind
Behind the start line

Chorus
Wake up this morning and tell the sun to rise
Play it your way, make a new start
Put it together, take it apart
Wake up inside
Tell the sun to rise

Aimless travels, in shifting sands
Trying to give with empty hands
Slipping through the growing haze
Nothing stays

Mornings meant for living dreams
Spent floating mindless streams
Nothing is as it seems
So...

Chorus

From the darkest night
Comes the dawn
The brightest light
A new day is born

The blessing of sleep
A new breath of life
Another chance to spread your light
Spread your light

The dreaming of dreams
A new breath of life
Another chance to spread your light
Spread your light

Chorus

🎧 I DAVEN

Chanale ©
Album: The Crown of Creation

I *Daven*, requesting
My small voice He hears
Hashem, can You bless me
With long happy years?

With each verse, I ask Him

Fulfill all my needs
Honor my merits
Reward my good deeds

Then before I close my *Siddur*
For one last thing, I'll pray
That He responds to my *Bakashos*
Even the ones my lips don't say

Chorus
For He can see a hidden part of me
Into my essence, at my core
And though I've asked for health and happiness
Hashem knows I need more
My soul inside is yearning
It cries, please bring me close
Shema Tza'akoseinu Yodeyah Ta'alumos
[*שמע צעקתנו, יודע תעלומות]

Swaying, I whisper
His praise on my tongue
I depend on His blessing
To provide for my young
Grant me my portion
A life free from pain
Judge with me with favor
Remember my name

Chorus

When my heart is broken, I trust He will mend it
When my troubles overwhelm me, He will know
When I need a hand to guide me He will send it
When uncertain, He will show me where to go

Chorus (x2)

...שמע צעקתנו, יודע תעלומות

Hear our cry, You Who knows secrets of the heart. -Prayerbook Liturgy

🎧 MIRACLES
Dovid Pearlman ©
Composed by Chayala Neuhaus
Album: Miracles

Do you close your eyes, and stop for a minute, just to imagine a scene?
Come take a walk, and see yourself standing in a beautiful garden, serene
See the vibrant rose as it comes to life
Smell the orchids, white like snow
A breath-taking picture, perfection beyond your dreams

One closer look, catch every detail, explore every petal with care
A dazzling array of countless bright colors, each shade is special and dear
And as the softest rain flutters to the ground, to awaken a sleeping world
Now the secret of its beauty soon unfurls

There's this feeling that takes hold of me
As I'm drawn into this picture, into this scene
And suddenly I seem to find my place in Your design

Like every sunset brings another sunrise, and every winter fades away
Into the spring, there's a whole new world each day
There's a whole new world in me

Chorus
So when I open up my eyes, I'll sing to you
The wonder of the world renewed each morning
For each breath of life, I'll sing to you
There's something new to see in every dawning
I'll praise in my own way,
For Your light shines on every day
As I'm learning how to see all Your miracles unfold
And with the rising sun, my soul has wings
I'm grateful for this chance You've given me
To lift up my own voice in harmony
To join as one with all of Your creations
Singing for eternity, reflecting Your glory
As I'm learning how to see all Your miracles unfold

Like every sunset brings another sunrise, and every winter fades away

Into the spring, and there's a whole new world each day
There's a whole new world in me

Chorus

ONE DAY AT A TIME

Shloime Dachs ©
Album: One Day At a Time

Waking every morning, I'm awed to see the way
Everything You made comes together
Opening my eyes to miracles each day
It helps to know; Your guiding light is here to stay
And as I'm rising slowly, I gather strength and say
"I am not alone; You are with me"
And one day at a time as I try to find my way
I'll reach for You and feel You near me as I pray

Chorus (x2)
Give me strength to grow and see
Who I am, who I need to be
And with You by my side
I have nothing to hide
If I can come to You honestly
And when it's all too much for me
I'll hold on tight, and You'll carry me
Just one day at a time
I'll look to You, and I'll find
All along You believed in me

So many new beginnings, so many times we fall
Each and every time is a chance to grow
But only when I search for the meaning in my day
I feel You close, I sense Your wisdom, and I know

That every test and challenge is only but a gift
A chance to seek You out and to find You
To try and see things clearly, to give my soul a lift
To feel Your strength, to see Your light come shining
through

Chorus

And when it's all too much for me
I'll hold on tight, and You'll carry me
Just one day at a time
I'll look to You, and I'll find
All along You believed in me

Give us strength to grow and see
Who we are, who we need to be
And with You by our side
We have nothing to hide
If we can come to You honestly
And when the burden's too much for us
We'll hold on tight, and You'll carry us
Just one day at a time
We'll look to You, and we'll find
You are all we have to trust

Chorus

One day at a time...

A RUSSIAN BOY'S HOPELESS PLIGHT

To the Tune of Avinu Av Horachamon

A certain young girl once heard the song "A Russian Boy's Hopeless Plight" at an overnight camp. The song concerns a young boy behind the Iron Curtain who wrote a heartfelt letter to the Lubavitcher Rebbe, seeking counsel on how he could strengthen his devotion in prayer; it evoked the Rebbe's tears upon his public reading of it. The campers told the girl the young boy was her father! When she returned home she asked him if this was true; he vaguely replied, "Ken Zeyn - Perhaps." She mentioned the letter, and with some coaxing, discovered the boy in the song was her father indeed: R' Y. Mishulovin. The song's deep message instilled within her lifelong strength, a deeper appreciation of prayer, and clarity about what's truly precious in life. Let us listen, and be inspired as well.

A Russian boy's hopeless plight
Dreariness fills his night
Hardship and pain befall him
His chance of survival is slim

Finding no source of true comfort
To the *Rebbe*, he turns, with a letter
Compelled to express to him
How life could have been so much better

Chorus
The boy did not beg for an easier life
Nor for a hope to be free

*"Vos zol ich ton, az es Davent zich nisht?"**
That was the Russian boy's plea (x2)

As the *Rebbe* spoke at a *Farbrengen*
The *Chassidim* gazed on in surprise
As the *Rebbe* choked with emotion
And tears came to his eyes

Chorus

What should I do, as my Davening doesn't come naturally?

🎧 EDGE OF PRAYER
Nechama Cohen ©

The spirit inside of me is hanging on by a thread
So I'm asking You, "Please G-d tell me when this will end"
Bruised and breaking, my heart is aching to be free
Begging you with all the strength I have left to help me

Chorus
I'm standing here on the edge of prayer
Trying not to look down as I'm waiting
Won't you come a little closer now?
Promise me things will turn around
Once I prayed all there's left to do is wait
Patiently for you to save me from falling down
I'll keep my ground on the edge of prayer

I'm all alone here in my world of endless tears to hide
Luckily I've got Someone who's always on my side
Through it all, every single painful fall
Knowing you're with me keeps me standing tall

Chorus

There's only one place to turn, and I know inside, it's true
Bring us home, I can't bear to be so far away from You
Standing up here with so much to fear
The world lays down below
I need you with me faithfully, I can't do this on my own

I'm standing here on the edge of prayer Looking at the heavens as I'm waiting
I can feel you coming closer now
Telling me things will turn around
Once I prayed all there's left to do is change
The way I view the world, stop the pain from holding me down
I'll keep my ground on the edge of prayer
I'll keep my ground, I'll keep my ground on the edge of prayer

🎧 GREATNESS
Nechama Cohen ©
Album: Heartbeat

As I'm lying down my head tonight
After a long day, I'm worn out and tired
I've let You down again, crossed those lines that were red
Without a care in my mind
Led by my heart, I didn't think twice

I wouldn't blame You
If today was my last
But I know You're not like that

Chorus

You give me another chance today
Though I failed
Your faith in me makes me believe
Every day comes and I still haven't changed
But You never give up on me

I wake up with determination
I've got a new day to fulfill your vision
So I try real hard, lift up my wings to fly
Like I've never done
Only to fall with all my broken aspirations

I wouldn't blame You
If today was my last
But I know You're not like that

Chorus

So I'll give all I have
Chase it down till it's in my hands
I'll find the greatness in me
I'll fight through the tests
Every day, take a step
Till I find my destiny
Every day's another chance for greatness
As long as you let me

Chorus

You give me another chance 'cause I haven't failed
I'm slowly working towards eternity
If G-d thinks I can, I'd be blind not to see
Yes, there's room for greatness in me
Oh, there's still room for greatness in me

SHMA YISRAEL ELOKAI

Composed by Shmuel Elbaz ©
Lyrics by Yossi Gispan and Arlet Tzfadia
Sung by Sarit Hadad

כְּשֶׁהַלֵּב בּוֹכֶה רַק אֱלוֹ-קַיִם שׁוֹמֵעַ
הַכְּאֵב עוֹלֶה מִתּוֹךְ הַנְּשָׁמָה
אָדָם נוֹפֵל לִפְנֵי שֶׁהוּא שׁוֹקֵעַ
בִּתְפִילָה קְטַנָּה חוֹתֵךְ אֶת הַדְּמָמָה

Chorus

שְׁמַע יִשְׂרָאֵל אֱ-לוֹהֵי אַתָּה הַכֹּל יָכוֹל
נָתַתָּ לִי אֶת חַיַּי נָתַתָּ לִי הַכֹּל
בְּעֵינֵי דִּמְעָה הַלֵּב בּוֹכֶה בְּשֶׁקֶט
וּכְשֶׁהַלֵּב שׁוֹתֵק הַנְּשָׁמָה זוֹעֶקֶת
שְׁמַע יִשְׂרָאֵל אֱ-לוֹהֵי עַכְשָׁיו אֲנִי לְבַד
חַזֵּק אוֹתִי אֱלוֹ-הֵי עֲשֵׂה שֶׁלֹּא אֶפְחַד
הַכְּאֵב גָּדוֹל וְאֵין לָאָן לִבְרוֹחַ
עֲשֵׂה שֶׁיִּגָּמֵר כִּי לֹא נוֹתַר בִּי כֹּחַ

כְּשֶׁהַלֵּב בּוֹכֶה הַזְּמַן עוֹמֵד מִלֶּכֶת
הָאָדָם רוֹאֶה אֶת כָּל חַיָּיו פִּתְאוֹם
אֶל הֲלֹא נוֹדַע הוּא לֹא רוֹצֶה לָלֶכֶת
לֵא-לוֹהָיו קוֹרֵא עַל סַף תְּהוֹם

Chorus

Translation:
When the heart cries, only G-d hears
The pain rises out of the soul
A man falls down before he sinks down
With a little prayer [he] cuts the silence

Chorus
Hear Israel my G-d, You're the Omnipotent
You gave me my life, You gave me everything
In my eyes a tear, the heart cries quietly
And when the heart is quiet, the soul screams
Hear Israel my G-d, now I am alone
Make me strong my G-d; make it that I won't be afraid
The pain is big, and there's no where to run away
Make it end, for no more strength is left within me

When the heart cries, time stands still
All of a sudden, the man sees his entire life
He doesn't want to go to the unknown
He cries to his G-d right before a big fall

🎧 I GIVE THIS DAY

Rivka Leah Popack ©
Lead and backing vocals by Taliah Bloom
Album: Silent Prayer

A crack of sunlight enters my world on a dreamy
morning
The unknown lies on the brink of a new day
Here I am gathering the thoughts inside my mind
A distant song plays over and over and over

Chorus
I give this day to you
Unlived, unwalked, undone
I give this day to you
A song that no ones sung
A dream that's just begun
Find your space, a homely place, within the light of day
A garden bright, pure delight, stay

Outside my window a million colors dance in the
waking sun
Deep within a single light shines bright
Can I live the play that lies beyond the script?
An empty stage calls me over and over and over

Chorus

A magic sunrise sweeps across the dawn horizon
Wraps the sky, the gift that's mine to give
Grasp the brush, to bring this canvas world to life
And paint the day, over and over, over and over

Chorus

🎧 SOMETHING ABOUT YOU

Shaindel Antelis ©
Album: Heart & Soul

As the sun comes up
The first thing I do
Is open up my heart and soul to You
You're so far, at the same time so near
I wonder are You really here

Chorus
There's something about You
I can't describe
Can I be close to You?
I would have nothing to hide
Though I don't understand
The reasons behind Your plan
I'm putting my life in Your hands

Please accept my words
Everything I say
I beg of You, don't turn me away
You're the only One
Who knows my hopes and my fears
So please accept my prayers

Chorus

Shema Kolainu, Hashem Elokeinu
Chus Veracheim, Veracheim Aleinu
[שמע קולינו, ה' א-לוקינו]
[חוס ורחם, ורחם עלינו]*

Chorus

Hear our voice, O Lord our G-d; spare us and have compassion upon us. -Amidah Prayer Liturgy

🎧 GAM KI EILEICH

Psalm 23
Shaindel Antelis ©
Album: Live Today

מִזְמוֹר לְדָוִד ה' רֹעִי לֹא אֶחְסָר
בִּנְאוֹת דֶּשֶׁא יַרְבִּיצֵנִי עַל־מֵי מְנֻחוֹת יְנַהֲלֵנִי
נַפְשִׁי יְשׁוֹבֵב יַנְחֵנִי בְמַעְגְּלֵי־צֶדֶק לְמַעַן שְׁמוֹ

Chorus
גַּם כִּי־אֵלֵךְ בְּגֵיא צַלְמָוֶת לֹא־אִירָא רָע כִּי־אַתָּה עִמָּדִי (x2)

שִׁבְטְךָ וּמִשְׁעַנְתֶּךָ הֵמָּה יְנַחֲמֻנִי
תַּעֲרֹךְ לְפָנַי | שֻׁלְחָן נֶגֶד צֹרְרָי דִּשַּׁנְתָּ בַשֶּׁמֶן רֹאשִׁי כּוֹסִי רְוָיָה

Chorus

אַךְ טוֹב וָחֶסֶד יִרְדְּפוּנִי כָּל־יְמֵי חַיָּי וְשַׁבְתִּי בְּבֵית־ה' לְאֹרֶךְ יָמִים

Chorus

Translation:
A song of David. The Lord is my shepherd; I shall not lack
He causes me to lie down in green pastures; He leads me beside still waters
He restores my soul; He leads me in paths of righteousness for His name's sake

Chorus
Even when I walk in the valley of darkness, I will fear no evil for You are with me (x2)

Your rod and Your staff - they comfort me
You set a table before me in the presence of my adversaries; You anointed my head with oil; my cup overflows

Chorus

May only goodness and kindness pursue me all the days of my life, and I will dwell in the house of the Lord for length of days

Chorus

BESIYATA DISHMAYA

Miami Boys Choir
Composed by Yerachmiel Begun ©
Album: Besiyata Dishmaya

Have you ever felt there's nowhere to turn?
Things seem confused, no one's concerned
The times we live in are oh, so dark
A little faith though light a spark
Clears our vision, eases the pain
Hope arises again, hope arises again

Chorus
Besiyata Dishmaya, whatever I do
When I need him to help me, He'll always come through
Never will I be alone
With His help I can stand on my own
I need *Siyata Dishmaya*, whatever will be
All the world that I hope for is open to see
I need Him to show me the way
Besiyata Dishmaya

Sometimes we feel the strength of our hand
Can bring us success, but we don't understand
It's not always the way it seems
Hashem alone provides our needs
And stands behind every circumstance
No, its not only by chance, it's not only by chance

Chorus

Prayer after prayer, tear after tear
Begging for help, for Heaven to hear

When *Hashem* is at our side
Every door is open wide
Our only hope is to look to the sky
Where He waits for our cry, where He waits for our cry

Besiyata Dishmaya, whatever we do
When we need him to help us, He'll always come through
Never will we be alone
With his help we can stand on our own
Besiyata Dishmaya, whatever will be
All the world that we hope for, is open to see
Just ask Him to show us the way
Besiyata Dishmaya

Chorus

FAR OVER DISTANT HILLS

To the tune of Erev Shel Shoshanim

There was once a young, orphaned Jewish boy, raised by a Gentile family. The boy was at peace with his life until a fateful mention of his Jewish identity reached his ears. Taken aback, he questioningly turned to his adoptive father, and thus began his emotional search to learn who his parents were, uncover more of his past, and find his place among his Jewish brethren.

His journey eventually led him to a synagogue congested with fervent worshipers, led by the saintly Baal Shem Tov on Yom Kippur. The opening service of Kol Nidrei had commenced, but a solemn expression rested upon the Baal Shem Tov's face. Amidst the crowd, the lad was ready to join the prayers but distressed by his illiteracy in Hebrew. With tears in his eyes, he lifted the book Heavenwards and implored G-d to have compassion on him, by arranging the holy letters in order and accepting them as his humble prayers. With this cry, the Baal Shem Tov's face lit up in satisfaction.

When asked about his sudden joy, the Tzaddik responded that a tragic event was decreed on High and the young boy's heartfelt supplication pierced the heavens and lifted the decree. This story illuminates the power of prayer, especially when we pray with the innocence and purity of a child to our Father in Heaven.

Far over distant hills
The air with anxiety fills
Yemei Haselichos already has come
Tefillos are directed to *Marom*

A young Jewish boy of five
His parents no longer alive
A Christian he has been brought up to be
A *Siddur* is his only memory

In a dream, his parents appear
They tell him *Yom Kippur* is near
Alas, the message he did not heed
The dream they had to repeat

Shuv El Yesod Amecha
Al Derech Hayashar Teilech
[שוב אל יסוד עמך]
[על דרך הישר תלך*]
For the *Mitzvos* of which he'd been deprived

The time for *Teshuvah* has arrived
To go to *Shul*, he does at last decide
He sees *Mispal'lim* standing side by side
Inspired by *Talleisim*, he stands by the door
Until his tears, he can hold back no more

Hashem, here is my *Siddur* in my hand
The words I do not understand
Accept these *Osiyos* as *Tefillos* to you
Open *Sha'arei Hashamayim* for every Jew

*Return to the foundation of your People; on the upright path shall you go.

🎧 ARIM ROSHI

Maccabeats ©
Composed by Ahuva Ozeri ob"m and Moshe Daabul
Lyrics by Shai Gabso
Album: Voices from the Heights

הוֹלֵךְ אֲנִי כָּעֵת בְּמִשְׁעוֹל הַהֹוֶה
כְּיֶלֶד הַהוֹלֵךְ לוֹ לְאִיבּוּד
כַּפּוֹת יָדַי הֵן מוֹשְׁטוֹת
מְבַקְשׁוֹת אֶת הָעֶזְרָה לְהַמְשִׁיךְ אִיתָךְ אֶת הַמַּסָּע

וּבְצִדָּדִים הַפְּרָחִים כְּאִילוּ אִיבְּדוּ אֶת זְהוּתָם
מְחַפְּשִׂים עוֹד קֶרֶן אוֹר שֶׁתַּעֲזוֹר
עוֹד לְגִימָה קְטַנָּה שֶׁל מַיִם מִמַּעְיְנֵי הַחוֹכְמָה
תָּבִיא לָהֶם אֶת הַתִּקְוָה

Chorus
אָרִים רֹאשִׁי, אֶשָּׂא עֵינַי אֶל הֶהָרִים בַּמֶּרְחַקִּים
וְקוֹלִי יִשָּׁמַע כְּזַעֲקָה, כִּתְפִילַת הָאָדָם
וְלִבִּי יִקְרָא מֵאַיִן יָבוֹא עֶזְרִי

עוֹבֵר אֲנִי כָּעֵת בֵּין נוֹפִים חֲדָשִׁים
הַצְעָדִים הֵם נַעֲשִׂים כֹּה אִיטִּיִּים
מַה יֵּשׁ שָׁם שֶׁאֵין פֹּה שָׁאַל אוֹתִי עוֹבֵר
מַה בְּלֵב אַתָּה שׁוֹמֵר

קָשִׁישׁ הָעִיר כְּשֶׁעַל גַּבּוֹ מוּנַח כָּל עֲבָרוֹ
מַבִּיט סָבִיב וּמְחַפֵּשׂ אֶת עוֹלָמוֹ
כְּשֶׁהַהֹוֶה כָּל כָּךְ קָשֶׁה
לֹא אוֹמֵר דָּבָר, אָרִים רֹאשִׁי אֶל הַמָּחָר

Chorus

Translation:
I walk now in the path of the present
Like a child walking into oblivion
My hands are extended
Asking for help to continue the journey with you

And on the sides the flowers as though they lost their
identity
Searching for a ray of light that would help
Another small gulp of water from the wells of wisdom
That will bring them the hope

Chorus
I will raise my head,
I'll lift my eyes to the mountains in the distance
And my voice will be heard as a scream, as a prayer of a
human
And my heart will call out, "From where will my help
come?"

I pass now between new landscapes
The steps are taken so slowly

"What is there that is not here?" I asked a passer-by
"What do you guard in your heart?"

The city senior whose whole past rests on his back
Glances around and looks for his world
When the present is so hard
He doesn't say a word; I will raise my head toward
tomorrow

🎧 ANI AVDECHO

Psalms 116:16
Song composed by Ari Goldwag & Yitzy Waldner ©
Song concept by Ari Goldwag

אָנָּה ה' כִּי־אֲנִי עַבְדֶּךָ אֲנִי עַבְדְּךָ בֶּן־אֲמָתֶךָ פִּתַּחְתָּ לְמוֹסֵרָי

Translation:
Please, O Lord, for I am Your servant! I am Your servant,
the son of Your maidservant; You have released my
bonds.

🎧 THE LETTER

Dovid Gabay
Composed by Yitzy Waldner ©
Lyrics by Idy Appel

Dear Yossef my friend, it's been a while
We were a team, untroubled and free
Yeshiva days, our youthful ways
Now but fond old memories
From time to time they cross my mind, what we were,
you and me '
Along with your wife you run a store
Helping the needy and the poor

Yet one thing weighs you down,
Like an anchor below sea
Will you ever hear the call of "Tatty"?

Chorus
Daven for me, and I'll *Daven* for you.
Oh I know, how I know your pain, I feel it too
So come take my hand
Stand beside me and *Hashem* will see
How I care for you and you care for me
Daven for me, and I'll *Daven* for you
Let's storm the gates of Heaven; we will break through

Kol Hamispalel Be'ad Chaveiro [כל המתפלל בעד חבירו*],
Yes it's true
Will you *Daven* for me?
'Cause I'll *Daven* for you

Oh Yossef I know, the tears sting so
So lonely so sad, no place to go
As the days turn to months,
And the months turn into years
Will there ever be an end to all the fear?
What I'm asking of you is not easy, I know
To be what we were so long ago
But with the help of *Hashem*, we won't give up our fight
Let's turn our darkest day into a beacon of light

Chorus
כל המתפלל בעד חבירו, of course, it's true
So you *Daven* for me, and I'll *Daven* for you

Five years have gone by; our Baruch is three

Yossef and his wife have their Chana and Tzvi
All the tears shed from despair,
Are now pure sounds of joy
From their sweet little twins and our beautiful boy

You *Davened* for me, and I *Davened* for you
We stormed the gates of Heaven;
Our *Tefillos* broke through
כל המתפלל בעד חבירו, we see it's true
You *Davened* for me, and I *Davened* for you
You *Davened* for me, and I *Davened* for you

Daven for me, and I'll *Daven* for you
Let's storm the gates of Heaven; we will break through
כל המתפלל בעד חבירו, we see it's true
So *Daven* for me, and I'll *Daven* for you
Just *Daven* for me, and I'll *Daven* for you
Oh, *Daven* for me, and I'll *Daven* for you

*Everyone who prays for his friend. -Talmud

🎧 SHOMER YISRAEL
Tachanun Liturgy

שׁוֹמֵר יִשְׂרָאֵל
שְׁמוֹר שְׁאֵרִית יִשְׂרָאֵל
וְאַל יֹאבַד יִשְׂרָאֵל
הָאוֹמְרִים שְׁמַע יִשְׂרָאֵל

Translation:
O Guardian of Israel
Guard the remnant of Israel
And let not Israel to perish
Who say, "Hear, O Israel"

HAMALACH HAGOEL

Genesis 48:16
Maccabeats ©
Album: Voices from the Heights

הַמַּלְאָךְ הַגֹּאֵל אֹתִי מִכָּל־רָע יְבָרֵךְ אֶת־הַנְּעָרִים
וְיִקָּרֵא בָהֶם שְׁמִי וְשֵׁם אֲבֹתַי אַבְרָהָם וְיִצְחָק
וְיִדְגּוּ לָרֹב בְּקֶרֶב הָאָרֶץ

Translation:
May the angel who redeemed me from all harm bless
the youths
And may they be called by my name and the name of
my fathers Abraham and Isaac
And may they multiply abundantly like fish in the midst
of the land

PITCHU LI

Psalms 118:19-25
Franciska ©
Album: Echad

פִּתְחוּ־לִי שַׁעֲרֵי־צֶדֶק אָבֹא־בָם אוֹדֶה יָ־הּ
זֶה־הַשַּׁעַר לַה' צַדִּיקִים יָבֹאוּ בוֹ
אוֹדְךָ כִּי עֲנִיתָנִי וַתְּהִי־לִי לִישׁוּעָה:

Chorus
זֶה־הַיּוֹם עָשָׂה ה' נָגִילָה וְנִשְׂמְחָה בוֹ:

אֶבֶן מָאֲסוּ הַבּוֹנִים הָיְתָה לְרֹאשׁ פִּנָּה:
מֵאֵת ה' הָיְתָה זֹּאת הִיא נִפְלָאת בְּעֵינֵינוּ:

Chorus

אָנָּא ה' הוֹשִׁיעָה נָּא, אָנָּא ה' הַצְלִיחָה נָּא
Chorus

Translation:
Open for me the gates of righteousness
I shall enter them and thank G-d.
This is the Lord's gate; the righteous will enter therein.
I shall thank You because You answered me, and You
were my salvation.
This is the day that the Lord made; we shall exult and
rejoice thereon.
The stone that the builders rejected became a
cornerstone.
This was from the Lord; it is wondrous in our eyes.
Please, O Lord, save now! Please, O Lord, make
prosperous now!

SOF DAVAR

Ecclesiastes 12:13
Sheves Chaverim
Composed and arranged by Ari Goldwag
Album: Sheves Chaverim

סוֹף דָּבָר הַכֹּל נִשְׁמָע אֶת־הָאֱ־לֹקִים יְרָא וְאֶת־מִצְוֹתָיו שְׁמוֹר
כִּי־זֶה כָּל־הָאָדָם

Translation:
The end of the matter, everything having been heard,
fear G-d and keep His commandments, for this is the
entire man.

ESSA EINAI

Psalms 121:1-2 & 4
Shalsheles
Composed by Yitzchok Rosenthal ©
Arranged and conducted by Yisroel Lamm
Album: Shalsheles, Volume 1

אֶשָּׂא עֵינַי אֶל־הֶהָרִים מֵאַיִן יָבֹא עֶזְרִי
עֶזְרִי מֵעִם ה' עֹשֵׂה שָׁמַיִם וָאָרֶץ
הִנֵּה לֹא יָנוּם וְלֹא יִישָׁן שׁוֹמֵר יִשְׂרָאֵל

Translation:
I shall raise my eyes to the mountains, from where will my help come?
My help is from the Lord, the Maker of heaven and earth.
Behold the Guardian of Israel will neither slumber nor sleep.

TZADIK

Psalms 92:13:16
Shalsheles
Composed by Yitzchok Rosenthal ©
Arranged and conducted by Yisroel Lamm
Album: Shalsheles, Volume 1

צַדִּיק כַּתָּמָר יִפְרָח כְּאֶרֶז בַּלְּבָנוֹן יִשְׂגֶּה
שְׁתוּלִים בְּבֵית ה' בְּחַצְרוֹת אֱ-לֹקֵינוּ יַפְרִיחוּ
עוֹד יְנוּבוּן בְּשֵׂיבָה דְּשֵׁנִים וְרַעֲנַנִּים יִהְיוּ
לְהַגִּיד כִּי־יָשָׁר ה' צוּרִי וְלֹא־עַוְלָתָה בּוֹ

Translation:
The righteous one flourishes like the palm; like a cedar in Lebanon he grows.

Planted in the house of the Lord, in the courts of our G-d they will flourish.
They will yet grow in old age; fat and fresh will they be.
To declare that the Lord is upright, my Rock in Whom there is no injustice.

HABEN YAKIR LI

Jeremiah 31:19
Composed and arranged by Abie Rotenberg ©
Sung by Label Sharfman
Album: Dveykus, Volumes 1/2/3

הֲבֵן יַקִּיר לִי אֶפְרַיִם אִם יֶלֶד שַׁעֲשׁוּעִים כִּי־מִדֵּי דַבְּרִי בּוֹ זָכֹר אֶזְכְּרֶנּוּ עוֹד
עַל־כֵּן הָמוּ מֵעַי לוֹ רַחֵם אֲרַחֲמֶנּוּ נְאֻם־ה'

Translation:
"Is Ephraim a son who is dear to Me? Is he a child who is dandled? For whenever I speak of him, I still remember him: therefore, My very innards are stirring for him; I will surely have compassion on him," says the Lord.

CHAPTER 9:
Israel

Israel is a land of fusion. It balances between rapid development in technology and breakthroughs reaching the larger contemporary world, and an enduring doctrine and culture faithful to its ancient roots. It dances tensely between war and peace. The Citadel of King David described by the prophet towers adjacent to a stylish new mall. Within its modest geographical borders, a diverse myriad of people mingle.

However, it is the one and only land we are intrinsically magnetized to as home; the land avowed to our Patriarch Abraham by G-d Himself, as an eternal possession. It is the setting to numerous of our most agonizing trials and our greatest joys. Through conflict and devastation we've never let go of it, even if hanging on by a thread. It is testament to the Divine miracle of Jewish survival: Israel, both the land and the nation, live on and shall remain.

We have stumbled, wept and mourned for our siblings tragically lost along the way. The suffering of our Holy Temple's destruction, of witnessing treasured Jerusalem, the "City of Gold" ravaged, and of our ensuing Exile, is reawakened. Yet, we have never truly been conquered. We unite in an unbreakable bond from the four corners of the earth and support one another, in festivity or under fire, all intensely yearning for the day we will all return to the home of our people. Indeed, since our earliest days we've battled; the brave soldiers of Israel's army, and notables in our history who stood for Torah and our convictions in spite of society's opposition, are but a few who have shown us the way. We pray and struggle for light and peace, when war will be no more and we can dwell in true harmony in our Promised Land.

QUESTION TO CONSIDER:
What can you do to show support for our brothers and sisters in the Holy Land, especially our soldiers — Chayalim who are protecting the country every day?

Dedicated to Frieda Geller

Birthday: July 17, 1922 | Yartzeit: 13 Cheshvan

Frieda was a Zionist, and often sung these songs about Israel.

SHNEI MICHTAVIM
Composed by Joel Engel ob"m and Avigdor Hemeiri ob"m ©

אמא:

עַל נְיַיר לָבָן וְצַח כְּשֶׁלֶג
בָּא מִכְתָּב מִן הַגּוֹלָה
כּוֹתֶבֶת אֵם בְּדִמְעַת עַיִן
"לִבְנִי הַטוֹב בִּירוּשָׁלַיִם
אָבִיךָ מֵת, אִמְּךָ חוֹלָה
בּוֹא הַבַּיְתָה לַגּוֹלָה!
בּוֹא הביתה לגולה!
נְחַכֶּה לְךָ בְּלִי הֶרֶף
מִן הַבּוֹקֶר עַד הָעֶרֶב
בּוֹא הַבַּיְתָה, בֶּן חָבִיב
בּוֹא הַבַּיְתָה לְאָבִיב
בּוֹא הַבַּיְתָה
בּוֹא הַבַּיְתָה
בּוֹא, בֶּן חָבִיב."

בֵּן:

הוֹלֵךְ מִכְתָּב אֶל הַגּוֹלָה
כּוֹתֵב חָלוּץ, בְּדִמְעַת עַיִן
שְׁנַת תרפ"ט בִּירוּשָׁלַיִם:

"סְלָחִי לִי, אִמִּי הַחוֹלָה
לֹא אָשׁוּב עוֹד לַגּוֹלָה!
לֹא אָשׁוּב עוֹד לַגּוֹלָה!
אִם אָהוּב תְּאָהֲבִינִי
בּוֹאִי הֵנָּה וְחַבְּקִינִי
לֹא אֶהְיֶה עוֹד נָע וָנָד!
לֹא אָזוּז מִפֹּה לָעַד!
לֹא אָזוּזָה
לֹא אָזוּזָה
לֹא!"

Translation:
Mother: On a white paper, white as snow, a letter comes from the diaspora
A mother is writing with tears in her eyes: To my son in Jerusalem, come home! Your father has died, your mother is sick, come home to the diaspora. We will wait for you ceaselessly, from morning till evening. Come home to spring. Come home dear son.

Son: On simple paper, simple and gray, a letter goes to the diaspora

A pioneer is writing with tears in his eyes in the year 1929:
Forgive me my sick mother. I will not return to the diaspora. If you love me, come here and love me, come here and hug me. I will not be a wanderer. I will never move from here. I won't move, I won't move, no!

NA HAGIDI
Composed by Hanina Karchevsky (1877-1925)
Adaptation: Gil Aldema (1928-1944)
From the CD "To the Top of the Mountain - Songs of Hanina Karchevsky", produced by the Hebrew Song Heritage Association (2004).

נָא הַגִּידִי, יַלְדָּתִי,
נָא הַגִּידִי, חֶמְדָּתִי,
אֵיךְ תִּסְּעִי, אֵיךְ תִּסְּעִי
לְאֶרֶץ יִשְׂרָאֵל?

יָם סוֹעֵר רְחַב יָדַיִם,
אֳנִיּוֹת טוֹבְעוֹת בַּמַּיִם,

אֵיךְ תִּסְּעִי, אֵיךְ תִּסְּעִי
לְאֶרֶץ יִשְׂרָאֵל?

הוֹי, אִמִּי, לִבִּי כַּיָּם הוּא;
הוּא סוֹעֵר, הוֹמֶה לְשָׁם הוּא,
רַק לְאָרֶץ, רַק לְאָרֶץ,
רַק לְאֶרֶץ יִשְׂרָאֵל!

Translation:
Please tell me, my daughter
Please tell me, my dearest
How will you travel, how will you travel
to Eretz Yisrael?

The sea is stormy and wide open
Ships are sinking in the sea
How will you travel, how will you travel
to Eretz Yisrael?

Oh, my mother, my heart is like the sea
It's stormy and noisy
Only to the land, only to the land
Only to the land of Israel!

🎧 I AM THE LAND

Chanale ©
Album: I Am the Land

Have you ever felt a calling?
A stir inside your soul
Until it gets so loud you can't ignore
Do you know the taste of freedom?
When you live a life of truth
And you finally close the miles
From you to her

Chorus
I am the land
I am her oceans
These are my mountains
I stand on my ground
I am the people
For we are the nation
Chosen by G-d
My home I have found
Her oxygen fills me
I breathe in her air
And no one can take it from me

The land that I love
The land that I need
The land of the land of *Yisrael*

Have you ever made a journey?
Like so many have before
Their footsteps aligning with yours

Do you know how she awaits us
To rebuild upon her throne?
When finally her kingdom is restored

Chorus

The land that I love
The land that I need
The land of my home
The land of the Jews
The land that is mine
The land that is ours, *Yisrael*

Yes, I am the land...

🎧 IM ESHKACHECH

Psalms 137:5-6
Yaakov Shwekey ©
Composed by Yochanan Shapiro

אִם אֶשְׁכָּחֵךְ יְרוּשָׁלַיִם, תִּשְׁכַּח יְמִינִי
תִּדְבַּק לְשׁוֹנִי לְחִכִּי אִם לֹא אֶזְכְּרֵכִי
אִם לֹא אַעֲלֶה אֶת יְרוּשָׁלַיִם עַל רֹאשׁ שִׂמְחָתִי

Translation:
If I forget you, O Jerusalem, let my right hand forget [its skill]
May my tongue cling to my palate if I do not remember you
If I do not elevate Jerusalem above my foremost joy

🎧 SHARM EL-SHEIKH

Ran Eliran
Melody composed by Amos Ettinger ©
Lyrics by Rafi Gabai

It was the Six-Day War of the Arabs against the Israelis in June 1967, and the Israeli public feared a dramatic defeat. Ran Eliran volunteered at the start of the war to uplift the troops. On the Sinai Desert road between one performance for the military to another, the song Sharm El-Sheikh — commemorating Israel's successful capture of Egypt's Sharm El-Sheikh during the War — was born.

גָּדוֹל הוּא הַלַּיְלָה וְלָךְ מְחַיֵּךְ
חָזַרְנוּ עִם בּוֹקֶר אֶל שארם אל-שייח
עָבַרְנוּ בַּלַּיְלָה, בַּיָּם וּבָהָר
וּבָאנוּ עִם בּוֹקֶר אֶל תּוֹךְ הַמֵּיצַר

Chorus
אֶת שָארָם א-שייח, חֲזַרְנוּ אֵלַיִךְ שֵׁנִית
אֶת בְּלִבֵּנוּ, לִיבֵּנוּ תָּמִיד
הַיָּם וְהַמֶּלַח יִרְאוּ אֶת הַשִּׁיר
חֲזַרְנוּ אֲלֵיכֶם, טִירָאן וְסַנְפִּיר
אוֹתָם הַשָּׁמַיִם מֵעַל לְבָבֵךְ
מֵיצַר, יָם וָמַיִם - אֶת שָארָם אל-שייח

Chorus

עוֹלָה לוֹ הַבּוֹקֶר בְּחוֹף אַלְמוֹגִים
עוֹבְרוֹת שׁוּב בְּמֵימֵי סְפִינוֹת דַּיָּגִים
יוֹרֵד לוֹ הָעֶרֶב, מֵבִיא עוֹד חֲלוֹם
מֵבִיא עַל הַמַּיִם תִּקְוָוה לְשָׁלוֹם

Chorus

הוי, שארם אל-שייח!

Translation:
Great is the night, and it smiles at you
We returned in the morning to *Sharm El-Sheikh*
We passed in the night, the sea and the mountain
Arriving in the morning at the straits

Chorus

The sea and the salt will view the song
We've returned to you, *Tiran* and *S'napir*
The same skies above your heart
Strait, sea, and water- you are *Sharm El-Sheikh*

Chorus
The morning rises in the coral beach

Fishing boats pass through the water again
The evening sets, bringing another dream
Brings on the water a hope for peace

Chorus

LU YEHI

Naomi Shemer ob"m ©
Sung by Chava Alberstein

When the Yom Kippur War broke out in 1973, it was Shemer's song "Lu Yehi" ("May It Be") that best expressed the feelings of both the battlefront and the homefront. The yearning lyrics reflect the mood and the distress of that difficult time.

עוֹד יֵשׁ מִפְרָשׂ לָבָן בָּאוֹפֶק
מוּל עָנָן שָׁחוֹר כָּבֵד
כָּל שֶׁנְּבַקֵּשׁ לוּ יְהִי
וְאִם בַּחַלּוֹנוֹת הָעֶרֶב
אוֹר נֵרוֹת הֶחָג רוֹעֵד
כָּל שֶׁנְּבַקֵּשׁ לוּ יְהִי

Chorus
לוּ יְהִי, לוּ יְהִי
אָנָּא לוּ יְהִי
כָּל שֶׁנְּבַקֵּשׁ לוּ יְהִי (x2)

מֶה קוֹל עֲנוֹת אֲנִי שׁוֹמֵעַ
קוֹל שׁוֹפָר וְקוֹל תֻּפִּים
כָּל שֶׁנְּבַקֵּשׁ לוּ יְהִי
לוּ תִשָּׁמַע בְּתוֹךְ כָּל אֵלֶּה
גַּם תְּפִלָּה אַחַת מִפִּי
כָּל שֶׁנְּבַקֵּשׁ לוּ יְהִי

Chorus

בְּתוֹךְ שְׁכוּנָה קְטַנָּה מוּצֶלֶת
בַּיִת קָט עִם גַּג אָדוֹם
כָּל שֶׁנְּבַקֵּשׁ לוּ יְהִי
זֶה סוֹף הַקַּיִץ סוֹף הַדֶּרֶךְ
תֵּן לָהֶם לָשׁוּב הֲלוֹם
כָּל שֶׁנְּבַקֵּשׁ לוּ יְהִי

Chorus

Translation:
There is still a white sail on the horizon
Opposite a heavy black cloud
All that we ask for - may it be
And if in the evening windows
The light of the holiday candles flickers
All that we seek - may it be

Chorus
May it be, may it be
Please, may it be
All that we seek, may it be

What is the sound that I hear
The cry of the *Shofar* and the sound of drums
All that we ask for, may it be
If only there can be heard within all this
One prayer from my lips also
All that we seek, may it be

Chorus
Within a small, shaded neighborhood
Is a small house with a red roof

All that we ask for, may it be
This is the end of summer, the end of the path
Allow them to return safely here
All that we seek, may it be

🎧 OHR

Naomi Shemer ob"m ©

אוֹר עוֹלָה בַּבֹּקֶר
עַל אֲגַם רָחוֹק זוֹכֶרֶת
כֵּן אֲנִי זוֹכֶרֶת
וְלֹא אֶחְדַּל וְלֹא אֶשְׁתּוֹק

אוֹר שֶׁמְבַשֵּׂר אֶת
הַהַשְׁכָּמָה וְהַזְרִיחָה זוֹכֶרֶת
רַק לִרְאוֹת עוֹד פַּעַם
יוֹתֵר מִזֶּה אֵינִי צְרִיכָה

Chorus
שֶׁמֶשׁ, הָבִיאוּ שֶׁמֶשׁ
עִם שָׁמַיִם מְעֻנָּנִים
עוֹצֶמֶת אֶת עֵינַי
אֲבָל הַשֶּׁמֶשׁ הִיא בִּפְנִים

אוֹר בְּצָהֳרַיִם
עַל הָאֲדָמָה זוֹכֶרֶת
עַל חֶלְקַת הַמַּיִם
וְעַל שְׁתִיל וְעַל קָמָה

אוֹר יוֹרֵד בָּעֶרֶב
עַל שְׂדוֹת חַיַּי זוֹכֶרֶת
עוֹד אֲנִי זוֹכֶרֶת
זֶה אוֹר יוֹמַי זֶה אוֹר יָמַי

Chorus

אוֹר יוֹרֵד בְּעֶרֶב שֶׁמֶשׁ
אוֹר בְּצָהֳרַיִם שֶׁמֶשׁ
אוֹר עוֹלָה בַּבֹּקֶר אוֹר

Translation:
Light comes up in the morning
On a far away lake, I remember
Yes, I remember
And I will not stop nor will I be quiet

Light that tells of
The waking and the sunrise, I remember
Just to see once more
I do not need more than that

Chorus
Sun, bring sun
With cloudy skies
I close my eyes
But the sun is inside

Light in the afternoon
On the earth, I remember
On the water
And on a seedling and on ripe grain

Light goes down in the evening
On the fields of my life, I remember
I still remember
It is the light of my day, it is the light of my years
Chorus

Light goes down in the evening, sun
Light in the afternoon, sun
Light comes up in the morning

🎧 YERUSHALAYIM SHEL ZAHAV

Naomi Shemer ob"m ©
Sung by Ofra Haza ob"m

אֲוִיר-הָרִים צָלוּל כַּיַּיִן
וְרֵיחַ אֳרָנִים
נִשָּׂא בְּרוּחַ הָעַרְבַּיִם
עִם קוֹל פַּעֲמוֹנִים

וּבְתַרְדֵּמַת אִילָן וָאֶבֶן
שְׁבוּיָה בַּחֲלוֹמָהּ
הָעִיר אֲשֶׁר בָּדָד יוֹשֶׁבֶת
וּבְלִבָּהּ חוֹמָה

Chorus
יְרוּשָׁלַיִם שֶׁל זָהָב
וְשֶׁל נְחֹשֶׁת וְשֶׁל אוֹר
הֲלֹא לְכָל שִׁירַיִךְ
אֲנִי כִּנּוֹר (x2)

אֵיכָה יָבְשׁוּ בּוֹרוֹת הַמַּיִם
כִּכַּר-הַשּׁוּק רֵיקָה
וְאֵין פּוֹקֵד אֶת הַר-הַבַּיִת
בָּעִיר הָעַתִּיקָה

וּבַמְּעָרוֹת אֲשֶׁר בַּסֶּלַע
מְיַלְּלוֹת רוּחוֹת
וְאֵין יוֹרֵד אֶל יַם-הַמֶּלַח
בְּדֶרֶךְ יְרִיחוֹ...

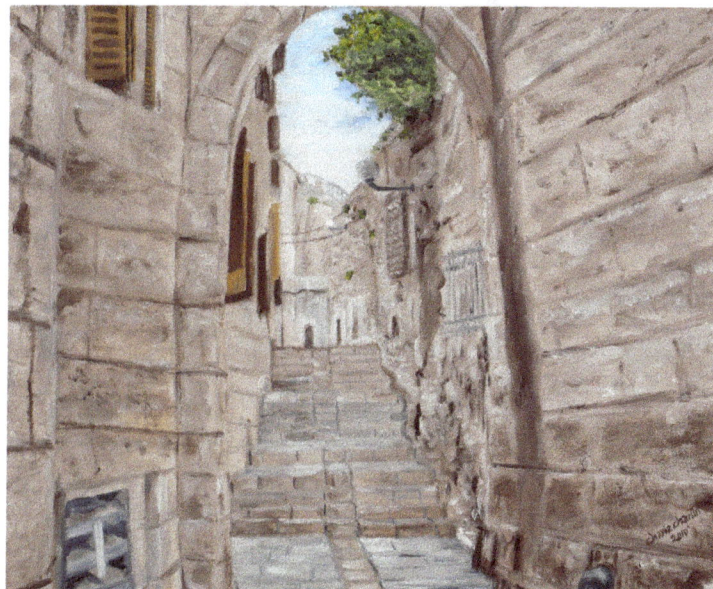

Chorus

אַךְ בְּבוֹאִי הַיּוֹם לָשִׁיר לָךְ
וְלָךְ לִקְשֹׁר כְּתָרִים
קָטֹנְתִּי מִצְּעִיר בָּנַיִךְ
וּמֵאַחֲרוֹן הַמְשׁוֹרְרִים

כי שמך צורב את השפתיים
כנשיקת שרף
אם אשכחך ירושלים
אשר כולה זהב

Translation:
The mountain air is clear as wine
And the scent of pines
Is carried on the breeze of twilight
With the sound of bells

And in the slumber of tree and stone
Captured in her dream

The city that sits solitary
And in its midst is a wall

Chorus
Jerusalem of gold
And of copper and of light
Behold, for all your songs
I am a lute (x2)

The wells are filled again with water
The marketplace with joyous crowd
The ram's horn rings out loud on the Temple Mount
Within the Old City

Within the caverns in the mountains
A thousand suns will glow,
We'll take the Dead Sea road together
That runs through Jericho

Chorus

But as I come to sing to you today
And to adorn crowns to you
I am the smallest of the youngest of your children
And of the last poet

For your name scorches the lips
Like the kiss of a fiery angel
If I forget you, O Jerusalem
Which is all gold

IT HAPPENED YOM KIPPUR

Mayer Rivkin ©
Album: Redemption

This song tells the story of a young Israeli soldier in need of special protection as he prepares to go into battle at the start of the Yom Kippur War.

It happened *Yom Kippur* as they were praying
A truck pulled up, and the Sergeants were saying
A war has broke out; we need all our men
To serve *Lema'an Hashem*

Young Mottel turned around to his father beside him
"Father, advise me before I go fight them
Give me a *Bracha* I should have *Hatzlocho*
And let's hope we'll meet again"

"Oh Mottel, my son, do not be dejected
We have a *Mezuzah*; you'll be protected

Set aside time during each day
To study the Torah and pray

"Speak to our soldiers that will be with you
Teach them *Bechol Derochecho De'eihu* [בכל דרכיך דעהו*]
Hashem Yishmor Tzeischa [** ה' ישמר צאתך], safe and
secure
Until you'll be with us once more"

*Know G-d in all your ways. -Proverbs 3:6
**G-d will guard your going out. -Psalms 121:8

🎧 AL KOL EILEH
Naomi Shemer ob"m ©

עַל הַדְּבַשׁ וְעַל הָעֹקֶץ
עַל הַמַּר וְהַמָּתוֹק
עַל בִּתֵּנוּ הַתִּינֹקֶת
שְׁמֹר אֵ-לִי הַטּוֹב
עַל הָאֵשׁ הַמְבֹעֶרֶת
עַל הַמַּיִם הַזַּכִּים
עַל הָאִישׁ הַשָּׁב הַבַּיְתָה
מִן הַמֶּרְחַקִּים

Chorus
עַל כָּל אֵלֶּה עַל כָּל אֵלֶּה
שְׁמֹר נָא לִי אֵ-לִי הַטּוֹב
עַל הַדְּבַשׁ וְעַל הָעֹקֶץ
עַל הַמַּר וְהַמָּתוֹק
אַל נָא תַעֲקֹר נָטוּעַ
אַל תִּשְׁכַּח אֶת הַתִּקְוָה
הֲשִׁיבֵנִי וְאָשׁוּבָה
אֶל הָאָרֶץ הַטּוֹבָה

שְׁמֹר אֵ-לִי עַל זֶה הַבַּיִת
עַל הַגַּן עַל הַחוֹמָה
מִיָּגוֹן מִפַּחַד-פֶּתַע
וּמִמִּלְחָמָה
שְׁמֹר עַל הַמְעַט שֶׁיֵּשׁ לִי
עַל הָאוֹר וְעַל הַטַּף
עַל הַפְּרִי שֶׁלֹּא הִבְשִׁיל עוֹד
וְשֶׁנֶּאֱסַף

Chorus

מֵרָשְׁרֵשׁ אִילָן בְּרוּחַ
מֵרָחוֹק נוֹשֵׁר כּוֹכָב
מִשְׁאֲלוֹת לִבִּי בַּחֹשֶׁךְ
נִרְשָׁמוֹת עַכְשָׁו
אָנָּא שְׁמֹר לִי עַל כָּל אֵלֶּה
וְעַל אֲהוּבֵי-נַפְשִׁי
עַל הַשֶּׁקֶט עַל הַבְּכִי
וְעַל זֶה הַשִּׁיר

Chorus

אֶל הָאָרֶץ הַטּוֹבָה...

Translation:
Over the honey and the stinger
Over the bitter and the sweet
And over our baby girl
Please guard, my good Lord
Over the burning fire
Over the crystal clear water
And over the man who is coming home
From afar

Chorus
Over all these things, over all these things
Please stand guard for me my good G-d
Over the honey and the stinger
Over the bitter and the sweet
Don't uproot a sapling
Don't forget the hope
May you return me, and may I return
To the good land

Save the houses that we live in
The small fences and the wall
From the sudden war-like thunder
May you save them all
Guard what little I've been given
Guard the hill my child might climb
Let the fruit that's yet to ripen
Not be plucked before its time

Chorus

As the wind makes rustling night sounds
And a star falls in its arc
All my dreams and my desires
Form crystal shapes out of the dark.
Guard for me, oh Lord, these treasures
All my friends keep safe and strong,
Guard the stillness, guard the weeping,
And above all, guard this song.

ELI, ELI

Lyrics by Hannah Szenes ob"m
Melody composed by David Zahavi ©
Excerpted from her poem Halicha L'Kesariya

אֵ-לִי, אֵ-לִי
שֶׁלֹּא יִגָּמֵר לְעוֹלָם
הַחוֹל וְהַיָּם
רִשְׁרוּשׁ שֶׁל הַמַּיִם
בְּרַק הַשָּׁמַיִם
תְּפִלַּת הָאָדָם

Translation:
My G-d, my G-d
May these things never end:
The sand and the sea
The rush of the water
The lightning in the heavens
The prayer of man

ANCIENT STONE

Rivka Leah Popack ©
Lead vocals by Carmella Lewis
Backing vocals by Taliah Bloom
Album: Silent Prayer

I'm ancient stone; I'm all alone, I stand here
And I pray that I'll be whole again one day
Hundreds of years have dried the tears on my golden
stone
And a thousand whispered prayers echo in my soul

I listen to the beating heart that knows it's not alone

In the place where heaven touches earth
And as each note is placed within, an angel sheds a tear
And its prayer is lifted high above on wings of love and fear

The gates of prayer open wide, the heavens part
To catch the perfect pieces of a solitary heart
I listen to the little child, so simple and so pure
To the lonely soldier, tired and torn
I listen to the father, worried for his child
To the mother as she prays into the night

Chorus
I listen to the voice of thanks, praise and prayer divine
To the voice of hope, that dreams a better time (x2)

🎧 SHMOR ELOKIM

Rivka Leah Popack ©
Lead vocals by Robin Aron
Backing vocals by Zahava Pinson
Album: Silent Prayer

Along a dusty path
Walking all alone
Knapsack on his back
Wanders far from home

Singing to the wind
Beneath the open skies
Silent in his thoughts
Tears in his eyes

Eyes that long for rest
A heart that hurts to feel

Relief so far away
A dream that can't be real

The sun slips through the sky
The day has come and gone
The world is deep in sleep
But he just wanders on

Shmor Elokim Al Chayal Haboded Sheli
Shmor Oto Misakanah Umikol Davar Shelili
Hadlek Loh Ner Boer Hanoten Shalvah Veshalom
Hamadrich Otoh Baderech B'cheshkat Hachalom

[שמור אלוקים על חיל הבודד שלי
שמור אותו מסכנה ומכל דבר שלילי
הדלק לו נר בוער הנותן שלווה ושלום
המדריך אותו בדרך בחשכת החלום*]

She thinks of him by day
Prays for him by night
G-d, watch him on his way
G-d, grant him strength to fight

And with each dawn and each dusk
Another tear is cried
To hear his gentle voice
His footsteps outside (chorus)

Oh, let it be a time of peace forevermore
From distant corners bring us back to homeland shores
We'll ride the dream of wings and let our spirits soar
Achakeh Lo Bechol Yom Sheyavo
[**אחכה לו בכל יום שיבא]

*Dear G-d, watch over this lonely soldier of mine. Guard him from danger and harm. Kindle within him the vision of serenity and peace to light his way through the darkest dream.
**I await his coming every day. -Rambam's Thirteen Principles of Faith, Article 12

🎧 HOMELAND

Rivky Saxon ©

Little Sarah's birthday was the fourth day of July
Her cowgirl hat always on, and her boots, they always shined
But somethin' nagged at her day and night
She couldn't figure what it was
Her horse, her farm, and the Tennessee charm never really felt enough

So she got off her horse and boarded a plane
Leavin' behind the ol' USA
To a homeland that she never had called home
Walkin' through the streets
Taking in her history
A southern girl, in a brand new world,
Found a new home to love

Chorus
And now it's a meaningful, beautiful life
Full of purpose and of pride
'Cause you know what you're standing for
And you know it's the good fight
Who am I to say it's easy?
I haven't moved there yet
But there's something special in the atmosphere
And it's somethin' you can't forget

Benny was a baseball star,
Been playing since he was three
Pledged every day to the stars and stripes,
American and free
But something just did not feel right
When he found he was a Jew
He put down the bat, and just like that;
He went to find out the truth

Chorus

So the Sarahs and Bennys all made their way
And I'm still here, in ol' USA
Wishing I had the strength to give it up
I won't lie and say it's simple
Leavin' this so-called home
But I know one day
I'll get on that plane
And call this land my own

Chorus (x2)

Yes, there's something special in the atmosphere
And it's somethin' you can't forget

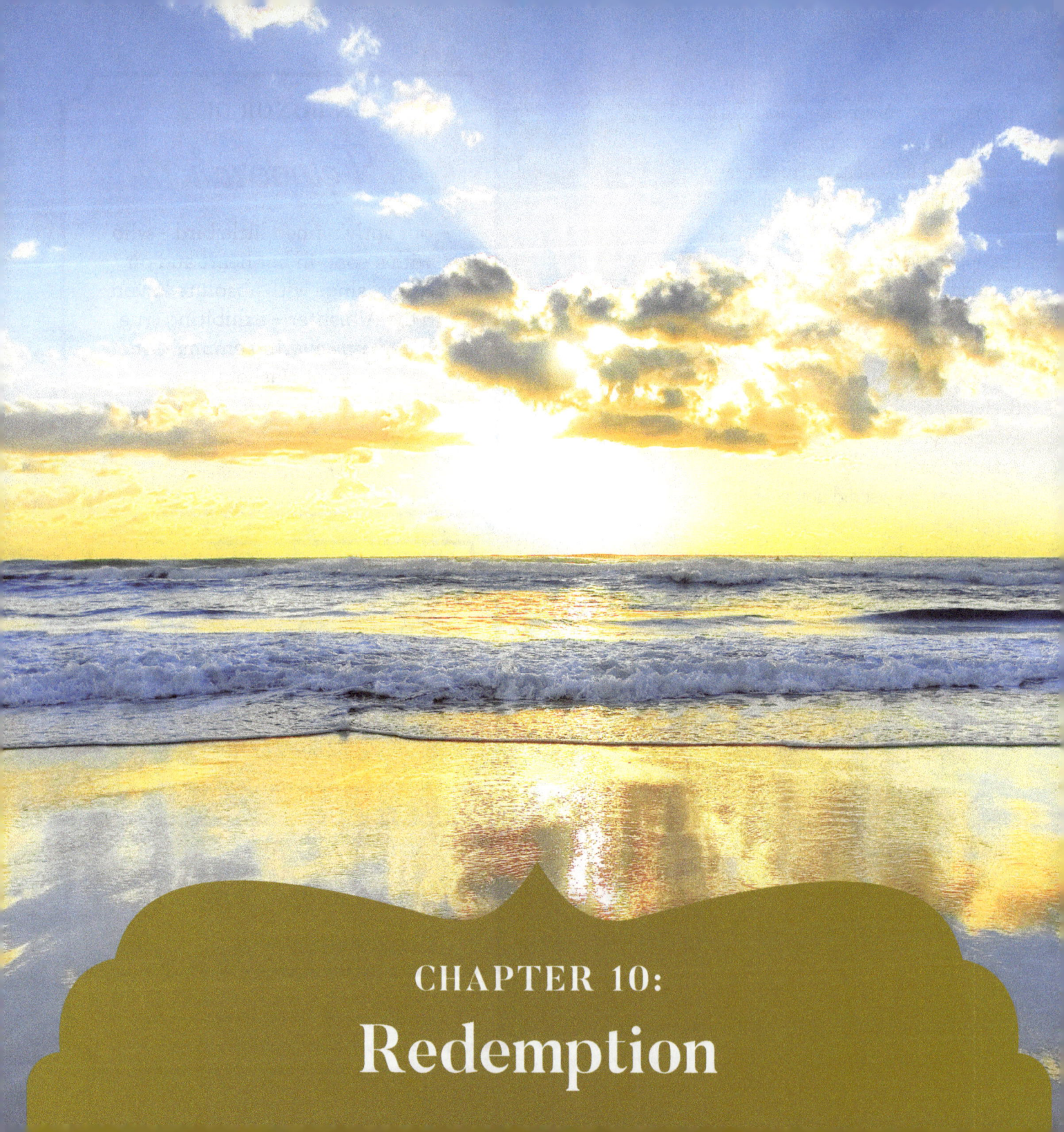

CHAPTER 10:
Redemption

The sun rises and sets in a seemingly endless cycle, yet our fiery longing for the coming of *Moshiach* is unquenchable. "*Achakeh Lo Bechol Yom Sheyavo* — I await his arrival every day." Perhaps, despite these hopeful yearnings, a concern may flit through one's mind: "Will the goals, successes, and relationships I've achieved in this world be nullified and forgotten in the era of redemption?"

The Lubavitcher Rebbe explains as follows that such shall not be: "*Geulah*" is Hebrew for "Redemption"; it is comprised of the word "*Golah* — Exile," referring to our present condition, plus an "*Aleph*," symbolizing the Oneness of G-d. This signifies that all positive elements of our exile existence will be included in the *Geulah*, but everything will be sanctified by the revelation of the One Above.

Our dream of over two thousand years will be actualized, with *Hashem*'s assistance, through our actions. *Moshiach* is already at our threshold; he's just waiting for us to open the door. Together, let's give him a royal welcome.

"שִׁיר הַמַּעֲלוֹת בְּשׁוּב ה' אֶת־שִׁיבַת צִיּוֹן הָיִינוּ כְּחֹלְמִים אָז יִמָּלֵא שְׂחוֹק פִּינוּ וּלְשׁוֹנֵנוּ רִנָּה"

"A song of ascents. When Hashem will return the exiles of Zion, we will be like dreamers. Then our mouth will be filled with laughter, and our tongue with joyous song." [Psalms 126:1-2]

QUESTION TO CONSIDER:

What can you do to strengthen and help prepare the world for the era of Redemption?

🎧 ANI MAAMIN

Rambam's Thirteen Principles of Faith, Article 12
Avraham Fried ©
Album: No Jew Will Be Left Behind

This haunting, traditional tune was written during the Holocaust, but its composer is unknown. However, it has been brought down that R' Azriel Dovid Fastag was divinely inspired to sing it, on a train destined for the Treblinka concentration camp. A fellow captive leaped from the train and escaped, and eventually reached the Modzitzer Rebbe, R' Shaul Yedidya Elazar, to whom he taught the stirring melody. The song reveals the unshakable soul of the Jewish People and our faith in a brighter future, even when presently engulfed by the darkest hour.

אֲנִי מַאֲמִין בֶּאֱמוּנָה שְׁלֵמָה בְּבִיאַת הַמָּשִׁיחַ
וְאַף עַל פִּי שֶׁיִּתְמַהְמֵהַּ, עִם כָּל זֶה אֲחַכֶּה לוֹ בְּכָל יוֹם שֶׁיָּבוֹא

Translation:
I believe with perfect faith in the coming of the Messiah.
Even if he delays, I will wait every day for him to come.

🎧 RACHEM BECHASDECHA

Shabbat Zemirot Liturgy
Mordechai Ben David ©
Album: MBD and Friends

רחם בחסדך על עמך צורנו
על ציון משכן כבודך
זבול בית תפארתנו
בן דוד עבדך יבא ויגאלנו

רוח אפינו משיח ה׳

יבנה המקדש עיר ציון תמלא
ושם נשיר שיר חדש וברננה נעלה
הרחמן הנקדש יתברך ויתעלה
על כוס יין מלא כברכת ה׳

Translation:
Have mercy in your kindness on your nation, our Rock
Upon Zion habitation of Your honor
The Temple of our splendor
May David's son, your servant, come and deliver us
The breath of our mouth, the anointed of G-d

The Temple will be rebuilt, the City of Zion will be filled
And there we will sing a new song and in exultation ascend
The Merciful and the Sanctified One will be blessed and exalted
Over a full cup of wine filled with G-d's blessing

🎧 ANI MAAMIN

Rivka Leah Popack ©
Lead vocals by Taliah Bloom
Backing vocals by Michelle Max and Taliah Bloom
Album: Silent Prayer

I don't want to play and sing this prayer
I just want to live Your song
A million years of asking
A million years too long

I don't want to close my eyes and dream

I want it here; I want it real
I want to touch it; I want to feel

To see the oneness
Feel the peace
The truth that's blowing in the breeze

Ani Maamin Be'emunah Sheleimah
Beviat Hamashiach
Ani Maamin, Ani Maamin
Ve'af Al Pi Sheyitmame'ah
Im Kol Zeh Achake Loh
Achake Loh, Achake Loh
Bechol Yom Sheyavo

[אני מאמין באמונה שלמה]
בביאת המשיח
אני מאמין, אני מאמין
ואף על פי שיתמהמה
עם כל זה אחכה לו
אחכה לו, אחכה לו
[*בכל יום שיבוא]

I believe with complete faith in the coming of the Messiah; and even though he may tarry, nevertheless I wait for him each day for his coming. -Rambam's Thirteen Principles of Faith, Article 12

🎧 ATA TAKUM

Psalms 102:14
Franciska ©
Album: Kol Haolam

(X4) אַתָּה תָקוּם תְּרַחֵם צִיּוֹן כִּי-עֵת לְחֶנְנָהּ כִּי-בָא מוֹעֵד

Chorus

(x4) כִּי-בָא מוֹעֵד

(x4) אַתָּה תָקוּם תְּרַחֵם צִיּוֹן כִּי-עֵת לְחֶנְנָהּ כִּי-בָא מוֹעֵד

Chorus

Translation:
You will arise, You will have mercy on Zion
For there's a time to favor it, for the appointed season has arrived (x2)

Chorus

🎧 MEHAIRA

Wedding Blessing Liturgy
Benny Friedman
Composed by Yitzy Waldner ©
Arranged by Tzvi Blumenfeld
Mixed by Eli Lishinsky
Album: Fill the World With Light

מְהֵרָה, ה' אֱ-לֹהֵינוּ, יִשָּׁמַע בְּעָרֵי יְהוּדָה וּבְחֻצוֹת יְרוּשָׁלַיִם,
קוֹל שָׂשׂוֹן וְקוֹל שִׂמְחָה, קוֹל חָתָן וְקוֹל כַּלָּה,
קוֹל מִצְהֲלוֹת חֲתָנִים מֵחֻפָּתָם וּנְעָרִים מִמִּשְׁתֵּה נְגִינָתָם

Translation:
Lord our G-d, let there speedily be heard in the cities of Judah and in the streets of Jerusalem the sound of joy and the sound of happiness, the sound of a groom and the sound of a bride, the sound of exultation of grooms from under their wedding canopy, and youths from their joyous banquets.

🎧 ACHAS

Psalms 27:4
Avraham Fried ©
Composed by Yossi Green
Arranged by Moshe Laufer
Album: Aderaba

אַחַת שָׁאַלְתִּי מֵאֵת־ה׳ אוֹתָהּ אֲבַקֵּשׁ
שִׁבְתִּי בְּבֵית־ה׳ כָּל־יְמֵי חַיַּי לַחֲזוֹת בְּנֹעַם־ה׳ וּלְבַקֵּר בְּהֵיכָלוֹ

Translation:
One [thing] I ask of the Lord, I seek that I may dwell in the house of the Lord all the days of my life, to see the pleasantness of the Lord and to visit His Temple every morning.

🎧 MOSHIACH

Kinderlach ©
Album: Kinderlach

Yo, yo, yo, yo!

Zehu Shir Atzuv Me'od, Al Echad Shemechakim Lo
Abba, Ima, Yeladim Eich Shehem Mispal'lim Lo
Eich Halev Nishbar Kol Boker, Lama Od Lo Higiyah
Ein Safek Ve'ein Dilmah Gam Im Hu Mitmame'ha

זהו שיר עצוב מאוה, על אחד שמחכים לו]
אבא, אמא, ילדים איך שהם מתפללים לו
איך הלב נשבר כל בוקר, למה עוד לא הגיע
[*אין ספק ואין דילמה גם אם הוא מתמהמה

Chorus

Everybody wants *Moshiach*, everybody wants
Everybody wants *Moshiach*
Shoyn Shoyn Sheyavo
[**שוין שוין שיבוא]
Everybody wants *Moshiach*, everybody wants
Everybody wants *Moshiach* now

Yo, yo, yo, yo!

This song comes right from our heart, about *Moshiach*, hear us out
We want him, and we wait each day
Never ever stop to pray
Children, parents, young and old
All the Jews around the world wait for him so he should come
Oy *Moshiach*, please come right now!

Moshiach (x6)
Ani Lo Yachol Yoter
[***אני לא יכול יותר]

Chorus

Ani Chai Bimitziut Hureset Turefet
Lo Ein Li Rega Kal, Kol Ha'aretz Mis'hafeches
Ubalev Yesheina Tefillah - Avinu Malkeinu
Shehinei Hu Magiyah Hamoshiach Eileinu
Ein Makom Leshum Yee'oush Amar Kavar Rabbi Nachman
Vehalev Shehu Shabur Hu Ba'etzem Mitukan Kavar
V'anachnu Lo Nishtok Ani Lachem Mavtiyach
Ro'im Kavar Merachok, Zeh Ha'ohr Shel Hamoshiach

[אני חי במציאות הורסת טורפת

לא אין לי רגע קל, כל הארץ מתהפכת

ובלב ישנה תפילה - אבינו מלכנו

שהנה הוא מגיע המשיח אלינו

אין מקום לשום ייאוש אמר כבר ר' נחמן

והלב שהוא שבור הוא בעצם מתוקן כבר

ואנחנו לא נשתוק אני לכם מבטיח

רואים כבר מרחוק, זה האור של המשיח****]

Chorus

*This is a very sad song, about one who is waiting for him. Father, mother, [and] children — how they pray for him! How the heart breaks every morning; why has he not arrived yet? There is no doubt, and there is no dilemma, even if he is tarrying.
**As of now he will come.
***I cannot take it anymore!
****I live in a destructive, consuming reality. I do not have a moment; the whole earth is turning over. And in the heart there sleeps a prayer — "Our Father our King!" Which is where the Moshiach approaches us. "There is no place for any despair," said R' Nachman, "and the heart that is broken in sadness is already mended." And we will not be silent, I promise you, having seen from a distance: this is the light of the Moshiach!

🎧 LITTLE KINDERLACH

Country Yossi ©
Album: Greatest Hits!

So you want to know who's gonna bring *Moshiach*?
Well I'll tell you, I'll tell you
It's not gonna be the businessman
Or the wealthy man or the famous man
Oh, no

Chorus (x2)

It's gonna be the little *Kinderlach*
The little, little, little *Kinderlach*
It's gonna be the little *Kinderlach*
Who'll make *Moshiach* come

The little boy who goes to *Yeshiva*
And learns *Hashem's* Torah and tries to understand
He'll make him come

The little girl who sings *Birchas Hamazon*
And says every word with holy *Kavanah*
She'll make him come

Chorus (x2)

The little boy who wears his *Tallis Katan*
And kisses his *Tzitzis* when he says the *Shema*
He'll make him come

The little girl who *Davens* each morning
And gives her allowance away for *Tzedakah*
She'll make him come

Chorus (x2)

The little boy who stays in *Shul*
And stands with his father to listen to the Torah
He'll make him come

The little girl who goes every *Shabbos*
To visit the sick and the lonely old people
She'll make him come

Chorus (x3)

DEDICATED TO

Rabbi Yitzi and Dina Hurwitz

You inspire us with your unwavering trust in Hashem. You encourage us to reach up higher and higher. You empower us to shine our little lights. As living examples of strength and joy despite all barriers, your dedication to shlichus has spread to the farthest reaches of the world. Your light gives strength to our light, and together we can bring Moshiach NOW.

REFUAH SHLEMAH B'KAROV!
LOVE MOTTY & MASHIE DONAT AND FAMILY

Rabbi Yitzi Hurwitz is battling ALS. He and his wife Dina are emissaries of the Rebbe in Temecula, California. For more info please visit yitzihurwitz.blogspot.com

SHINE A LITTLE LIGHT

Yitzi Hurwitz ©
Edits by Berry Cohen
Sung by various Jewish artists

For fourteen years as a Chabad emissary, alongside his wife Dina and their seven children, R' Yitzi Hurwitz faithfully served his fellow Jews in Temecula, California. Despite facing one of life's most difficult trials (R' Yitzi was diagnosed with ALS, accompanied by extreme bodily paralysis), he continues to inspire all those who come in contact with him to greater joy and faith. He shows us you aren't truly imprisoned by adverse circumstances in life, but rather your soul can always soar high and free.

Can't you see I'm trying to be all that you want of me?
But it's so cold now; it's so dark here
What could I do?
It's not very clear

Chorus (x2)
Shine a little light
Show us the way
Lead us to a brighter day

If I'm a little light, you're a little light
Together we are so very bright
A little light here, a little light there
See the smiles; it's so very clear

Chorus (x4)

When we stand together as one
There is nothing we can't do
So let's lead the way to a brighter day
And the whole world will join along

We can bring a brighter day for everyone
It's only up to me and you
We can see it, we all believe it
Let us shine our light right now

Chorus (x8)

DA MASHIACH MAN
(Shortened)

Waiting for so long now, waiting for so long now
Two thousand years, two thousand years
Waiting for so long now, waiting for so long now
We cannot wait no more; we cannot wait no more
Whom we be waiting for? Whom we be waiting for?
Da *Moshiach* man, da *Moshiach* man

And what will be, when he will come?
When he will come there will be lots of fun
On the trees will be growing candy
Everything will be nice and dandy
Don't you know the main thing of all
You're gonna be having peace in the Middle East
And we say

Chorus (x3)
Shalom in the east, *Shalom* in the west
Shalom in the north and *Shalom* in the south

Come on now
Whom we be waiting for? Whom we be waiting for?
Yes, da *Moshiach* man, da *Moshiach* man

Yehudah V'Shomron, Azzah V'Chevron
Tel Aviv, Yerushalayim, Ir Shel Shalom
[יהודה ושומרון, עזה וחברון]
[תל אביב, ירושלים, עיר של שלום]

Chorus (x2)

Come on now, all together now
Let me hear you, children, now, yes
Follow me, follow me now
Yes, yes, yes full time
All together now
Shalom in the east and *Shalom* in the west
Let me see your smile
We see *Shalom*
No more sorrow, no more sadness
Only happiness
Let me see you smiling, my man
Sing with me

🎧 SOMEDAY
Mordechai Ben David ©
Album: *The English Collection*

They learned in a dark, frigid cellar
Alone, just a small group of men
When in rushed the soldiers and led them all away
The flame of Torah flickered on that day
So many tears, so much sorrow
The pain has lasted thousands of years

But soon we'll stop crying; the cruelty will end
The *Melech Hamoshiach* will descend

Chorus
Someday we will all be together
Someday we'll be sheltered and warm
Never will we have to express any fear
Our scars and our wounds will disappear

Avraham and Yitzchak will be there to greet us
Yaakov and his sons will stand by and smile
Moshe *Rabbeinu* will meet us once again
In *Yerushalayim, B'Ezrat Hashem*

We learn every day and we *Daven*
We ask *Hashem*, "Please bring those old times back"
We all know that You're listening, of course, we know it's true
I received a promise and so have you

That *Hashem* will lead us out of this *Golus*
It won't be too much longer you know why
And then together we're all going to *Daven*
Together we're all going to sing
We're going to praise and thank You, *Hashem*, for everything

Chorus

Someday we'll all be together

DREAMS COME TRUE

Abie Rotenberg ©
Arranged and conducted by Leib Yaakov Rigler
Album: Journeys, Volume 4

Let me tell a tale; I beg you all to listen
I think you'll recognize that every word is true
It's the story that I tell about my brother
The brother that I loved but hardly knew

We were forced to live so far from one another
But it was more than distance keeping him from me
While I had the right to lead the life I'd chosen
All he yearned for was the day that he'd be free

Chorus
How I dreamed that one day we could be together
Doing all the things that brothers do
But I feared that I would have to dream forever
For only dreamers still believe that dreams come true

I fought with all my strength to gain his freedom
And challenged those who dared keep us apart
I begged them for compassion, "He's my brother"
But there's no mercy when the soul is cold and dark, cold
and dark

The years and decades followed one another
And I worried what they must have done to him
Though the flame that made us brothers was still
burning
I knew that tiny spark was growing dim

Chorus

But He who rules the world heard our prayers
How I wept the day they set my brother free
And I wondered, would he find faith with his freedom
In my heart I knew that it was up to me

Oh, I realized the first time that I embraced him
He's a stranger who feels awkward and alone
But I have just what it takes to make him welcome
A brother's love to make him feel at home

How I dreamed that one day we could be together
Doing all the things that brothers do
Now that day has come, and it will last forever
For I know and I believe, yes I know, and I believe
I'm a dreamer who believes that dreams come true

THE CITY STREETS WILL FILL

Chanale ©
Album: Believer

Where our holy house once stood
A fox roams in its place
In ruins, the mount forsaken
The sacred stones disgraced
In pain, the Sages cry
As Uriah's words ring true
And echoed through the night
"Woe unto the Jews
Akiva, don't you see?
We're faced with tragedy
But still, it seems that you deny

With laughter and with glee"
"No my sons," he's answering
"Half the promise now fulfilled
And soon He will rebuild only stronger"

Chorus
And the city streets will fill
Once more will children play
As prophecies unravel
And tomorrow starts today
So take comfort in these words
Let the tears dry from your eyes
For one day we'll see our *Mikdash*
One day these walls will rise
And the city streets will fill

Urechovos Ha'ir Yimalu
Yeladim Viyelados Mesachakim Birechovoseha
וּרְחֹבוֹת הָעִיר יִמָּלְאוּ[
[*]יְלָדִים וִילָדוֹת מְשַׂחֲקִים בִּרְחֹבֹתֶיהָ

When the old remains forever young
And the Torah's words shine as the sun
And the lion lays in peace aside the lamb
He'll bring us home on eagles' wings
And once again *Levi'im* sing
To a nation now rejoined only stronger

Chorus

*And the streets of the city shall be filled, with boys and girls
playing in its streets. -Zechariah 8:5*

TELL ME WHY?

Tzivia Kay ©
Album: Tell Me Why?

You were with us; You gave us the powers
You were with us; You gave us the strength
It's been long now, and we're still stuck in *Golus*
It's been long, and we won't stop to pray
It's been long now, and we're still stuck in *Golus*
It's been long, and we won't stop to pray

Chorus
Tell me why; can You give me a reason?
Tell me why there is so much pain?
Tell me why You're so near but so distant?
Tell me how it all happened this way?

Only birds keep flying in circles
And the leaves keep drifting away
It is stunning; the sky's almost purple
It's been long, and we won't stop to pray
It is stunning; the sky's almost purple
It's been long, and we won't stop to pray

Chorus

Who am I to ask You such questions?
Who am I, who am I to bring out such words?
I just know I'm another creation
You're the Master of this universe
You're the Master

🎧 ACHEINU

Avraham Fried ©
Morning Weekday Torah Reading Liturgy
Composed by Yossi Green
Arranged by Moshe Laufer
Album: Forever One

אַחֵינוּ כָּל בֵּית יִשְׂרָאֵל, הַנְּתוּנִים בְּצָרָה וּבַשִּׁבְיָה,
הָעוֹמְדִים בֵּין בַּיָּם וּבֵין בַּיַּבָּשָׁה,
הַמָּקוֹם יְרַחֵם עֲלֵיהֶם, וְיוֹצִיאֵם מִצָּרָה לִרְוָחָה,
וּמֵאֲפֵלָה לְאוֹרָה, וּמִשִּׁעְבּוּד לִגְאֻלָּה

Translation:
Our brothers the whole house of Israel, who are in distress and captivity, who wander over sea and over land — may G-d have mercy on them, and bring them from distress to comfort, from darkness to light, from bondage to redemption.

🎧 ON GIANTS' SHOULDERS

Avraham Fried ©
Composed by Yossi Green
Arranged by Moshe Laufer
Album: Shtar Hatnoim

When I was young, I heard a tale
Of a giant standing tall
And his son, oh so small
They shared a dream to see the king
They hungered for the day
And hurried on their way

As they neared, the two despaired

A wall rose to the skies
Above the giant's eyes
"Wait, my son," said he
"Climb upon me
And after you arise
You will be my eyes"

Chorus
And we will do it, brothers
After us, there'll be no others
You and I will do
What giants wanted to
So stand and take the credit
We will be the ones to end it
Though we're small
We're standing tall like soldiers
Riding high, because we're on our fathers' shoulders

Holy and pure, our fathers were
Giant righteous men
We are small compared to them
But our deeds, upon their deeds
Together they will bring
Moshiach, our king
Moshiach, Moshiach, our king

Chorus

It's up to us
To hammer home that final blow
Our fathers started long ago
Compelling us to follow

So stand and take the credit

Golus - we're about to end it
Though we're small
We're standing tall like soldiers
Riding high, because we're on our fathers' shoulders

🎧 HAPPY DAYS

Mordechai Ben David ©
Album: The English Collection

Do you stop and wonder what's going on?
Can you remember happy days?
Where have they gone?
Life goes by so fast; nothing seems to last
People feel the squeeze is on
It's really a shame

Can you hear the thunder?
Do you feel the pain?
So many tragedies, disasters - so insane
There seems to be no end
To this terrifying trend
And everyone you talk to feels the same

Chorus
But many happy days are coming now
So won't you please listen to me?
We'll be singing, dancing, laughing
Everybody - just you wait and see
Miracles, amazing wonders
Like no one's ever seen before
Finally that magic moment
We have all been waiting for

All the senseless hating, who knows why?

When there is so much good to see
Shouldn't we try?
And rather than reject
Just admire and respect
Must we feel like strangers, when we really are one?

It's so irritating, like a thorny rose
A generation all confused
Where everything goes
Where right and wrong's the same
Even sin has lost it's shame
Perhaps the final chapter's just begun

Chorus (x2)

There's no denying the feeling's low
You feel the pressure, got the blues
What do you know?
We seek a helping hand
It's so hard to understand
How life can turn so vicious, so absurd and unfair

We saw millions dying
We were left to cry
While the nations of the world just turned an eye
Despite the raging tears
We have suffered all these years
Never we'll surrender to despair

Chorus

Miracles, amazing wonders
Like no one's ever seen before
Finally that magic moment
We have all been waiting for

BRING THE HOUSE DOWN

Avraham Fried ©
Composed by Avraham Fried and Yitzy Waldner
Lyrics by Avraham Fried
Album: Bring the House Down

Sheyiboneh Beis Hamikdash Bimhaira Beyameinu,
Ahhh...
Sheyiboneh Beis Hamikdash Bimhaira Beyameinu,
Ahhh...
Sheyiboneh, Beis Hamikdash, Bimhaira

שיבנה בית המקדש במהרה בימינו, אהההה]
שיבנה בית המקדש במהרה בימינו, אהההה
(x2) [*שיבנה, בית המקדש, במהרה

Bring the House down
It's time; it's time
We can bring, gotta bring
Let's bring the House down
Bring the House down
It's time; it's time
It's about time

שיבנה בית המקדש במהרה בימינו, אהההה
שיבנה בית המקדש במהרה בימינו, אהההה
(x2) שיבנה, בית המקדש, במהרה

Bring the House down
It's time; it's time
We can bring, gotta bring
Let's bring the House down
Bring the House down

It's time; it's time
It's about time (x2)

You bring it down, down, down
And we'll go up, up up
To *Yerushalayim, Yerushalayim* (x2)

Bring the House down
It's time; it's time
We can bring, gotta bring
Bring it down, bring it down
Bring it, bring it, bring it down
Bring the House down
It's time; it's time
It's about time

Bring the House down
It's time; it's time
We can bring, gotta bring
Let's bring the House down
Bring the House down
Oh, it's coming down
It's time; it's time
It's about time

*May the Holy Temple be rebuilt speedily in our days. -Amidah
Prayer Liturgy

YERUSHALAYIM OUR HOME

Mordechai Ben David ©
Album: Yerushalayim Our Home

In a village near our home, works a carpenter alone
He's been carving wood for years, *Shtenders*, shelves and chairs
Daily buyers come and go, but there's one thing they don't know
His thoughts, so far away, while waiting for a special day

Chorus
There is a dream, a vision, deep within his heart
That he'll rebuild the *Beis Hamikdash* part by part
Doing *Mitzvos*, adding precious stones
Our dream, our palace, *Yerushalayim* our home

Yes, there's a dream, a vision, deep within his heart
That he'll rebuild the *Beis Hamikdash* part by part
Doing *Mitzvos*, adding precious stones
Yerushalayim, our home

In a crumbling little home, lives a fiddler all alone
His inheritance so dear, for many ancient years
It's this instrument he holds; his great-grandfather he's told
Would hurry off each day, to the courtyards of *Hashem* to play

Chorus

On a mountain, on a stone, sits *Moshiach* all alone

Suffering for years, from all our sins he bears
While so painfully he cries, prayers piercing through the skies
He's pleading to *Hashem* to take us all back home again

Yes, there's a dream a vision deep within his heart
That we'll rebuild the *Beis Hamikdash* part by part
Doing *Mitzvos*, adding precious stones
Our dream, our palace, *Yerushalayim* our home

Chorus

Ani Ma'amin, Ani Ma'amin, Ani Ma'amin...

SONG OF MOSHIACH

Shloime Gertner
Composed by Motty Ilowitz ©
Album: Imagine

In a world filled with music
Where spirits fill the air
Melodies bring us closer to that special day

The songs of David we hold so dear
Have kept us going for all those years
The sound of Torah, with every note
Singing songs that give us hope

Though we've held on so very long
With our *Emunah* and with our song
Still, we're awaiting that happy tune
How we hope to hear it soon

Yes, that song will top it all
Once we hear the *Shofar's* call
A melody so pure
Will open every door
We will sing and dance – rejoice like never before!

Chorus
Let us sing the song of *Moshiach*
Let us hear the voice of *Moshiach*
Shir Chodosh – it's a brand new song
Soon we'll sing along with *Moshiach!*

Mir varten shoin azoi*, to sing the song of joy
Achakeh loi b'chol yom sheyovoi
[**אחכה לו בכל יום שיבוא]
Very soon, you'll see, we'll be hearing *Kol Dodi*
And together we will sing in harmony!

Chorus

*We are already waiting
***I wait for him each day for his coming. -Rambam's Thirteen
Principles of Faith, Article 12*

🎧 SHABBAT LIGHTS - I HAVE HOPE

*Composed, produced and music by Mista Spoz
Lyrics and sung by Yossi K.*

**Dedicated by Michael and Ariella Sapoznik to our
parents and teachers who have guided us to sing the
song of our soul.**

I can't cry no more
Distracted from the pain
iPod, iPhone, I go insane
So blind have our eyes become from the truth
We hide our minds from what we're put here to do
To love each other
To bring redemption
To hear the whole world scream out *Hashem* is One
To cry when we look at the *Kosel* wall
Don't know who we are our or how far we fall

Chorus
But I have hope when I see
In *Yerushalayim* kids playing in the streets
The sounds of family on Friday night
And my sister lighting *Shabbos* lights for the first time

I have hope when I hear
My brothers and sisters asking me why am I here
This life can't be
Only money makes you happy
It must be, us Jews have got responsibility
Moshiach's coming now
What can we do to help him out?

Unveiled in a second I reckon
If only we open our eyes to what life's about

Chorus

I have hope when I hear
My brothers and sisters asking me why am I here
This life can't be
Only money makes you happy
It must be, us Jews have got responsibility
Come and pray with me
Moshiach soon we'll see

Chorus

THE LITTLE BIRD IS CALLING

Tzlil V'Zemer Boys Choir ©
Album: Wake Up Yidden
Recording by Chaviva Tarlow

The little bird is calling, it wishes to return
The little bird is wounded, it cannot fly but yearn
It's captured by the vultures, crying bitterly
Oh, to see my nest again, oh, to be redeemed

The little bird of silver, so delicate and rare
Still chirps amongst the vultures, outshining all that's there
How long, how long it suffers, how long will it be?
When will come the eagle and set the little bird free?

The little bird is *Yisroel*
The vultures are our foes
The painful wound is *Golus*
Which we all feel and know
The nest is *Yerushalayim*
Where we yearn to be once more
The eagle is the *Moshiach*
Whom we are waiting for

MIRACLES GO ON
Tzivia Kay ©

With Your help, I stay strong
I dedicate another song
To You my Lord, to You my Lord
Every moment is a gift
And every chance I get I lift
My eyes to Your throne
But only You can see us all

Chorus
Every second miracles go on
You send them down, You send them down
And if only people noticed
There would be mercy, peace and love
All over this chaotic world

With Your help, I stay strong
As my soul sings this song
To You my Lord, to You my Lord
I am brave, when You're here
You're beside me
I've felt You all along
I'm not alone

Chorus

You've given me all I have
You've helped me through each way
You are so good to me
And all I do, and all I do is pray

Chorus

I PRAY
Tzivia Kay ©
Album: Tell Me Why?

I'ma tie a ribbon, on a holy tree
I'll recite a prayer to Gracious Lord under it
I'ma sing a soft song, by the crystal lake
Asking G-d to forgive us all
Oh for heaven's sake...

Chorus
And for peace in this world
For some light, for some love
For the sick and the poor
And for my soul to stay humble and pure
To stay humble and pure

I'ma speak to angels, in the deepest night
Asking them to save this world
Oh for you and I
I'ma greet the nightfall, and the sunrise too
Till *Moshiach* comes this way
Oh I pray to You...

Chorus

Sponsoring Artists

Tzivia Kay

Tzivia Kay was born in the Former Soviet Union, Uzbekistan, in the city of Tashkent in 1983, and was raised in a secular, Russian-speaking Jewish home. Tzivia remembers demanding for pen and paper and making up songs in her backyard since early childhood. "As a child, I remember dancing around the trees in my backyard and composing my own songs. I pretended to be a singer on stage." Tzivia foresaw herself on a big stage and knew that she would become an artist one day.

In 1993, Tzivia and her whole family migrated to New York, where she grew extremely nostalgic for her former country and friends. She kept writing songs and poems in her native language. "I wrote my first song in Russian on a sheet of paper and repeatedly sang it over. I called my friends and shared it with them. To my surprise it was a big hit in my neighborhood," she says. At around fourteen, Tzivia felt very comfortable with expressing herself in English and started composing songs and poems in English as well as in Russian.

Today, Tzivia Kay is a bilingual poet, singer, songwriter, actress, inspirational, speaker, parodist, artist, producer and performer for women and girls only. Tzivia writes inspirational songs to bring herself, her family and others closer to G-d.

Tzivia Kay released her first CD album, *Tell Me Why?* in November, 2014 and is currently working on her second album. Tzivia enjoys working and inspiring all Jewish communities. However, her main focus remains outreach as she herself became *Baal Teshuva* and can highly relate to the *Kiruv* community, hoping to make a difference in people's lives by bringing them closer to *Hashem*. "I had a spiritual wakeup call and realized that my mission is to exalt G-d through my poetry, songs and art."

Franciska

Franciska is a composer, singer, and performer. She creates her masterpieces by weaving eternal words of prayer into soulful guitar melodies. Raised in religious school and in musical academy, Franciska's compositions reflect her commitment to bridging both worlds. Franciska started playing the piano at six years old. She began composing after she mastered the guitar at the young age of twelve. While studying in high school, she toured in the US and Europe with the musical ensemble Ilanit. Currently, Franciska works on her music production and is on tour with her new show Reinvention, in addition to highlight performing and DJ'ing. She recently produced her fifth solo album titled *Kol Haolam* and currently hosts a podcast titled *The Franciska Show*, interviewing women in the Jewish entertainment world.

www.franciskamusic.com

Rivky Saxon

Rivky Saxon is a seventeen-year-old singer and songwriter from Pittsburgh, Pennsylvania. She has taken voice lessons from the age of ten, and in January of 2017 released her first single, "Honey, You'll Survive," available on iTunes, along with a music video available on YouTube. Since that time, she has released many more songs, and performs concerts for women and girls. Rivky hopes to impact and inspire the lives of her listeners with relatable messages for today's teenage girls.

To listen to or purchase Rivky's music, or contact her, visit RivkySaxon.com.

Leah Caras

Leah Caras founded YALDAH magazine for Jewish girls at age 13, which she published and directed for ten years. Through YALDAH, she became involved with the Jewish Girls Retreat, spending many summers and winters as a counselor and program director, in addition to managing all the graphic and web design needs of the retreat.

Together with Nechama Laber, Leah envisioned the Jewish Girls Unite community, and eventually designed the JGU website so many girls enjoy today. She continued in her role as graphic designer for JGU, and designed this songbook, as well as the "One More Light" book.

Through her graphic design business, Carasmatic Design, Leah and her husband Michael do print and web design for organizations and businesses around the world.

Leah grew up in Massachusetts and now lives with her husband and four children, K"H, in Albany, NY.

For more information visit
www.carasmaticdesign.com.

CARASMATIC
DESIGN

WITH GRATITUDE TO
Chanie Chanin

FOR THE BEAUTIFUL PAINTINGS FEATURED THROUGHOUT THIS BOOK

Chanie Chanin
Chanie Chanin (nee Raskin), grew up in London, England in a Chabad-Lubavitch home. She has always loved to use her creative talents in art and song since she was a young child.

She received an A in her Art GCSE (English government exam) when she graduated. After marrying Mendy she moved to Brooklyn, New York and continued to pursue her creativity in art by joining the NY Art Student League. She also joined art classes by Chaya Pellin in Crown Heights and Andrew Reiss in Park Slope. Chanie is a mother of eight children K"H and still finds the time to paint in her home studio.

When she paints she puts her essence into her art. Chanie has a program for women called "A Journey Through My Art" where she presents her paintings through story, poems and song. Chanie says she uses her talent in art as her *Shlichus* to inspire people.

To order any of the artwork in this book, visit
www.frommyartandsoul.com.

Chaviva Tarlow has a passion for authentic Jewish music. Over the years she has brought that passion to various groups of women and girls through guitar lessons, music and movement classes, drum circles, concerts and choirs. She currently serves as the music coach for Jewish Girls Unite. As a professional and trained singer, Chaviva aims to inspire and empower Jewish women and girls through her roles as teacher and musician.

To book email Chavivamusic@gmail.com.

Shaindel Antelis has been singing since she learned how to talk, and started writing her own songs at ten years old. From when she was a young girl she dreamed about releasing albums of her own. Well, that time has come! Shaindel just released her fourth album, *The Sun Is Rising*! Shaindel's albums contain songs with a pop feel and meaningful messages. Her aim is to inspire women and girls everywhere to feel good about themselves. With songs ranging from the pursuit of happiness, to connecting to G-d, and getting through hard times, there is definitely something for everyone. The lyrics to Shaindel's songs are like excerpts from her diary which make them easy to enjoy and relate to!

To check out Shaindel's music and videos head to www.ShaindelAntelis.com.

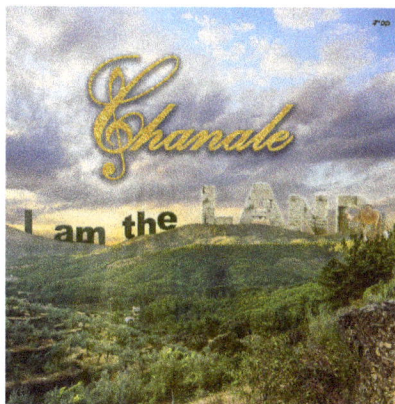

Chanale

Singer, Songwriter & Mother
facebook.com/ChanaleSings

Kerry Bar-Cohn has many passions. She is married to David and together they are raising four sons ages ten to twenty years in Israel. She is a doctor of chiropractic and spends a big part of her day helping people get out of pain. Kerry loves to sing and dance and one of her favorite creative projects is performing as "Rebbetzin Tap." As Rebbetzin Tap, she has starred in five DVDs and performed for children and women around the world. She is also the founder of the "Kol Isha" Facebook group and Radio Station.

You can watch her videos and more at: www.rebbetzintap.com

Kol Isha Radio! 24 hours of Jewish Women's Music: www.rebbetzintap.com/kolisha

Racheli Jacks has always been singing, for as long as she can remember. She still has an old tape of herself at three years old singing a family tune of *Shir Hama'alos*! Racheli had her first solo in a production in elementary school, and has been involved in choirs and productions ever since. As choir head in high school, Racheli wrote lyrics to songs, many of which girls around the world are singing today. In seminary, Racheli began arranging tunes to facilitate the memorization of the first twelve chapters of *Tanya* by heart, a feat that was considered almost unachievable for girls at that time. She has completed six CDs, but she is not stopping there. Racheli hopes to continue producing her CDs, using melody, harmony and rhythm to help girls achieve their goal.

Mista Spoz - Michael Sapoznik

Music Producer - Composer - Audio Engineer

Michael 'Mista Spoz' Sapoznik is a multi-instrumentalist in Southern Florida playing piano, guitar, percussion, and drums. He's cooking up live performances of some of his original creations, such as using a loop pedal to create a five-piece band in front of your eyes. He has a unique ability to fuse flavors from every genre. His love for film and the art of storytelling beams through his productions and compositions. His eclectic flair and creative approach to music production makes Mista Spoz a must-have for collaborating music connoisseurs. It wasn't long before he began recording his debut album, *The Résumé*.

Chaya-Bracha Rubin is an inspirational speaker, singer and songwriter. She has performed in the U.S. and Israel, and most notably for a crowd of over 3,500 at the *Kinus HaShluchos* in Manhattan. In intimate settings or formal events, she moves her listeners to joy and strength through her original compositions and personal stories.

Rivka Leah Popack's music combines both folk, soul and classic pop, and her poetic lyrics are deeply touching and upbeat. In her performances, Rivka Leah enjoys sharing her own experience of music as one that evokes the spiritual dimension of life's journeys, offering comfort, inspiration and strength.
www.rivkaleahmusic.com

Shoshana Levin Bander is a singer, songwriter, and storyteller who has touched and inspired female audiences around the United States and Israel with her heart-warming, soul-touching melodies and breathtaking stories. She is fun and deep at the same time, leaving the crowd not only with melodies to hum, but with something to think about long after the performance.

SINGERS & COMPOSERS

FEMALE ARTISTS:

Chava Alberstein
Shaindel Antelis
Idy Appel
Shoshana Bander
Suri Berman
Sarah Chana Biren
Sheira Brayer
Nechama Cohen
Sorah Leah Eber
Rivky Feld
Chanale Fellig-Harrel
Franciska
Sophia Franco
Esther Freeman
Debbie Friedman
Robin Garbose
Sarit Hadad
Thalia Hakin
Ofra Haza
Miriam Israeli
Racheli Jacks
Tzivia Kay
Rivkah Krinsky
Chaya Aydel Lebovics
Surie Levilev
Chany Levy
Leah Namdar
Chayala Neuhaus
Mali New
Ohel Chana High School
Ahuvah Ozeri

Rivka Leah Popack
Rebbetzin Tap
Mirele Rosenberger
Chaya-Bracha Rubin
Rivky Saxon
Shayna Mushka Saxon
Miriam Leah Shaw
Naomi Shemer
Chavie Sobel
JGR Camp Staff
Hannah Szenes
Chaviva Tarlow
Arlet Tzfadia
Chana Yerushalmi

JGU GIRLS:

Chana Mandella
Malkie Peiser
Neshama Sari
Rachael Tahir

MALE ARTISTS:

8th Day
Mordechai Ben David
Avremel Blesofsky
Baruch Chait
Yossi Cohen
Country Yossi
Moshe Daabul
Shloime Dachs
Dedi
Suki & Ding

Shmuel Elbaz
Yoni Eliav
Ran Eliran
Joel Engel
Yitzy Erps
Amos Ettinger
Avraham Fried
Benny Friedman
Eli Friedman
Rafi Gabai
Dovid Gabay
Shai Gabso
Eli Gerstner
Shloime Gertner
Yossi Gispan
Sam Glaser
Eyal Golan
Ari Goldwag
Yossi Green
Avigdor Hemeiri
Yitzchok Hurwitz
Yitzi Hurwitz
Motty Ilowitz
Kinderlach
Moshe Kravitsky
Shmuel Kunda
Yisroel Lamm
S. Levertov
Dov Levine
Maccabeats
Shmuel Marcus
Matisyahu

Sheya Mendelowitz
Chony Milecki
Miami Boys Choir led by Yerachmiel Begun
Uncle Moishy
Yossi Newman
Dovid Pearlman
Yehuda Piamenta
Lew Pollack
Michoel Pruzansky
Leib Yaakov Rigler
Mayer Rivkin
Yitzchok Rosenthal
Elie Schwab
Shalsheles
Yochanan Shapiro
Mordechai Shapiro
Label Sharfman
Yaakov Shwekey
H. M. Spalter
Shlomo Sternberg
The Kapelle
Tzlil V'Zemer Boys Choir
Yitzy Waldner
M. M. Warshawsky
Jack Yellen
Yeshiva Boys Choir
Moshe Yess
David Zahavi

GLOSSARY

Heb. - Hebrew; Yid. - Yiddish; Ara. - Aramaic

Abba - Heb. Father

Adar - Heb. The twelfth month of the Hebrew (lunar) calendar

Ad Mosai - Heb. Until when?

A"H - Heb. Abbreviation of "aleha/alav hashalom - peace be upon her/him"

Aishes Chayil - Heb. A woman of valor; a traditional song of King Solomon's proverbs praising the Jewish woman, sung on Friday evenings

Aleh Katan - Heb. A small leaf

Aleph - Heb. The first letter of the Hebrew alphabet

Aleph Beis - Heb. The Hebrew alphabet

Am - Heb. Nation

Am Segulah - Heb. A treasured nation

Amen - Heb. A response to a prayer or blessing, signifying acceptance and belief in the words of praise recited

Ani Ma'amin - Heb. I believe

Avinu - Heb. Our father

Avodah - Heb. Service; worship

Avodah Shebalev - Heb. Service of the heart

Baal Teshuva - Heb. Literally, "master of return;" one who returns to the path of Torah and Jewish observance, or rises higher in their service of G-d

Beis Hamikdash - Heb. The Holy Temple, which stood in Jerusalem. The first was built by King Solomon and lasted for 410 years before ravaged by Nebuchadnezzar of Babylon. The second remained 420 years, and was destroyed by the Romans in 70 C.E. Established upon Mount Moriah, it was the meeting place of heaven and earth through which all blessing emanated to the world, and called "a house of prayer for all peoples" by the prophet. It is where the entire Jewish People could congregate to worship G-d, and the Divine Presence rests until today.

Bakashos - Heb. Requests

Bar Mitzvah - Heb. Literally, "Son of the Commandment;" a Jewish boy who's reached the age of 13 and attained majority as an adult bound to the observance of Jewish Law

Bas Mitzvah - Heb. Literally, "Daughter of the Commandment;" a Jewish girl who's reached the age of 12 and attained majority as an adult bound to the observance of Jewish Law

Bas Yisroel [Pl. Bnos Yisrael] - Heb. Literally, "Daughter of Israel;" a Jewish girl

Beinoni [Pl. Beinonim] - Heb. An average person

Beis Rivkah - Heb. Literally, "House of Rebecca;" a Jewish girls' school with branches all over the world, established by the Lubavitch Educational System

Beracha - Heb. Blessing

Besiyata Dishmaya - Ara. With the help of Heaven

B'Ezrat Hashem - Heb. With G-d's help

Bimheirah - Heb. Speedily

Birchas Hamazon - Heb. Grace After Meals

Bitachon - Heb. Trust (in G-d)

Biyas Hamoshiach - Heb. The coming of the Messiah

Bizchus Nashim - Heb. In the merit of women

Bnei Avraham - Heb. Children of Abraham

Borei Ha'olam - Heb. Creator of the Universe (a title of G-d)

Bubby - Yid. Grandmother

B'Yachad - Heb. In unity; as one

Challah [Pl. Challos] - Heb. Literally "loaf;" the traditional, often-braided bread blessed and partaken of at Jewish celebrations and festive meals; originally the portion separated from the dough and given to the priest as a gift in Temple times

Chanukah - Heb. Literally, "dedication;" the 8-night festival originating in Temple times which celebrates G-d's miracles, light and religious freedom, and commemorates the rededication of the Holy Temple which had been defiled by the Syrian-Greeks

Cholent - Yid. A traditional, long-cooking type of stew, originally created as a way to have a hot meal on the Sabbath when the act of cooking is prohibited

Chossid [Pl. Chassidim] - *Heb.* Literally, "pious one;" a Jew who goes beyond the letter of the law in his Torah observance and service of G-d, with great self-discipline and joy; a follower of a Chassidic Rebbe

Chassidishkeit - *Yid.* The nature and practice of Hasidism

Chassidus - *Heb.* Hasidism; the mystical secrets and inner dimension of Torah sanctifying and directing every aspect of one's life, as taught by the movement's founder, the Baal Shem Tov

Chayalim - *Heb.* Soldiers

Chayus - *Heb.* Vitality

Chessed - *Heb.* Lovingkindness; acts of kindness

Cholent - *Yid.* A long and slow-cooking stew, originating centuries ago as a suitable dish for Shabbos, when cooking is forbidden in Jewish law

Chuppah - *Heb.* Marriage canopy

Daven - *Yid.* Pray

Derech - *Heb.* Literally, "path;" especially denoting the upright path of Torah observance

Dirah - *Heb.* Dwelling place

Dovid Hamelech - *Heb.* King David

Eimasai - *Ara.* When?

Emes - *Heb.* Truth

Emunah - *Heb.* Faith (in G-d)

Eretz Yisroel - *Heb.* The Land of Israel

Erev Shabbos - *Heb.* Sabbath Eve

Farbrengen - *Yid.* A joyous gathering brimming with unity, song, and strengthened resolve to Torah and

Mitzvos

Fartzik yor - *Yid.* Forty years

Gan - *Heb.* Garden; also a common reference for a Jewish preschool or kindergarten

Gan Eden - *Heb.* The Garden of Eden

Gedolah - *Heb.* Eminence

Gematrios - *Heb.* Numerical equivalents of the letters of the Hebrew alphabet

Geulah - *Heb.* Redemption

Golah - *Heb.* Exile

Golus - *Heb.* Exile

Hachein - *Heb.* The grace

Hakadosh Baruch Hu - *Heb.* The Holy One, Blessed be He

Hakohen - *Heb.* The priest

Hamotzi - *Heb.* Literally, "The One Who brings forth;" a reference for the blessing said over bread

Har Sinai - *Heb.* Mount Sinai, site of the Giving of the Torah

Hashem - *Heb.* Literally, "the Name;" G-d

Hashgocha Protis - *Heb.* Divine Providence

Hiskashrus - *Heb.* Bond

Hatzlocho - *Heb.* Success

Havdala - *Heb.* Literally, "separation;" the ritual performed following the Sabbath to signify the holy day's end and the transition into the mundane week

Ima - *Heb.* Mother

Imeinu - *Heb.* Our mother

Im Yirtzeh Hashem - *Heb.* If G-d wills it

Ir Shel Shalom - *Heb.* City of peace

Kallah - *Heb.* Bride

Kavanah - *Heb.* Focus; intention

Kedushah - *Heb.* Holiness

Kever Rochel - *Heb.* Rachel's tomb; the resting place of our Matriarch Rachel on the road to Bethlehem, where countless people come to pray

K"H - *Yid.* Abbreviation of "*keyn ayin hora* - no evil eye," meaning no negative influences (e.g. jealousy or harm) should be aroused by tidings of this person's good fortune

Kiddush - *Heb.* Literally, "sanctification;" the blessing(s) recited, typically over wine, to declare the holiness of a special occasion, such a Sabbath, Festivals and weddings

Kinderlach - *Yid.* Children

Kinus HaShluchos - *Heb.* Conference of Chabad-Lubavitch Women Emissaries

Kiruv - *Heb.* Literally, "bringing close;" outreach

Kiyor - *Heb.* Laver; the copper washbasin at which the priests cleansed and sanctified their hands and feet in the Holy Temple

Klal Yisroel - *Heb.* The entire community of Israel; the Jewish People

Kodesh Hakodashim - *Heb.* The Holy of Holies; the innermost sanctum of the Holy Temple where G-d's Presence rested upon the Ark of the Covenant, which the High Priest alone was permitted to enter, on Yom Kippur only

Kol Dodi - *Heb.* The voice of my Beloved

Kol Nidrei - *Heb.* Literally, "all vows;" the opening prayer of the Yom Kippur service, during which we nullify all our vows made during the past year

Kosel Hama'arovi - Heb. The Western Wall

Kossi Mar - Ara. [When...] will the Master come?

L'Chayim - Heb. To life; a toast made as a blessing for life

L'chi Lach - Heb. You shall go

Lecha Dodi - Heb. Come my Beloved; a portion of the liturgy penned by the Kabbalist R' Shlomo Halevi Alkabetz (16th century) sung to welcome in the Sabbath

Lech Lecha - Heb. Go for yourself

Lema'an Hashem - Heb. For G-d's sake

Levi'im - Heb. Levites; the tribe and descendants of Levi, our Patriarch Jacob's third son, who merited priesthood and served the spiritual needs of the Jewish nation

Lichtelach - Yid. Candles

L'Simchat Chayim - Heb. For joy in life

Malachim - Heb. Angels

Malach'l - Yid. Dear angel

Manhig Hador - Heb. Leader of the generation

Marom - Heb. Above; on High

Mayim Rabim - Heb. Literally, "many waters;" a euphemism for the myriad temptations of this physical world distracting us from fulfilling our soul's essential purpose here

Megillah - Heb. Literally, "scroll;" in the holy Writings, the Song of Songs, Ruth, Lamentations, Ecclesiastes and Esther are each canonized as a Megillah

Melava Malka - Heb. Literally, "escorting the Queen;" the festive meal partaken of immediately following the Sabbath, to demonstrate our love for the Sabbath Queen and our reluctance to her departure

Melech Hamoshiach - Heb. The King Messiah

Melech Malchei Hamelachim - Heb. The King of all kings; a title of G-d's

Menorah - Heb. Candelabra; the seven branched lamp kindled daily in the Holy Temple; also a common term for our nine-branched Hanukkah lamps

Mesiras Nefesh - Heb. Self-sacrifice

Mezuzah - Heb. Literally, "door post;" the scroll we affix

Midbar - Heb. Wilderness

Midrash - Heb. The homiletical interpretation of the Torah as brought down in Rabbinical literature

Mikdash - Heb. Sanctuary

Mikdash Hashlishi - Heb. Literally, "the third sanctuary;" the third Holy Temple which will be built with the coming of the Messiah

Mishna - Heb. Literally "review;" the first major work of Rabbinic literature and collection of Jewish Law, also known as "Oral Torah," canonized by R' Judah HaNasi in approximately 70 C.E.

Mishkan - Heb. Literally, "dwelling place;" the portable Tabernacle which served as a resting place for G-d before the more permanent Holy Temple's erection

Mispal'lim - Heb. Prayer-goers

Mitzrayim - Heb. Egypt

Mitzvah [Pl. Mitzvos] - Heb. Connection;

one of the 613 divine commandments transmitted in the Torah

Moshiach - Heb. The Messiah; the progeny of the tribe of Judah, future redeemer and king of the Jewish people, who will usher in universal peace and awareness of the One G-d

Moshiach ben Dovid - Heb. Messiah son of David

Moshiach Tzidkeinu - Heb. Our righteous Messiah

Muktzeh - Heb. Literally, "set aside;" objects purposeless or prohibited on the Sabbath and Festivals, which we abstain from using

Mun - Heb. Manna; the delicate, Heaven-sent food G-d sustained the Children of Israel with during their 40 years in the Wilderness

Nachas - Heb. Satisfaction; a common expression for parental pride and joy in one's children and their accomplishments

Nasi - Heb. Prince; leader

Nechama - Heb. Comfort

Neshama [Pl. Neshamos] - Heb. Soul

Neshomo'le - Yid. Dear soul

Nessius - Heb. Leadership

Niggun [Pl. Niggunim] - Heb. Melody

Osiyos - Heb. Letters

Parsha - Heb. Passage; a common term for the weekly Torah portion

Peirushim - Heb. Explanations; commentary

Perek Tanya - Heb. Chapter of Tanya

Plotz - Yid. Collapse

P'tach Libi - Heb. Open my heart

Rabbeinu - Heb. Our Rabbi

Refuah - Heb. Healing; recovery

Ruach - Heb. Spirit; energy

Seforim - Heb. Books; a common term for Torah books in particular

Sha'arei Hashamayim - Heb. The Gates of Heaven

Shabbatons - Heb. Inspiring events or retreats held over the Sabbath

Shabbos [Alt. Shabbat] - Heb. Sabbath

Shabbos Kodesh - Heb. The Holy Sabbath

Shabbos Mivorchim - Heb. Literally, "the week they bless," referring to the final Sabbath before entering the new Hebrew month, which we bless

Shalom - Heb. Peace; a twofold expression of greeting and farewell

Shammesh - Heb. Caretaker

Shechina - Heb. G-d's manifested Divine Presence - referred to in the feminine gender

Sheitel - Yid. Wig

Shema - Heb. Literally, "hear;" a common reference for the Biblically mandated, twice-daily, verbalized acceptance of G-d's Kingship and our faith

Shema Yisroel - Heb. Hear O Israel [the opening of the Shema prayer]

Shir Hama'alos - Heb. Literally, "a song of ascents;" a common reference for the introductory psalm to Grace After Meals on festive occasions

Shliach - Heb. Emissary

Shlichus - Heb. Mission; a common reference especially for the initiative

of Chabad emissaries to ignite and strengthen Torah and Jewish life worldwide

Shlomo Hamelech - Heb. King Solomon

Shlucha - Heb. Female emissary

Shofar - Heb. A ram's horn, blown to mark significant occasions, and evoke atonement, such as on the High Holidays

Shtenders - Yid. Lecterns, typically employed in studying and prayers

Shul - Yid. Synagogue

Shviger - Yid. Mother-in-law

Siddur - Heb. Prayerbook

Simchas - Heb. Joyous and celebratory occasions

Sinas Chinam - Heb. Baseless hatred

Siyata Dishmaya - Ara. Help of Heaven

Sukkah'le - Yid. Little hut; referring to the hut built on the holiday of Sukkos

Tallis [Pl. Talleisim] - Heb. A fringed shawl worn by Jewish men during prayers, adorned with 613 tassels and knots to remind the wearer of the 613 commandments

Tallis Katan - Heb. Small fringed shirt worn under the garments throughout the day, similar to a prayer shawl, including 613 tassels and knots reminiscent of the 613 commandments

Talmidim - Heb. Students

Tanya - Heb. Literally, "we have learned;" the seminal masterwork of Chabad Chassidic philosophy, penned by its founding-father R' Schenur Zalman of Liadi

Tefillah [Pl. Tefillos] - Heb. Prayer

Tehillim - Heb. Psalms

Teshuvah - Heb. Repentance; return

Tzaddikim - Heb. Righteous ones

Tzedakah - Heb. Charity

Tzedakah B'Guf - Heb. Charity with the body

Tzitzis - Heb. Shirt with ritual fringes at the corners worn throughout the day as prescribed in the Torah, including 613 tassels and knots reminiscent of the 613 commandments

Tznius - Heb. Modesty

Yachad - Heb. Together

Yartzeit - Yid. Anniversary of one's death

Yemei Hamoshiach - Heb. Days of Messiah

Yemei Haselichos - Heb. The period we recite special penitential liturgy prior to the High Holidays

Yerushalayim - Heb. Jerusalem

Yeshiva - Heb. Academy of Torah and Talmudic study

Yetzer Hara - Heb. Evil inclination

Yid [Pl. Yidden] - Yid. Jew

Yiddishe Mameh - Yid. Jewish mother

Yiddishkeit - Yid. Judaism

Yirat Hashem - Heb. Fear [i.e. awe] of G-d

Yisrael - Heb. Israel

Zaidy - Yid. Grandfather

Zemiros - Heb. Songs

Zohar - Heb. Literally, "radiance;" the foundational masterwork of Jewish mysticism penned by R' Shimon bar Yochai.

ACKNOWLEDGMENTS

Thank You *Hashem* for being our Partner and bringing us together to create *Voices in Harmony*.

No great endeavor comes to fruition by a single person. We want to thank the following people for helping to bring this songbook to light. Each of you is an angel whispering to a Jewish daughter. This book would not be in the hands of generations of Jewish women and girls without you.

With thanks to:

• My husband, Rabbi Avraham Laber, for his patience and support for the endless hours while this book was being created

• Susan Axelrod, JGU Strategy Advisor, for your guidance in conceptualizing and structuring this book

• Tzipporah Prottas for the eloquent introductions, glossary, and help compiling the songs

• Leah Caras of Carasmatic Design for the graphic design in this beautiful book

• Chanie Chanin for the stunning artwork that adds so much beauty to the book

• Chana Shloush for your editing expertise and attention to detail

• Chaviva Tarlow, JGU Music coach for her help with compiling and recording JGU songs

• The Seymour Fox Foundation for sponsoring JGU recordings at the WAMC studio

• Bonnie Chavin for her support and encouragement of this project

• Singers and composers, who have contributed your moving songs, and joined together to create *Voices in Harmony*

• Tribute and legacy page donors, for sharing your loved ones with us and for supporting Jewish girls worldwide

• JGR campers and staff for singing and composing songs at camp throughout the years

So many were involved in creating this songbook; we fear that we might have left someone out. If we did, we ask your forgiveness. Please let us know, and we will revise the next edition.

THANK YOU TO ALL SPONSORS OF THE VOICES IN HARMONY
2018 CAMPAIGN & PRE-LAUNCH CELEBRATION

Sara Abikasis	Pierre Bouskila	Chanie Chanin
Regis Attuil	Shoshana Brenenson	Bonnie Chavin
Fanny Miara Attuil	Arthur & Nanette Brenner	Itty Chazan
Susan Axelrod	Eta Chaya Brummel	Dina Cohen
Shoshana Bander	Michael & Leah Caras	Yehudis Cohen
Devorah Barnett	Yehudah & Chana Chakoff	Motti & Mashi Donat
Ruth Benarroch	Philip & Linda Chandler	Sorah Leah Eber
Basha Botnick	Riki Chanin	Iris Emmer

Leah Ezagui
Jacob & Raizel Feder
Franci Feld
Miriam Feldman
Masha Feldman
Chanale Fellig-Harrel
Dena Fox
Jody Fox
Tzirel Frankel
Mushky Fuchs
Leah Gaies
Yitzchok & Leah Gniwisch
Debbie Grashin
Sue Ann Grosberg
David & Dora Gurevitch
Rabbi Mayer & Shaindy Gutnick
Dina Halpern
Shimon & Sarah Hecht
Dr. & Mrs. Leah Chava Hertzberg
Julie Hintz & Abi'l-Khayr
Aliza Horowitz
Shalom Huber
Miriam Hurwitz
Miriam Ilyayev
Sylvia Ivry
Dr. Ed & Laura Jacobs
Judy Kahn
Balor Kalendareva
Yalena Kalendareva
Baila Kamman
Yitzchok & Daniella Katzenberg
Tzivia Kay
Franciska Kay

Avraham & Nechama Laber
Shmuel & Gittel Laber
Chani & Shimon Laber
Shprintza Ladaev
Mayor & Sara Langer
Chana Lazar
Zelda Lerner
Bracha Levertov
Chana Lew
Sofia Lewitt
Chaya Mushkah Lezak
Daniella Lezell
Jerome & Joyce Lichtenstein
Loren Lichtenstein & Arie Ferber
Aryeh & Esther Mandella
Mazaliya Mardakhayeva
Malkie Marrus
Micki & Norman Massry
Laura Melnicoff
Chana Zelda Minkowitz
Raizel Nissim
Anita Katz Peiser
Chaya Feiga Pellin
Chaya Pinson
Josh Prottas
Leslie & Joseph Prottas
Miriam Ravnoy-Frimerman
Chana Hinda Rivkin
Chana Rogatsky
Dr. Eli & Mrs. Chana Rosen
Henya Rosenberg
Rochel Rosenberg
Chana Rosenberger

Tzivia Chaya Rosenthal
Sharna Rosenzweig
Perel Rotenberg
Chaya-Bracha Rubin
Hinde Devorah Saltzman
Nechama Dina Samuels
Michael & Ariella Sapoznik
Rivka Sari
Mordechai Saxon
Ory & Linda Schwartz
Seymour Fox Foundation
Esther Shagalow
Lea Shemtov
Mendy & Chaya Shepherd
Chana Shloush
Sara Shollar
Susanne Shulman
Shalom & Dina Simon
Dinie Sufrin
Laurie & Rachael Tahir
Orit Taksir
Chaviva Tarlow
Nechama Tauber
Joyce Teitelman
Mairav Vaknin
Leonard Wasserman
Ezzy & Chana Wasserman
Yedida Wolfe
Miriam Yerushalmi
Chana Zuckerman
Sterna Zwiebel

With apologies, please let us know if we have misspelled or omitted your name.

JGU GLOBAL TEAM

JGU Founders
Linda & Ory Schwartz

JGU Global Director
Nechama Laber

CFO
Rabbi Avraham Laber

JGU Global Advisor
Susan Axelrod

Webmaster & Graphic Designer
Leah Caras

Art Coach
Ahuvah Coates

Music Coach
Chaviva Tarlow

Writing Coach
Yedida Wolfe

Admin
Chaya Shepherd

Art Consultant
Rivka Sari

Resource Provider
Miriam Yerushalmi

Video Editor
Esther Mandella

JGU ADVISORY BOARD

Michelle Arko

Ilana Bassman

Nanette Brenner

Joanne Caras

Chana Chakoff

Bonnie Chavin

Yehudis Cohen

Yocheved Daphna

Mashi Donat

Sorah Leah Eber

Gita Gammal

Dinie Greenberg

Julie Hintz

Racheli Jacks

Daniella Katzenberg

Tzivia Kay

Evelyn Krieger

Gittel Laber

Chana Laber

Sara Langer

Mazal Mardakhayeva

Sofia Muhlmann

Leah Namdar

Geulah Newman

Raizel Nissim

Rivka Leah Popack

Chana Hinda Rivkin

Mirele Rosenberger

Ariella Sapoznik

Devorah Schulman

Rae Shagalov

Chana Wasserman

Miriam Yerushalmi

Nechama Dena Zwiebel

JGU PROGRAMS

BEYOND BAT MITZVAH

Unlock the treasures entrusted to Jewish women and girls through a combination of text study, lively discussion and games. We will delve into the lives of women in the Torah and explore related topics and contemporary issues that will guide us in our role as women in modern times. Discover the tools to blossom into a true Bat Mitzvah, a life long goal.

MIRROR REFLECTIONS FOR TEENS

Join the quest to discover tools and techniques to find your sense of self and achieve inner joy and peace. Using a mirror as a tool for exploration, we will look beyond the mere reflection that is skin deep, share life lessons from Jewish women of our history and focus on a vision for your future that will reveal your inner beauty and strengths today. Integrated throughout the course are life-skills and resume-building opportunities and an integrated opportunity for connecting with other Jewish high school girls from around the country.

CREATIVE ONLINE CLUB

Cultivate your natural talents in art, music, writing and science! Unite with talented Jewish girls from around the world. Discover your Jewish self through the arts. Meet Jewish artists online. Become a JGU Shining Star!

FROM ROSES TO PEARLS WOMEN'S WORKSHOPS

Find joy and meaning in our Jewish holidays and prayers. Discover transformitive tools, tips and meditations from the wisdom of Chassidus. Join a community of women who see through the thorns, smell the roses and transform irritations into pearls.

JGU EDUCATORS FORUM

Join our free monthly educator's forum, a community dedicated to bringing creativity and innovation into Jewish education. Your students will benefit from inter-school broadcasts and JGU curricula.

JEWISH GIRLS RETREAT

Summer and winter retreats provide a safe and loving environment where Jewish girls of all backgrounds explore Judaism through the arts and nature. The camp provides girls with a variety of opportunities to explore and strengthen their musical, dramatic, dance and creative writing abilities as well as guide them to discover new talents. Each girl shines in her unique way and builds pride in her artistic and spiritual self. The fun and warm family-like atmosphere at camp enables girls to feel comfortable expressing their personalities and interests. At JGR, everyone is family!

www.ingramcontent.com/pod-product-compliance
Lightning Source LLC
Chambersburg PA
CBHW061955090426
42811CB00006B/943